THE LIBRARY OF ENGLISH ART
GENERAL EDITOR: C. M. WEEKLEY

ENGLISH POTTERY AND PORCELAIN

THE LIBRARY OF ENGLISH ART

General Editor: C. M. Weekley

First Titles

ENGLISH WATER-COLOURS
LAURENCE BINYON, C.H.
Lately Keeper of Prints and Drawings, British Museum

ENGLISH POTTERY AND PORCELAIN
W. B. HONEY
Assistant Keeper, Department of Ceramics, Victoria & Albert Museum

ENGLISH NEEDLEWORK
A. F. KENDRICK
Formerly Keeper of the Department of Textiles, Victoria & Albert Museum

In Preparation

ENGLISH SILVER
C. C. OMAN
Assistant Keeper, Department of Metalwork, Victoria & Albert Museum

ENGLISH GLASS
W. A. THORPE
Author of 'A History of English and Irish Glass', etc.
Assistant Keeper in the Victoria & Albert Museum

ENGLISH FURNITURE
JOHN GLOAG
Author of 'Time, Taste, and Furniture', etc.

PLATE I   *See pages* 10, 11

(*a*) JUG. 14TH–15TH CENTURY
The London Museum

(*b*) JUG. 13TH–14TH CENTURY   (*c*) JUG. 14TH–15TH CENTURY
The London Museum   *The London Museum*

ENGLISH POTTERY AND PORCELAIN

BY

W. B. HONEY

ASSISTANT KEEPER, DEPARTMENT OF CERAMICS
VICTORIA AND ALBERT MUSEUM

With twenty-four pages of illustrations
from photographs
and twelve from line drawings

A. & C. BLACK LTD
4, 5 & 6 SOHO SQUARE LONDON W.1
1933

The United States
THE MACMILLAN COMPANY, NEW YORK

Australia and New Zealand
THE OXFORD UNIVERSITY PRESS, MELBOURNE

Canada
THE MACMILLAN COMPANY OF CANADA, TORONTO

South Africa
THE OXFORD UNIVERSITY PRESS, CAPE TOWN

India and Burma
MACMILLAN AND COMPANY LIMITED
BOMBAY   CALCUTTA   MADRAS

PRINTED IN GREAT BRITAIN
BY R. & R. CLARK LTD. EDINBURGH

TO
W. W. WINKWORTH

PREFACE

THE purpose of this book is to provide a concise history of English ceramic art, that is to say, an account of the sequence of the various kinds of distinctively English wares, of their authorship or derivation, and more especially of their aesthetic charm—of those qualities in fact which make their study and collection worth while. Matters of purely archaeological interest have naturally been excluded, and space has not allowed the citation of authorities or a full discussion of many controversial matters; these have, however, been pointed out, as subjects of special concern to the collector, and the reasons for any departures from customary opinions have been briefly explained. The reader wishing to pursue in greater detail the difficult study of the porcelain is referred to my *Old English Porcelain* (Geo. Bell & Sons), where the arguments for and against the attributions are more fully discussed, and references to authorities and more numerous illustrations are provided. A classified bibliography has been added here, for both pottery and porcelain.

I wish to thank Mr. C. C. Oman for several references to old inventories, and to record my great indebtedness to Mr. Bernard Rackham, for much instruction and many suggestions.

CONTENTS

PART I

EARTHENWARE AND STONEWARE TO THE END OF THE EIGHTEENTH CENTURY

PART II

ENGLISH PORCELAIN OF THE EIGHTEENTH CENTURY

ix

CONTENTS

LIST OF PLATES

xi

LIST OF PLATES

xii

xiv

Figures in the Text

LIST OF FIGURES

xvi

ENGLISH POTTERY AND PORCELAIN

INTRODUCTION

THE appreciation of English ceramic art requires a
breadth of mind and an adaptable taste which the
purist will hasten to tell us are not taste at all. To admire the
noble forms of the mediaeval pottery and at the same time
not to despise the frivolous amusements of *rococo* porcelain
will seem inexplicable perversity to those arbiters of taste
whose admiration for none but the earliest Chinese pottery
has set the fashion for to-day. Yet the historian knows well
that the varying aspect of works of art in different periods
is not necessarily due to the presence or absence of genuine
artistic worth, or even evidence of alternating spells of
good and bad taste. There were (and are) artists in every
age, but the social and technical conditions under which
they worked have constantly varied, and allowance must
be made for these. A type of art that unites beauty and usefulness without redundancy may perhaps imply a moral
excellence in the society that produces it, and may indeed
be the highest form of art; and it may well be argued, too,
that the artist is more fortunate if he works in a period of
simple taste—in a primitive period, in fact—rather than
in a sophisticated age, when an over-ripe technique or a
luxurious society may seduce him into a pointless, artistically irrelevant naturalism or into 'amusing' baroque extravagance. But even when 'allowance has been made' it
is extremely doubtful whether the essential art thus arrived

at can or should be judged by a single standard. A full discussion of this question would be out of place here, and I must be content to affirm that to me the different sorts of beauty in art are so many modes of expression of a creative force which I am content to call vitality, something I can recognise, but of which I can give no explanation whatever; that the several modes are as distinct and insusceptible of comparison in point of merit as are the modes of expression of that same force in Nature, where an attuned sensibility may indeed receive impressions of beauty not differing in essence from the impressions given by art; and that to pare down to a greatest common measure those varying modes, in the interests of a barren logic and consistency or a comprehensive theory of art, is, to me, to rob them of all that makes them vivid, sharp, and moving.

Nowhere is the single standard in criticism that seeks a common measure more misguided than in the ceramic art. It implies a single 'ideal pottery' towards which all the diverse types are assumed to aspire. The ideal pottery is, I believe, a linguistic fiction, the single word suggesting the single thing. Rough galena-glazed clay pots, smooth enamelled wares, painting with a big brush, enamel-painting in miniature style, figure-modelling of many kinds, each is *sui generis* and demands independent consideration. An educated taste will show suppleness and a point-of-view perpetually adjusted to each of these and many other sorts of accomplishment. This is indeed a test of education; those severe critics who make 'pure form' their criterion, or attempt to apply some *a priori* test of unity or fitness, in my experience invariably fail to distinguish the most admirable works in the modes they disapprove of from the crudest and most insincere imitations. They confuse Chelsea-Derby with Chelsea, and Thuringian with Meissen. The Germans have generally been aware of these necessities, and the great critic Lessing once wrote, in a passage which I owe to my friend Professor Max Sauerlandt: 'He has no taste whose taste is for one thing only. . . . True taste is all-embracing, comprehending beauty of every kind, never expecting from any a greater or different delight or satisfaction than it can by its nature give.'

But to impugn the single standard is not to abandon the right of criticism. Forms, though not supposed to aspire to 'right proportion' or an imagined 'perfection', must still be vital, true to themselves, and, as we say, sincere. Painting, though it may or may not derive an added grace from its fitness to a form or its relation to its framing, must delight us by its vigour or delicacy, charged with that life and significance which alone entitle it to be called art. Modelling may be still and monumental or it may be full of movement, but always making profiles and a composition of masses that have beauty and 'meaning' to a sensibility capable of judging it. And a piece of pottery may have some or all of these good qualities, even though it may have been derived, in details or in its entirety, from some other work, ceramic or engraved, as was so often the case. As Ruskin said in one of his inspired moments, 'Originality is not newness but genuineness'.

This book, then, is devoted to the description of the varying aesthetic qualities in English ceramic wares and their elucidation by history and classification. To help the collector to separate into groups the multifarious wares that confront him, each with its special qualities, is to go a long way in helping appreciation. This is the service which an historical study of the arts, and especially museums of art, should always render. Archaeology has different aims.

No general summary of the course of English ceramic history need be given here; it is sufficiently indicated in the chapter headings of this book. After a first mediaeval period it shows a constant reflection of European excitements, yet withal achieved a notable originality. Maiolica had relatively little influence, but Dutch Delftware inspired much, and the Chinese fashions were as potent here as elsewhere. Staffordshire in its rising time produced a distinguished and highly original body of work, and Wedgwood of course left his mark on the whole world.

. . . . . .

Technique in its various aspects is dealt with in the chapters following, but a few general notes may be useful here. Pottery is essentially clay baked to a certain degree of hardness, a quality varying as a rule with the intensity and duration of the firing. Clay may be either 'short' and non-plastic or 'fat' and cohesively retentive of its form, when shaped by throwing on the wheel, by modelling, by moulding, or by casting. White clays, unlike the commoner red ones, are usually lacking in plasticity. Clay may shrink much or little in the baking, and ground-up old pottery ('grog') is sometimes added to it to lessen the shrinkage of a body. Clays may be refractory, or they may be easily fusible from the presence of a flux, either metallic (such as an oxide of iron) or alkaline (such as lime); refractoriness may be increased by adding silica in the form of sand or quartz or (most notably in the case of the Staffordshire wares) calcined flints, which also increase whiteness. Firing may be light, or carried to a point where the clay fuses to a hard, impervious, vitrified mass, at which point earthenware becomes stoneware. Glazes are glasses usually containing lead and silica, sometimes made white and opaque by the addition of oxide (ashes) of tin, in which case they are called enamel. In recent times white

4

clays have been added to glazes with a similar effect. Pigments added over a glaze at a separate firing are also called enamel colours or, for brevity, enamels. Porcelain is strictly a special kind of stoneware made of a white refractory clay, produced by the decay of a feldspar and called after the Chinese *kaolin*, or, in England, 'china clay'; it is fused at a high temperature with the help of a less decayed feldspathic material called (again after the Chinese) *petuntse*, or china stone; the latter acts as a sort of cement, binding the particles of refractory clay. It is glazed with the *petuntse*, fluxed as a rule with lime and potash. Such 'true' porcelain is white and translucent and shows a conchoidal, or shell-like, fracture; it was called hard-paste by Alexandre Brongniart apparently because it requires a 'hard fire' (that is to say, a high temperature in the kiln) to fuse it, but the name is customarily taken to refer to its characteristic hardness to the file. 'Soft-pastes' are imitations of true porcelain made of ground-up glass of various composition mixed with white clay or other substances; they fuse at a low temperature and are glazed with easily fusible lead glazes. The white ash of calcined bones was a characteristic ingredient in some English soft-pastes, and was mixed with the ingredients of hard-paste in the nineteenth-century English 'hybrid' porcelain. Painting may be *under* a translucent glaze, *in* an opaque glaze (as in maiolica and delftware), or *over* either of them. In the first case it must be capable of withstanding the heat of the glaze-firing; in soft porcelain this limited the colours to cobalt blue and a rarely used manganese purple; in true porcelain, blue, and a copper red understood only by the Chinese and by modern European potters, virtually alone of colours used for painting (as distinct from coloured glazes) will withstand the very high temperature at which the glaze is fired. (Greens, browns, and blacks from iron have been used only in modern times in imitation of the early Chinese, and modern chemistry has of course provided other colours.) The maiolica- and delft-colours painted on the unfired enamel and fused into it ('high temperature colours') are limited to yellow, orange, and red from antimony and iron, cobalt blue, manganese purple, and copper green. The overglaze enamel colours are melted and caused to adhere to the glaze by refiring at a low temperature in a muffle-kiln; they provide an almost unlimited range of tones. Lustre colours are also added over the fired glaze, and consist of metallic films reduced from their oxides by re-firing in a smoky atmosphere; if thin they are iridescent, if thick they commonly show the colour of the metal used.

PART I

EARTHENWARE AND STONEWARE TO THE END OF THE EIGHTEENTH CENTURY

CHAPTER I

MEDIAEVAL AND EARLY RENAISSANCE
POTTERY

THOUGH fragments have occasionally been found
on sites of earlier date, it is not until the thirteenth
century is reached that pottery appears in England with
enough character and in sufficient quantity and complete-
ness to reveal a definitely national style. One may suppose
that it was little made. It is not merely that it was not
valued and preserved (the admirable wares dating from
the thirteenth to the fifteenth centuries are known only
from material found in excavations), but that an English
idiom in pottery had not been created. To account for the
origin of that art is as difficult as to explain the birth of
English poetry with Chaucer in the century following; it
is tempting to ascribe it to the genius of some individual
potter. It is remarkable that the French wares of the same
period, though made of much the same materials and
comprising vessels intended for the same purposes, show
an entirely different form-rhythm and proportion; and
this almost unanalysable character in form which distinguishes the national groups is something to be particularly noted. It persists throughout the history of English
pottery, and many instances will be given in the following
pages of foreign types imitated in England in which the
forms and decorations have been translated into an indefinable English idiom.

One of the earliest English styles has an easily recog-

9

nised character. The tall, slender pitchers of this group, with rim and base spreading about equally, are for the most part devoid of decoration, often indeed of bare grey or buff earthenware or thinly and partially covered with an imperfect green or yellow lead glaze. The common yellowish glaze was doubtless produced by dusting the raw clay pot with powdered galena (a natural sulphide of lead); the green probably by a dusting of copper filings before the application of the glaze. A find of coins of Henry III and Edward I in a jug now in the British Museum helps to confirm the dating of this 'slender' class. Many masterpieces could be cited. An exceedingly graceful buff pitcher with incurved lip, known to its admirers as the 'lady pot', is an old possession of the Victoria and Albert Museum and doubtless familiar to discerning visitors. One of the best of several in the London Museum, richest of all collections of mediaeval wares, is figured in Plate I, B. Some exceptionally slender green-glazed specimens in the Yorkshire Museum are thought by Mr. Arthur Hurst to have been 'dipping jugs', for lowering into wells. It is natural to assume that decoration, even of roulette-marked bands, implies a later date; but this is hazardous. On rare occasions a lighter or darker (probably ferruginous) clay was used on this 'slender' class for painting of bold stripes or trellis, or in scrolls recalling the thirteenth-century ironwork, but it is prudent to ascribe the group as a whole to a wide period, covered by the thirteenth and early part of the fourteenth century.

Whether any of the more capacious vessels can be of this early period is doubtful, though some good authorities have claimed certain classes as of twelfth- or thirteenth-century date. In my own opinion, there are usually technical features linking these supposedly early pieces with those undoubtedly of the fourteenth century and later, to be described presently. There is, I fear, a general tendency to date the mediaeval wares too early.

One curious class of vessels, for example, is often cited as of early thirteenth- or even twelfth-century date. This comprises the water-vessels or ewers, unnecessarily called aquamaniles, in the form of various beasts, such as a stag found at Seaford, two rams now at Scarborough, and the like. One at Salisbury is in the form of a knight on horseback and from the style of the armour has been confidently ascribed to the period mentioned. But this armour was probably rendered deliberately in archaic fashion, and the character of the decoration on most pieces of this class links it rather with the fourteenth-century wares described below. In style these animal-shaped ewers often recall the brass vessels of the time, kindred of the well-known *dinanderie*.

No finer use of clay in earthenware could well be found than in the best of the fourteenth-century jugs. The slender early type now gives place to more sturdy vessels of many fine shapes (Plate I, A and C), often boldly thumbed down at the base to provide a steady supporting 'foot-ring' and at the same time giving a free and pleasant wavy outline. Decoration takes the form of devices impressed in the clay of the pot itself—such as stars and circles, crosses and cross-hatching, as well as wheel-made lines and rouletted bands; or flat strips or bits of clay have been worked up with the fingers and applied to the body of the vessel and afterwards impressed with various patterns of the kind mentioned. Some of the most charming designs are made of very simple rosettes. The placing of this decoration in the finest pieces shows a masterly feeling for proportion and emphasis of form, and coloured clays, chiefly reds and buffs, serve to give life and accent to the admirable designs (Fig. 1). Some jugs have bits of clay applied all over, like scales, to form a sort of pine-cone pattern; on others, more ambitious, heraldic beasts and even figures were shaped and applied in low relief; or the pots themselves were formed into stylised human figures or

FIG. 1. MEDIAEVAL JUG. 14TH CENTURY

faces. A quite exceptional but noteworthy pot of this order is in the Nottingham Museum, in the form of a double-head cleanly stylised in almost a negro idiom. For glazes dull yellow-browns and speckled greens are characteristic; the green was sometimes used with fine judgement to colour the vertical bands only. Many of the forms show the simple use of an art, seen at its most elaborate in some of the Rhenish stonewares, by which the profile is built up 'architecturally' of subtly contrasted members brought into vital relation, now smoothly melting together, now breaking away in sharp angles. This is the potter's art at its highest. A lack of precision in workmanship or of refinement in material does not in the least diminish the aesthetic merit of the best of these fourteenth-century wares. Painting, strictly so called, was quite exceptional. Strong scrollwork in thirteenth-fourteenth-century style, in dark brown slip on a lighter body, is seen notably on some wares found in excavations at Cheam, in Surrey, but the technique was doubtless used in other places. A quite exceptional and rare class of jugs, claimed also as of French origin, shows painting of rough arabesque foliations over a white slip (that is, a thin wash or coating of white clay) in green, brown, and manganese-purple in a style which astonishingly recalls the so-called Orvieto maiolica of Italy; their forms, too, with large and ugly projecting lip-spout, are quite similar. The chief examples are a jug found in London, at the Guildhall Museum, and several others (London Museum, Cardiff Museum, and elsewhere) found at seaport towns, a circumstance suggesting that they were importations. One of the most remarkable is a fragmentary jug said to have been found at Exeter, with figures of bishops and musicians in full relief. In spite of features suggesting an earlier date, I believe this to be an archaistic work, certainly not made before the fourteenth century. In spite of their evident kinship with them, they differ markedly from the wares of Italy and Spain, and, whether English or French, are evidence of the extraordinarily wide vogue of this 'green and purple' decoration in the latter part of the fourteenth and the fifteenth centuries. In the Mediterranean area it was almost universally in favour.

The fifteenth-century wares are distinguishable, if at

all, from those of the preceding period, chiefly by shape. The thumbed-down foot is less common; a cylindrical-necked form of globular jug apparently belongs to this period, and the green glaze becomes usual (Fig. 2). In the sixteenth century, with the movement towards refinement that came with the Tudors, smaller, neater jugs are

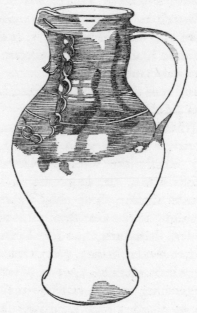

FIG. 2. MEDIAEVAL JUG. 15TH CENTURY

found, as well as many entirely new shapes. The green glaze, now generally richer in tone but still inclined to be speckled, enjoyed the same popularity as on the Continent, where in Germany, at Nuremberg and elsewhere, it was used very notably on the great stoves of the period, and in France the Saintonge peasant-pottery provided the ground from which the more famous Palissy wares were developed. The French and German pottery with elaborate moulded relief decoration finds its counterpart in England in some rare cisterns, flat pilgrim-bottles, candle-brackets, and stove-tiles, with Tudor arms, roses, and other devices, which have sometimes been regarded as actually foreign work. But the style of lettering and other details point to an English origin. The green glaze was, of course, not exclusively in favour. A clear buff (again recalling the German) is found as well as the green on the relief-decorated wares, and some brown- and black-glazed vessels are important as providing a link with some of the most distinctive of all English pottery—the slipware of the seventeenth and eighteenth centuries. A notable piece, almost unique as a nearly complete survivor of what must have been a numerous class, is a jug in the Victoria and Albert Museum, found at Wittington (Bucks), with a grape-vine pattern trailed in thick white slip over a red body under a yellow glaze. More numerous are the wares loosely grouped under the name Cistercian, commonly but by no means exclusively found on abbey sites. Fountains and Kirkstall were excavated by Mr. J. T. Micklethwaite, who first called attention to the class. These wares have a hard red body with a very dark brown, almost black, glaze, which in one sub-variety often survives in mirror-like brilliance, though much of the ware must date back to the sixteenth or, at latest, early seventeenth century. Wide double-curved cups and tall mugs (Fig. 3) provided with several loop handles, of the form known as tygs (a word supposed to be derived from the Anglo-Saxon *tigel*, a tile or brick, or anything made of clay), are the most usual shapes, but some tall cylindrical mugs with hoops, apparently imitating wooden tankards, are also distinctive and are of the true Cistercian type with a glaze of metallic or blacklead-like appearance. A decoration of small circular patches of white clay, appearing yellow under the glaze, anticipates the later slipware. A large collection of the tygs, which are commonly of fine proportions, is in the London Museum; they were perhaps the secular imitations of Cistercian ware.

Artistically of slight importance and possibly of French origin are some long pear-shaped pilgrim-bottles with suspension loops, known as costrels, with marbled decoration in mingled red and white slips. These are often found

FIG. 3. TYG. 16TH OR 17TH CENTURY

in London excavations, and are apparently of sixteenth-century date.

Little can be affirmed at present as to the places of manufacture of this pottery, though the results of Mr. G. C. Dunning's researches, which it is hoped may shortly be published, will doubtless throw much light on this question. The London-found specimens are the most numerous, as the collections in the Guildhall and London Museums bear witness, and include most of the types

16

found elsewhere. Kiln-sites have been explored at Cheam, Nottingham, and various places in Cambridgeshire, but I think it likely that the finer pieces were taken to distant markets, and a local origin cannot be presumed for any of the finds on other than the kiln-sites.

Something must be said about the English mediaeval tiles, though they are a large subject by themselves. By far the most important of these were decorated by inlaying with white clay a pattern impressed apparently with wood-blocks into the surface of the tile, in a technique sometimes quite inappropriately called 'encaustic', which merely means burnt. It would be out-of-place here to specify the multitude of heraldic, foliate, and pictorial designs found on these over a period of three centuries or more, or to mention the many abbey and other sites where they have come to light. Some of the earliest have admirably stylised beasts, shields of arms, and scrolled foliage. Perhaps the most famous of all are the Chertsey Abbey tiles with elaborate designs illustrating the Tristram story and the life of Richard Cœur de Lion; their recurrence at Halesowen together with an inscription referring to Abbot Nicholas of that place gives a precise date (about 1290) for the series, and suggests that the craftsmen carried their wood-blocks from place to place. Other patterns commonly recur at widely separated places. It is less likely that the tiles themselves were distributed so far and wide, since their technique readily allowed of their local manufacture. Some delightful hunting-scenes with clowns and dogs (from Neath Abbey), and some firmly drawn maple and other foliage are among the best designs on the fourteenth-century tiles, while the fantasies on the profuse crocketed pinnacles of the Perpendicular architecture (as on the fine tiles from Great Malvern Priory) may be cited as typical of the fifteenth century, after the close of which the inlaid type went quickly out of favour. A rare fourteenth-century class found at Tring Church (specimens in the British Museum and Victoria and Albert Museum) is decorated in *sgraffito*—that is to say, the designs were cut with a pointed instrument through a coating of white slip—with scenes from the Apocryphal Infancy Gospels. Tiles with designs in countersunk relief were never as popular in England as in France and Germany. But specimens with relief designs of the same character as the inlaid are found from the thirteenth century onwards; they were in fact made by a kindred technique of impressing with wood-blocks, and the type remained in favour long after the others had ceased to be made. Some examples from Devonshire, surprisingly bearing the date 1708, prove the late continuance of this mediaeval style.

CHAPTER II

SLIPWARE AND OTHER PEASANT POTTERY OF THE SEVENTEENTH CENTURY ONWARDS

MENTION has already been made of the mediaeval use on occasion of slip and of clays of contrasting colour. These were the resources by which the village potters of England in the seventeenth century developed a number of elaborate and often fantastic styles which are of the greatest importance in English ceramic history. Elaborate slipware was, it is true, made abroad in the same period and is sometimes of much merit, but none of it shows quite the same appreciation of the possibilities of the pure clay technique it employs, and certain devices, such as combing and feathering and the accenting of designs with white dots, were seldom or never used outside England. It is natural, therefore, that collectors and lovers of English pottery should value slipware perhaps more than any other type, and that the contempt of such foreign critics as Hannover and Hudig should seem to them misguided and absurd. To a generation accepting the genius of Henri Matisse, for example, it should be obvious that vitality and freedom of drawing are virtues heavily outweighing 'refinement' and mechanical finish. They, and a rare charm of colour, are the virtues of the best slipware.

It must not be supposed, however, that the elaborately made pieces now treasured by collectors were anything but the occasional work of the potters, whose regular output was doubtless such undecorated crockery as flower-

19

pots and bread-pans, or even bricks and tiles. Staffordshire butter-pots—plain rough cylinders—were well known in the Midlands in the seventeenth century, and on the site of the Wrotham potteries were found amongst other things many plain glazed cups and plates with raised concentric rings for feeding chickens. The now-valued slipwares were the show-pieces of these village potters, made as gifts to patron or landlord, or for weddings, christenings, or other special occasions. The common pots if we could recover them would no doubt show the same sure craftsmanship and fine proportions as the earlier mediaeval wares.

The earliest and most easily defined group is formed by the wares of Wrotham (pronounced Root-ham), a village in Kent between Sevenoaks and Maidstone. The late Dr. Glaisher made excavations in the village, extracted the names of potters from the parish registers, and tabulated the initials which occur on the surviving pieces, with the result that we can trace the activity of two remarkable artists—George Richardson (*d.* 1687) and Nicholas Hubble (*d.* 1689), who flourished from about 1640 onwards. It is clear, however, that the initials inscribed on the pottery were not always those of the makers, and it is important to bear this in mind in the case of the Staffordshire slipware to be discussed presently. One recorded Wrotham pot of 1642 is of special interest since it bears the initials of George Richardson, together with those of Mary Hubble, whom he married a few months after the date on the pot. Nicholas Hubble may have been his partner. The pot has a further interest as evidence of the complete untrustworthiness of the self-styled historian of Staffordshire pottery, 'Dr.' Simeon Shaw, whose statements have been uncritically accepted by almost all writers on the subject. Shaw declared that this undoubted Wrotham tyg, now unfortunately lost, was made 'at the Green

Head, Burslem', and (in familiar words) had been in some local person's family 'for over a hundred years'.

How soon Wrotham pottery began is a matter of interesting conjecture. A rare class of sixteenth-century tin-enamelled jugs, to be discussed in the next chapter, commonly bearing silver mounts, is in several instances associated with this district and is often thought to be of Kentish origin. Now one of the earliest of these mounted jugs (bearing the hall-mark for 1547–48), though of the usual form, is not of enamelled ware but has a greenish-brown lead-glaze, and its close resemblance to an undoubted Wrotham-marked jug in the Glaisher Collection was pointed out by Mr. Bernard Rackham. The latter jug, however, bears the initials of George Richardson and therefore dates from the mid-seventeenth century; Mr. William Ridout has suggested to me that the other is a replacement of that or later date. No other sixteenth-century pieces of this kind are known, and the matter must remain undecided. It may prove that Richardson's immediate predecessors 'I L' (perhaps a John Livermore) and 'H I' (probably Henry Ifield) were not the first Wrotham potters, but only the first to mark their wares. The dated and well-authenticated pieces begin with a tyg of 1612 marked 'I L', in the Liverpool Museum. This is a good representative of the cleaner productions of the earlier period. Applied pads of white pipe-clay were stamped with flowers, stars, 'raspberries', rosettes, and devices sometimes apparently moulded from metal-work (such as bronze mortars and bells) or from the Rhenish stoneware, which had enjoyed a market in England since the sixteenth century. The shield of arms of Amsterdam on a tyg in the British Museum was probably moulded in this way from a Rhenish piece. A curious device seen only on Wrotham ware is the 'stitching', in short strokes of white round the thick reliefs, suggested no doubt by the stump-work embroidery of the time. The handles were some-times similarly stitched over or inlaid with twisted double ropes of red and white clay. But these wares in their total effect arc in no way copies of anything. Their aesthetic value is not always great. At their best it depends largely on the freedom, boldness, and fine spacing of the inscrip-tions and large dots of white which were 'trailed' on (*i.e.* poured at close range from a spouted vessel) in semi-liquid state, in the true slip technique. The process is very similar to that of icing a cake and requires as much dexterity. The longest of the Wrotham inscriptions is on a huge 'cistern' of 1678 in the British Museum; it reads 'THE RIT GENNRAL CORNAL OF ER THE DROUNKEN REGMENT', with a letter or two appropriately displaced. One would like to know the identity of the $\frac{W}{WE}$ for whom this was made by Nicholas Hubble. The second oldest dated piece (1614) is quite un-usual. It is a large globular jug in the Victoria and Albert Museum with a grotesque mask on the front touched with white clay but elsewhere covered with a lustrous dark brown glaze. Among the applied reliefs are the initials 'I L'. Apart from this the Wrotham wares show the warm deep red-browns and yellows of the typical galena-glazed red earthenware. The forms of the early tygs (which again recall mortars), posset-pots, cups, and other pieces are dis-tinctive, but of no special beauty in themselves. The candle-sticks, which are peculiar to Wrotham, are among the most effective. The later pieces with dates down to 1721 were apparently the work of an unidentified successor of Richardson and Hubble—one 'I E'—and are decidedly less skilfully made; but there are some simple trailed designs chiefly of lettering and formal flowers (as on a posset-pot of 1703 at S. Kensington) which are admirably set out. The only recorded Wrotham dish (in the British Museum), made by 'I E' in 1699, is also unique in being decorated by incising the design, of formal flowers, through a coating of white clay slip, in the *sgraffito* technique.

Contemporary with the best Wrotham is the pale red-brown and white 'Metropolitan' slipware, found in London excavations, with dates from 1630 to about 1670, the later being the commoner. For decoration, if it can be so called, they bear inscriptions in trailed slip, most often of scriptural texts and pious exhortations, with some very plain flowers, stars, and coils, in lettering that is without much grace. They serve to remind us that this was the period when an overmastering Puritanism brought a distrust of beauty. Cups, mugs, and jugs are the most usual forms, but Richard Jocelyn's posset-pot ('FEAR GOD', 1633) in the Glaisher Collection, though decorated in Wrotham style, is undoubtedly Metropolitan, and there is a porringer of 1659 in the British Museum inappropriately inscribed 'FAST AND PRAY'. Mr. Lomax conjectured that the manufacture came to an end with the Great Fire in 1666.

Next in sequence comes a great and varied body of pieces most of which may be associated with Staffordshire, though several groups are still persistently ascribed to places in Derbyshire and elsewhere. The ascription of some pieces to Cockpit Hill in the town of Derby was apparently due to the local patriotism of William Bemrose, and to the absurd supposition that the subject of a cock indicates this factory. Pottery was undoubtedly made at Cockpit Hill, but at a much later date; Mr. F. Williamson has, I think, finally disposed of the legend of the Derby slipware. Most of the dishes with notched edge confidently ascribed to Tickenhall by Bemrose and Jewitt can be definitely associated with Staffordshire potters, as will be shown presently. Some peculiar early seventeenth-century

tygs may, however, have been made at Tickenhall, and
these are interesting as close followers of the Cistercian
wares described in the previous chapter. Pads of white
clay were applied and cut out to the desired shape—
rosettes and stags' heads are common motives—and the
whole covered with yellow glaze. The material was a
relatively hard red earthenware appearing dark brown
under the rough glaze. The characteristic form was a
two-handled, nearly cylindrical mug. Some globular jugs
with cylindrical neck and simple trailed decoration are also
doubtfully ascribed to Tickenhall. A Staffordshire origin
seems more probable for these, and for some very attractive
covered pots or honey-jars with simple patterns of dots
and stripes of slip placed with a nice sense of proportion,
which fully maintain the tradition of the mediaeval wares.

The Staffordshire slipwares are an intricate study, with
many problems still to solve. The whole class (or group of
classes) was at one time broadly called Toft ware, from the
name occurring on some of the most elaborate and characteristic pieces. But it is certain that much was the work of
other potters, and indeed it cannot be proved that the
Tofts were potters at all, or at any rate that they worked in
Staffordshire. No trace of the name has yet come to light
in the Potteries (Solon's Tinker's Clough was a pure invention), while the researches of Mr. S. A. H. Burne and
Mr. G. P. Mander have shown that several Tofts (including a Thomas and a Ralph) were living at Leek and
Rushton Spencer, near Macclesfield, during the period in
question, and were not described as potters. Since other
closely similar dishes bear the names of known Burslem
potters, it is at least possible that the Toft dishes were
made for and not by the persons of that name; the presence
of women's names alone would make it clear that those of
recipients were sometimes inscribed. On the other hand a

dish at Chester has Thomas Toft's name as well as those of 'Filep' and 'Elesabath Heves'.

Before passing to the consideration of the numerous slipwares grouped under the name of Toft, I must mention some odd green-glazed puzzle-jugs which are usually cited as the earliest dated Staffordshire pottery. Two of these have sixteenth-century dates in applied relief: one of 1569 is in the Lomax Collection, the other of 1571 is in the Victoria and Albert Museum, while another in the latter collection bears the name of 'John Wedgwood' and the date 1691 incised. This Wedgwood was not, however, of the Staffordshire branch of the family, but a potter of Walmgate, York, whose history has been recorded by Mr. Oxley Grabham. Much of this mediaeval-looking green-glazed Yorkshire ware survives in the form of big jars or milk-pots decorated with rosettes. The close similarity of the dated jugs mentioned makes it almost incredible that they are of such widely separated periods, and but for the fact that the South Kensington Jug was acquired for the Jermyn Street Collection before 1871 it would be tempting to regard it as a more than usually successful production of the infamous Castle Hedingham.

The 'Toft wares' in general owe their attractiveness not to any special beauty of form but to the vitality and freedom of their decoration, in which new resources unknown to the Wrotham potters were employed. Not only white slip on dark grounds but red and brown clays were used on a ground made light-coloured by a wash of white, while in some rare cases a greyish olive-green appears, curiously marked with a pattern of canvas mesh. The colours were trailed on with the utmost skill, and the designs were as a rule charmingly accented with lines of white dots, while the alternation of light on dark and dark on light gave a further resource. The wares actually bearing the name of

25

Toft are for the most part large dishes, though there is a loving-cup in the Yorkshire Museum, and Mr. Lomax had a jug. The designs range from the rampant lion of the well-known South Kensington dish to formal patterns of foliage, as on another dish belonging to Mr. Lomax. Grotesque heads were a favourite motive, and Adam and Eve, a mermaid (Plate II, A), a spread eagle, and King Charles in the Oak are among the subjects drawn on the dishes, always in an entirely unacademic style. Surely executed borders of criss-cross in warm red are very characteristic, and, as on the Wrotham wares, the bold inscriptions are particularly effective. The pieces with the name of Toft are seldom dated; there is, however, a Thomas Toft dish of 1671 at Chester and another in Mr. Cyril Andrade's collection dated 1674, while there are Ralph Toft dishes of 1676, 1677, and 1683. The closely kindred pieces with other names (which include those of the well-known Burslem potters' families of Simpson, Glass, and Meir, amongst others) bear dates between 1676 and 1707; survivors of 1707 and 1709 (John and William Wright) can scarcely be separated from the main body. It is impossible in most cases to be sure whether a name is that of maker or recipient. I think it is significant that in a list of Burslem potters of about 1710, compiled by Josiah Wedgwood, only Richard and J. Simpson are described as makers of red dishes.

In the latter part of this period and for a few years later appear some even more attractive wares employing a similar technique, in the form of wide-mouthed posset-pots and loving-cups with several handles and crinkled vertical bands, globular jugs usually small, cups or mugs (Plate II, B and C), cream-piggins, jugs in the form of owls, gadrooned and other dishes, and miniature cradles, made doubtless for christenings. They are inscribed with many

PLATE II   *See pages 26, 27*

(*a*) DISH. STAFFORDSHIRE SLIPWARE. ABOUT 1675
Victoria and Albert Museum

(*b*) POSSET-POT. STAFFORDSHIRE SLIPWARE   (*c*) CUP. STAFFORDSHIRE SLIP-
EARLY 18TH CENTURY   WARE. ABOUT 1700
Victoria and Albert Museum   *Victoria and Albert Museum*

good Staffordshire names—such as Joshua Heath (Plate II, B), William Chatterley, 'Robart' Shaw, etc. Tulips and formal flowers are new and favourite motives, and to the technical resources of trailing, dotting, striping, and counterchange of colour are added a wealth of impressed patterns, usually circular and enclosing wheels, crosses, rosettes, and mushroom-like devices, and (most notably) a free use of feathering and combing of the slip. This last process is closely similar to that used for the marbling of paper, the semi-liquid clay colours being worked into a pattern with a brush or stick. In this class of slipware it was commonly done with great delicacy and discretion; in some instances nearly symmetrical patterns like the barbs of a feather were produced. The combing technique in its simpler forms continued in use in many places until quite recent times, for the decoration notably of large concave oval meat- or pie-dishes, made for country markets. But the late seventeenth- and early eighteenth-century feathered posset-pot class (as we may call it), with its varied resources and abundant fancy, in my opinion represents the highest level of quality reached in English slipware.

Designs simply trailed in white or red slip, without dots or counterchange of colour on the same piece, gave the greatest opportunity for the display of skill in the swift application of the fluid slip. There is a famous dish in the Lomax Collection with an admirably stylised running hare (white on brown); a dish at Northampton with a strong floral design shows the same mastery. These and others similar are almost certainly of late seventeenth-century date, but the type persisted at least until 1796, the date on a dish with a cock and the initials of Enoch Wood (Lomax Collection). Some of these have been called Tickenhall and (quite absurdly) Cockpit Hill, though the characteristic notched edge is a link with the class of moulded dishes

27

described below of which the Staffordshire origin is practically certain. It is not impossible, however, that these late 'trailed' dishes were made outside the Potteries, where by this time a much more civilised type of ware was being made. To the end they retained the rich colour of the original type, with the warm red and brown slips admirably harmonising with the soft yellow glaze.

The moulded dishes bear dates between about 1725 and 1755. The designs were outlined in relief in such a way as to limit the flow of the slip, which was applied in patches rather than trailed. This skill-saving device robs the work of much of its vitality, though the charm of colour and unsophisticated design still remains. A mould in the British Museum, inscribed '*William Bird made me 1751*', with a design of a man in a frockcoat, and a dish apparently made with it, in the Manchester Art Gallery, clearly illustrate the technique, with curious notched grooves giving a 'milled' edge to the outlines; while another similar mould at the Victoria and Albert Museum with the name of Thomas Wedgwood (perhaps Dr. Thomas, *d.* 1737) is virtually proof of its Staffordshire origin. The initials of Samuel Meir (of a well-known Staffordshire family), and the 'R S' for Ralph Shaw or Ralph Simpson, also point in the same direction. The designs of birds and formal plants ('*One burd: in The: hand* . . .'), crude sun-faces, horsemen (including St. George), Charles in the Oak Tree, etc., have at least a primitive simplicity. Depressions are generally seen at the back of the dishes where the clay was pressed into the hollows of the mould. A pattern of pomegranates usually signed 'I S' is of a kindred but not quite certainly the same class. The mark 'S I' (or 'S F') cited in many books is a fiction due to the reversing of 'I S' in Solon's etching of one of these designs.

A very distinct class, undoubtedly of Staffordshire

origin, with dates from 1747 to 1779, is usually, but in my opinion wrongly, associated with Ralph Shaw, who left for France after the failure in 1736 of a lawsuit in defence of his patent of three years earlier. The lawsuit is well known in Simeon Shaw's comic account. In it Ralph was refused, 'with acclamations and strongest ebullitions of satisfactions' from the other potters, the exclusive right to make a 'strip'd ware' formed of clays 'mix't and incorporated together', and 'glazed with salt', by processes stated in the suit to have been in common use at the time. I think that the so-called solid agate ware (to be described in a subsequent chapter) was probably in question. The specimens now to be described are with one known exception (in Mr. Wallace Elliot's collection) lead-glazed, and as stated above bear dates much later than the lawsuit. The usual forms are bowls and jugs, decorated with simple *sgraffito* designs of animals and birds, flowers and foliage, and occasionally vertical stripes. These last cannot very well be the 'stripes' of Shaw's patent, which were not a pattern but a process. A line of moulded beading is sometimes found, and bands of checker were very effectively used. The class lacks the variety of colour of the earlier wares, and its effect is in comparison a little hard; its generally tidied-up appearance, in fact, proclaims its kinship with the already half-commercialised wares of Wedgwood and his contemporaries.

Another class of *sgraffito* wares, of much greater merit, consists of cylindrical mugs, dishes, and globular posset-pots with designs of animals and formal foliage cut through a rich dark-brown slip and covered with a warm glaze of lighter brown. In colour and freedom of drawing these are particularly charming. Though generally ascribed to Staffordshire, they show some affinity with Tickenhall. They date from the early eighteenth century.

A small class of great interest is associated with the name of Hugheson (or Hucheson). There are some Samuel Hugheson jugs dated 1677 and 1678, and a John Hugheson posset-pot of 1691; a John Wenter jug of 1686 (British Museum) and an Ann Benom posset-pot (1687) are of the same origin. The characteristic decoration is of bands of slip stamped with lozenges and crosses and clusters of radiating lines; and the glaze shows patches of bright green. The impressed patterns closely correspond with those on a Toft piece, and a Staffordshire origin was therefore suggested by Mr. Rackham, but the admirable shape of the jugs and the use of green recall the Devon and Somerset wares, and they may prove to have been made in the West of England.

The Devonshire (Bideford, Fremington, and Barn-staple) wares, chiefly 'harvest' jugs of generous capacity, with a characteristic bold coil at the base of the handle, are more noteworthy for their excellence of form than for their decoration, which consists of somewhat untidy *sgraffito* designs, amongst the motives of which a mariner's compass is perhaps not surprising. Some yellow-glazed large loving-cups with amusingly crude figures applied should also be mentioned.

The wares of Crock Street and Donyat in Somerset and of Pencoed and Ewenny in Glamorgan show a similar technique, but are more varied—puzzle-jugs and dishes of peculiar form being made in Somerset, as well as the usual harvest jugs. The bright yellow glaze was some-times stained with patches of green. The finest Somerset piece known to me is a dish in the Taunton Museum with wide-skirted figures; this is dated 1685, but most of the surviving specimens are of eighteenth- and early nineteenth-century date. A pottery at Honiton in Devonshire also made similar *sgraffito* wares with deep yellow glaze: there is a marked jug apparently of early nineteenth-century date in Mr. W. W. Winkworth's collection.

The so-called Fareham posset-pots, which also may prove to be of West of England origin, are decorated with large-lettered inscriptions, bars and bands, of various coloured clays (including green) applied and stamped with a crinkled chain-pattern, under a greenish toned glaze. The dates 1706, 1707, and 1711 are recorded.

The dark purple-brown (manganese-glazed) Wiltshire wares, made by one W. Zillwood probably at Clarendon or Amesbury, or elsewhere in the neighbourhood of Salisbury, include the well-known and delightful christening goblets (*'Here is the gest of the Barly Corne Glad Ham I the cild is born 1692. I G. R K. S K'*).

Apart from the distinctive classes so far described, a great many specimens of slipware survive which cannot be ascribed to any locality, while others with traditional ascriptions conform to general types of the period. This is true of most of the wares of Sussex and the Kentish border, which are of many types, never very elaborate but sharing to the full the warm colour of their class. Rye, Dicker, Chailey, and Burgess Hill were (and still are) centres of manufacture. One type only, formerly called Brede, but now ascribed to Bethersden, is outstanding, with very charming patterns of sprays of foliage or stylised trees, stars, and printer's type inscriptions impressed in the red body and filled with white clay. (These colours were sometimes reversed.) Dates range from the late eighteenth century until about 1810 or later. At Gestingthorpe in Essex and Buckland Common near Aylesbury ('Thomas Brackley, potter') dark-brown wares were made, and at Howcans and Swill Hill near Halifax, Burton in Lonsdale, Midhope near Sheffield, Blackburton in the West Riding, Polesworth in Warwickshire, Gorsty Hill in

Worcestershire, Bolsover in Derbyshire, and many other places in the Midlands and North, simple trailed, striped, and marbled slipware continued to be made for local markets until quite recent times. The dark-brown-and-white Howcans wares include some curious wide-mouthed salt 'kits', sometimes called ballot-boxes, usually with dates about 1850 to 1890. Combed and feathered oval meat-dishes continued to be made under the name of 'Welsh ware' at Isleworth, and some marked Sunderland pieces (Scott's 'Superior Fireproof') show the type taken over by the modern industrial potter.

All the wares described in this chapter belong to peasant pottery and have the virtues usually found in it, of sincerity and freedom from fashionable affectations. Not all of them attain the rank of works of art, since the potters were not necessarily always artists. But at their best they show a fresh uncramped feeling for shape and rhythm, notably in the irregular and quite unacademic lettering. Their colour is that of true earthenware, with predominating warm tones of golden yellow, amber, red, and brown. Apart from its intrinsic merit, the outstanding Staffordshire slipware is also important as the ground from which sprang the great industry which takes so overwhelmingly important a place in the later history of ceramic art in England, and indeed in all Europe. But the attempts sometimes made to 'revive' such peasant art in England to-day must fail, in my opinion, for two reasons: on the technical side the potters are virtually compelled to work with factory-refined materials, lacking the 'impurities' which gave quality to the old wares, and on the other hand their sophisticated productions, made for a luxury market, must lack the economic necessity which made the crafts-manship of the old potters so genuine a thing in its day.

CHAPTER III

ENGLISH MAIOLICA AND DELFTWARE CHIEFLY
OF THE SEVENTEENTH AND EIGHTEENTH
CENTURIES

THE latter part of the fifteenth and the sixteenth
centuries witnessed the rise in Italy, and the rapid
spread over most of the countries of Europe, of the craft
of tin-enamelled pottery, and (more significantly) of the
art of painting it in bright colours. In France and Spain,
in Tyrol, at Nuremberg, and above all in the Netherlands, this novel painted white pottery was greatly in
vogue, and distinct national styles were developed for its
decoration. In England, however, the wave of fashion did
not come until considerably later, when the force of the
original Italian outburst was almost spent. The Netherlands potteries (which were at first situated chiefly in
Antwerp and by the second half of the seventeenth century
were centred in Delft) soon took the lead in northern
Europe, and their example was paramount in the relatively
few English wares of recognisably Italian derivation.
There is in fact record, in Stow's *Survey*, of a Jasper
Andries and a Jacob Janson settling in Norwich in 1567
and moving to London, by the river-side, in 1570. They
were described as of Antwerp, but the former was almost
certainly a kinsman of the Italian Guido Andries (Guido
da Savino of Castel Durante) by whom the Netherlandish
maiolica industry was founded. Nothing is yet certainly
known of their work. A cleanly painted tile in the Victoria

3

and Albert Museum, one of two known examples, with the crest, arms, and motto of the Bacon family, came from Gorhambury, near St. Albans, a house which was building in 1563–68, just after Andries and Janson came to Norwich, and it may be their work. These two tiles stand alone, however; they do not closely resemble anything else surviving, and the 'gally paving tiles' and 'vessels for apothecaries' said to have been made by the two potters remain for the present unidentified.

For the sixteenth century besides there is Solon's statement that a Netherlands potter was at Sandwich in 1582, and Chaffers' reference to another at Maidstone in the same year; neither writer gives any authority, and one was perhaps copying the other. If there actually were maiolica potters in Kent at this time and earlier, and it is not at all improbable in view of the geographical situation of the county, this would give a possible origin for the much-discussed class of silver- and pewter-mounted jugs already referred to in connection with Wrotham. These are imitations in a very different material of the Rhenish stoneware ('tiger-ware') jugs with globular bodies and wide cylindrical necks, then being imported into England and apparently much prized. The tin-enamelled (pompously, 'stanniferous') ware of which they are made is technically similar to maiolica, which may be defined as a more or less soft, low-fired earthenware covered with a lead-glaze made white and opaque with oxide (ashes) of tin; painting may be added on this tin-enamel before firing, and the absorbent character of the surface exacts a sure and unhesitating touch on the part of the painter. The 'high-temperature colours' thus used are limited to cobalt-blue, manganese-purple, yellows and browns from antimony and iron, green from copper, and more rarely a red, again from iron. The Delft ware was made in the same way but

34

with the object of imitating porcelain, necessitating greater care and refinement in the preparation of the materials; it was at first devoted to blue-painting in the Chinese style, but in the eighteenth century painting in enamel colours over the already fired glaze came into use (though never in England) in emulation of European porcelain. In English usage the terms maiolica and delftware (with a small initial) are conveniently adopted to distinguish respectively the polychrome wares more or less in the Italian tradition, and those following the Chinese mode introduced by the potters of Delft. As Mr. Bernard Rackham has pointed out, the customary term 'Lambeth delft' is a misnomer, since the most characteristic pottery attributed to 'Lambeth' in the seventeenth century is in styles derived from the Italian, and much of it dates from before the rise of Delft. It should be noted that the maiolica dishes are in general much heavier in build than the delftware, and are enamelled only on the front, the back being covered with a yellowish lead-glaze. In Holland they were the work of a distinct class of potters (who also made tiles), opposed to the 'porselein'-makers.

It is a remarkable fact that the earliest of all English specimens in this technique should be these mounted jugs, which are neither Italian nor Netherlandish in style. They are disclaimed by the Dutch and German authorities, and their mounts and provenance make their English origin almost certain. In my opinion, moreover, their shapes have already acquired something of an English character. Besides those with enamel splashed with blue and purple, blue, yellow, and brown, or with blue only, in distant imitation of the markings on the stoneware, they sometimes show enamels coloured in their substance deep blue or turquoise, the latter in a specimen in the silver collection at South Kensington being of great beauty; a brown lead-glazed specimen was also mentioned in the previous chapter. The dates on the mounts range from 1549–50 (on one in the Franks Collection at the British Museum) onwards into the seventeenth century. The Kentish provenance of at least three specimens, of which

FIG. 4. SILVER-MOUNTED TIN-ENAMELLED-WARE JUG. 16TH CENTURY

that formerly at West Malling Church gives its name to the type, has caused the class to be linked both with the supposed Sandwich-Maidstone potter of 1582 and with the later Wrotham industry. But all this is conjecture. A 'Malling jug' of 1550 in the Swaythling Collection (Fig. 4) was sold for five hundred and sixty guineas. With their fine silver mounts they are very beautiful things.

That maiolica potters were established early in the

PLATE III

See pages 38, 39, 41

(*a*) JUG. LAMBETH DELFT
DATED 1628
Victoria and Albert Museum

(*b*) WINE-BOTTLE. LAMBETH DELFT
DATED 1647
Victoria and Albert Museum

(*c*) DISH ('BLUE-DASH CHARGER'). BRISLINGTON OR BRISTOL
SECOND HALF OF 17TH CENTURY
Brig.-General Sir Gilbert Mellor's Collection

seventeenth century on the southern bank of the Thames, not only at Lambeth but at Southwark and Bermondsey also (though 'Lambeth' is a convenient designation for all), seems certain from Stow's record and from the results of excavations. The few surviving early specimens in Italian-Dutch style, doubtless made in this locality, have often been discussed and need detain us here only for their interest as the source of more purely English types.

The earliest dated piece is a dish of 1601, in the London Museum, with a much stylised rendering of a town supposed to be London, within a border of strap-work and arabesques somewhat in Antwerp style. No other similar piece is known. A dish in the Glaisher Collection in the Fitzwilliam Museum at Cambridge with a Faenza-Venice design of parti-coloured foliage is inscribed 'ANNO DODN 1620'; and a dish, dated 1640, formerly in the J. H. Taylor Collection, bears a Netherlands version of another Venetian decoration in a sumptuous design of fruit—pomegranates, grapes, etc.—within a border of painted gadroons. A jug in Colonel John Parker's collection with the same sort of decoration has a portrait of a young man in early seventeenth-century costume. All these are distinguishable as English and not Dutch by slight indications hardly amounting to national characteristics.

A beautiful undated dish in the British Museum, with the subject of Adam and Eve and the Tree of Knowledge, though rendered almost in Italian style, is important as the first of a series of many less accomplished but very characteristic English versions. One of the earliest of these, dated 1635, is in the Victoria and Albert Museum, and ranks with a beautiful plate in the same collection painted with the Magdalen in a stylised landscape (1637) among the first purely English pictorial pieces. Their full-toned colour, dominated by a splendid green, is as strong and vital as their drawing. Another dish, also at South Kensington, with a family group dated 1614, is the forerunner of a considerable class, most of them with much later dates. Such big dishes, archaistically named 'chargers' by the late Father Downman, who so devotedly collected them, are the seventeenth-century English bourgeois equivalents of the *piatti da pompa* of Italian maiolica, used to decorate sideboard or chimney-piece, and are a most important class whose popularity lasted for at least a hundred years. But before they are further considered an account must be given of some other 'Lambeth' types of shorter duration.

A small class, very English and simple, is well represented by a beautiful little mug at South Kensington with the name of 'ELIZABETH BROCKLEHURST' and the date 1628 (Plate III, A). This is speckled all over, save for the band of inscription at the top, with manganese-purple, and provides a possible link with the Malling jugs, though the long interval makes the comparison inconclusive. Then there are the adopted Chinese motives of the early seventeenth century, amongst which a starry flower is conspicuous and easily remembered; WILLIAM AND MARY BURGES' mug of 1631, at South Kensington, is typical of this early blue-painted class, which must be distinguished from the later blue-and-white of the great Delft movement. These Chinese motives are sometimes queerly mixed with the bastard Italian grotesques, sphinxes, fantastic birds, etc., in a weak polychrome, of another class (ANN CHAPMAN's mug, again, at South Kensington is typical). These borrowed motives never developed into a really national style and are of but slight artistic importance, though there is a peculiar charm about the medleys on such a dish as the big one at South Kensington presented by the National Art-Collections Fund, which has also a panel in the middle with a subject thought to be the Queen of Sheba. Much more important, and developing an individual style, are the Lambeth wine-bottles, ranging in date from 1639 to 1672. These are now believed to have held samples of the wines, the names of which, such as 'SACK', 'WHIT', 'RENISH', etc., written in blue with the date and a flourish, are often their only and very effective decoration (Plate III, B). Shields of arms gave the opportunity for the addition of touches of yellow, and occasionally a figure, sketchily drawn, reminds us that this class stands as the English analogue of the important seventeenth-century Italian blue-and-yellow maiolica. The beautiful milky-white enamel of the wine-bottles is seen again in some puzzle-jugs of about 1675, with open-work neck, painted with a formal blue-and-orange flower, of which the English origin is much disputed. Specimens with *fleur-de-lys* and with green-splashed enamel are also known. The mid-seventeenth-century Lambeth wares also include a great many pieces moulded in metal-, chiefly silver-, forms, often very elaborate; candlesticks, two-handled bleeding-bowls, flower- and hyacinth-vases, and salt-cellars are examples of these, which often bear names and occasionally arms in blue. A fragment of a cup of 1659, at South Kensington, is of a very charming baluster form. The florid mantling in blackish blue on a dish of 1654 with the arms of London, in the same collection, is a pure crib from the Netherlands. Perhaps the most numerous of all the mid-seventeenth-century London wares were the drug-pots, mostly broad little ointment-jars; many pill-slabs were also made, and sometimes bear the arms or motto of the Apothecaries' Company. The little pots are frequently found in London excavations, with the white enamel discoloured to a glossy dark-brown or black that has often puzzled people unacquainted with this pro-

stylised tulips, carnations, and other flowers often growing in pots, perhaps suggested originally by some piece of 'Rhodian' ware. Their strong rhythm, and the rich green, blue, and orange of their colour (in one class), make these perhaps the finest of all English painted pottery. A quieter palette of green, purple, and yellow is seen in another class, no less attractive. The only known dated 'tulip dish' is one of 1676 in the Glaisher Collection. Some charming designs, of spirals and formal clusters of brush-strokes mainly in blue and purple, are also seen on dishes to be ascribed to the London potteries. The task of separating these and other 'Lambeth' pieces, however, from those made at Bristol or the neighbouring Brislington, is not at all an easy one.

The Bristol potteries making tin-enamelled ware began not later than 1669, when a 'gallipot maker' is mentioned in the local records. The term 'gallipot' in this is of disputed significance; it is plausibly said to be derived from a similar Dutch word occurring in contemporary documents and supposed to mean pottery brought by sea in galleys from Italy and Spain. A fragment found in Mr. William Pountney's excavations on the pottery site at Brislington, a few miles from Bristol, is dated 1652, though the first mention of a gallipot-maker there (Edward Ward) is thirty years later. It is thus clear that the chargers made before about 1650 are most probably London productions. On the other hand, most of the later chargers, which often show a strong red in their colouring, seem to be Bristol. The red was apparently never used at Lambeth. For the rest there is much room for difference of opinion. Trees with foliage added by means of a sponge dipped in colour are believed to indicate Bristol, and a burnt-looking orange and brown-shaded yellow (as opposed to a lemon yellow) perhaps distinguish the 'Lambeth' chargers. The great aesthetic merit, however, of this truly English painted ware is of course not affected by the doubts which must often exist as to its exact place of origin.

What I have called the phase of Delft ascendancy came with a new wave of importations from China; and with the stabilisation of the Kingdom under K'ang Hsi (1662–1722) vast quantities of blue-and-white and polychrome porcelain of the *famille verte* began to be made for export to Europe and supplied new models for the potters, those of England included. Some trace of Chinese influence (direct or indirect) is in fact evident in most English delftware from the late seventeenth century onwards. But many delicious variants were invented. Lambeth had now lost the lead, and Liverpool entered the field as a rival to Bristol.

The chief Bristol potters in this period were Thomas Frank (*fl.* about 1703 to 1770), successor to the Edward Ward of Brislington already mentioned, who in 1683 started a pottery in Bristol itself, and Frank's pupil Joseph Flower (*fl.* 1743 to 1785). Thomas Taylor, originally of Brislington (1739 to 1769), and William Pottery and others of Limekiln Lane (1706 to 1746) owned other less important works in Bristol. The potteries at Wincanton in Somerset conducted by the Lindslees and Nathaniel Ireson, about 1737 to 1748, were offshoots of Bristol, the first-named having come from Limekiln Lane. The sequence of their productions follows, roughly speaking, that of the Chinese types that inspired them. Thus some of their earliest pieces are blue-and-white covered posset-pots, sometimes of elaborate form, with a spout for sucking, painted with figures after the mid-seventeenth-century (pre-K'ang Hsi) Chinese model. These pots often come close to the Dutch and the very similar Frankfort pieces; but the English body is as a rule considerably harder, more highly fired than the others. I think it likely that the Chinese influence operated as much through the medium of imported Delft as directly. At all events the Bristol decoration is as a rule utterly different in feeling from the Chinese and has a fantasy all its own. The early K'ang Hsi blue-and-white designs were very much simplified, and European figures like those on Dutch tiles, with heavy outlines, were added. Dutch forms were also in evidence for flower-vases, tea-caddies, and puzzle-jugs. The earliest eighteenth-century derivatives of K'ang Hsi polychrome are mainly in blue, dull green, and a red which is often rather dark and sticky-looking but occasionally of fine strong quality. Punch-bowls, at first of characteristic straight-sided form, succeeded the posset-pots of the earliest period. Light compound foliage rather like that of the acacia is a common motive, and panels with flowering plants and sprays in blue, red, green, and yellow occur on a typical covered bowl with the arms of the Carpenters' Company, dated 1709 (W. R. Acland Collection). In another type very distinctive 'square' leaves were drawn with short strokes of a broad brush. These leaves are associated with some fantastic designs with Chinese figures adapted from the *famille verte* and treated in an angular but rhythmical and effective style. These are attributed to a John Niglett on the evidence of a dish in the Bristol Museum dated 1733 with the initials $\frac{N}{J\ E}$, presumed to stand for 'Niglett, John and Esther', but I confess that the inferences it is customary to draw from such initials (their triangular placing, by the way, is almost peculiar to English wares) seem to me of doubtful value; such initials may as well be those of the recipient as of the painter. Whoever he may have been, the supposed Niglett was a delightful artist, and the most individual of all those working in the early part of the eighteenth century.

PLATE IV   *See pages* 45, 46

(*a*) PLATE. BRISTOL DELFT
MIDDLE OF 18TH CENTURY

Brig.-General Sir Gilbert Mellor's Collection

(*b*) PLATE. BRISTOL DELFT
MIDDLE OF 18TH CENTURY

Dr. F. H. Garner's Collection

(*c*) DISH. BRISTOL DELFT. PAINTED BY JOHN BOWEN, ABOUT 1760

Brig.-General Sir Gilbert Mellor's Collection

Nevertheless it may be said that the art of Bristol delft did not attain its full maturity until later.

In the mid-eighteenth-century figure-pieces in blue several individual styles were developed. Processions and the like, with many figures, were sketched in with a beautifully light touch, as on a tea-tray at South Kensington with painting of a tea-party. One hand, believed to be that of John Bowen, who worked for several potters, is recognisable in many pieces (Plate IV, c); river-scenes and landscapes and a not uncommon theatre subject all show a gift of delicious *rococo* design, with skilful, almost dramatic, use of heavy masses in the foreground to balance the airy tufts which stand for trees in his convention, and frame as in a fairyland atmosphere his swiftly drawn and slender figures and delicately painted ships. To Joseph Flower the potter are attributed several styles which are surely by different hands. There is no reason to regard the flower mark sometimes copied on Bristol delft from Chinese porcelain as his particular device, and little indeed for supposing that he sometimes (but not always !) marked his pieces with an ' F'; other initials to be interpreted at will as painters' or potters' marks are equally unsafe as a guide. The painting on two large dishes of the taking of Chagre by Admiral Vernon (1740) and Burleigh House is attributed to him on the authority of a descendant, but is poor and laboured. One noteworthy type of decoration, however, to be associated with his factory if not his hand employs an opaque white enamel for painting, chiefly on borders, on a lavender-blue or greyish-toned ground (the technique is often called *bianco sopra bianco* though not directly derived from Italian maiolica), and his factory work thus identified includes much of the best Bristol delft. Some punch-bowls and plates of about 1750–70, made for ships calling at Bristol, gave the opportunity for a very sensitive rendering of sails and rigging: the names of foreign ships and skippers have sometimes obscured the Bristol origin of these. Some rapidly drawn figure-pieces are delightfully sure in touch and soft in colour, with blue outlines washed over with indefinite green, purple, and yellow. By the same hand, I think, are some firmly stylised portraits in central circular panels, such as that of the King of Prussia formerly in Mr. Mundy's collection. Another gifted hand painted within the opaque white borders some exceedingly delicate landscapes and *chinoiserie* subjects with fantastic steepled churches, sometimes in blue only or in a soft polychrome without red. I think the same painter may also have done the shields of arms in blue with feathery mantling on plates which are frequently met with. Flower-pieces from the same factory show a full-toned polychrome with a bluish grey-green, a purple, and a rich orange—a palette coming near to a well-known Liverpool type associated with the name of Fazackerley. The versions of Chinese flower and landscape subjects (Plate IV, A and B) invariably surpass their originals in spontaneity and grace; the grey-green and purple tonality of one class is very distinct. A wealth of charming narrow border patterns made up of trefoils, checkers or 'bricks', and the like, also give a special character to the best of the Bristol ware from Flower's factory.

Much is talked of the work of Michael Edkins, an interesting and versatile person whose history happens to be recorded. The specimens of his handiwork identified by his grandson differ so much among themselves (even after allowance has been made for difference of material) as to raise doubts as to the value of the tradition. A plate at South Kensington with a *chinoiserie* subject in blue has an inscription $\frac{E}{MB}$ and the date 1760, and is therefore said to have been painted by him—for himself and his wife Betty! A Bristol white glass tea-canister with a goldfinch on a spray was also said to be his but shows a different style. Whoever painted the Chinese subjects in question they remain among the liveliest on Bristol delft, especially in the vivid polychrome versions, which are lit up by a fine red.

More of the nature of peasant pottery, but no less charming, are the Bristol plates of this period with boldly sponged trees and simply stylised houses, commonly in panels reserved on a ground sprayed with manganese-purple. This ground was often inclined to have a pinkish tone and was effectively decorated with linear patterns scratched through it or otherwise caused to appear white. In general the Bristol potters showed a sensitive appreciation of the beauty of this manganese colour, which is one of the most distinctive in the ceramic palette and almost peculiar to it. To the same peasant class belongs the so-called mimosa-pattern of formal flowers each consisting of a circle enclosing a dot. This is one of the patterns done at Wincanton, as was shown by Mr. Pountney's excavations; most of the inscribed and dated pieces from that factory are laboriously painted 'special efforts', and the common wares are much better. A pinkish manganese-purple ground-colour seems to have been a special favourite at Wincanton.

Numerous inscribed and dated Bristol pieces survive and have sometimes caused people to invent mythical factories, such as that supposed to have existed at Yarmouth, on the evidence of plates with the names of persons of that place and of Norwich, Wivernhoe, and Harwich, some of which may even be Dutch. Election bowls and plates are not uncommon. 'Calvert and Martin for Tewkesbury, 1754', and 'Wenman and Dashwood for ever, 1755', are examples certainly of Bristol origin. Lunardi's balloon

ascent of 1784 was for some reason repeatedly com-
memorated.

The rivalry of English as well as Continental porcelain
must have been felt at this time, and we find tea-pots and
tea-cups surviving in this unserviceable delftware; but to
their credit we never find the potters deserting their high-
temperature colours for enamel-painting over the glaze in
porcelain style.

Tiles for walls and fire-places were an important part
of the Dutch industry, and tiles were naturally much in
demand from the English potters. Several of the types of
decoration described above are found on the Bristol tiles,
and Bowen's little landscapes and the single blue-painted
figures in circles are especially charming. Other noteworthy patterns are some of goats in manganese-purple
monochrome, and of birds partly stencilled in green and
painted over in colours; specimens of both types are in
the Schreiber Collection. Tile pictures in the Dutch
manner with designs continuously painted over a number
of tiles include one in the Victoria and Albert Museum
depicting in blue the church of St. Mary Redcliff at
Bristol and bearing the arms of Bishop Butler (1738–50).
A very large single 'tile', more than three feet long, also
in the Victoria and Albert Museum, is painted in blue
with a roadstead with shipping and wooded islets and
figures in the foreground, all rendered with the utmost
delicacy and feeling. In style it comes very close to
Bowen's best work, though the trees are differently treated;
it was perhaps a piece done by him to a special order, with
unusual care. It is in any case one of the masterpieces of
Bristol delft.

The delftware of Liverpool made by Thomas Shaw,
Lawrence Harrison, Richard Chaffers and his successor
Philip Christian, Seth and John Pennington, and Zach-

ariah Barnes, follows the same sequence as at Bristol but is much less attractive. The common wares have less character, and in those with figure-subjects made for special occasions a certain crudeness and uncivilised humour is to be noted, and they are laboriously painted. The common delft was made largely for export to America. The punch-bowls with ships and bold flower-pieces, however, are equal to the best Bristol, and resemble it very closely. They can best be distinguished by their colour, in which the green is not so bluish-toned and the orange-red more brownish. Two well-known mugs with flowers in these colours are said to have been made for Thomas Fazackerley and his wife, at Shaw's Liverpool pottery. These 'Fazackerley' colours also point to Liverpool as the place of origin of some charming tiles with figures of sailors and their ladies, given to the Victoria and Albert Museum by that devoted student of delftware, the late Mr. Theodore Charbonnier, who disclaimed them for Bristol. The Chinese flowers and rocks are often recognisably by the same hand as much Liverpool porcelain: a characteristic shower of dots surrounds the familiar peony. It is said that borders and outside-painting of nautical apparatus and arms appear only on the Liverpool ship-bowls, which are often of great size. A famous specimen with a whole fleet (in the Hanley Museum) is traditionally said to be the work of one John Robinson, done at Seth Pennington's pottery. Another, equally big, with a single ship, is at South Kensington. Some shallow pots boldly painted with large fishes, said to have been made for pre-served char from the Lake District, also deserve mention. A bright red-brown edge is noticeable on these and may be a sign of Liverpool origin in delftware in general.

There is no evidence that the Liverpool delft manu-facture began before the eighteenth century; apart from tile-panels dated 1716 and 1722, the earliest documentary piece is of 1724—a gigantic blue-and-white covered punch-bowl on high foot, in the Glaisher Collection, painted in Delft-Chinese style and bearing the inscription 'THOMAS BOOTLE ESQUIRE MEMBER OF PARLIAMENT FOR LIVERPOOL'.

Perhaps the most characteristic Liverpool decoration was transfer-printing. Of the invention of this process more will be said on later pages dealing with Bow and Worcester porcelain. It is certain, I think, that it was not invented by John Sadler and Guy Green, who claimed to have done so when they opened a Printed Ware Manufactory, and proposed a patent for it, in 1756. That they never took out their patent is perhaps proof of this, and their reference to six years' previous experience is not confirmed by any actual specimens. Their 1200 tiles printed in six hours is evidence of the commercialising tendency evident at Liverpool even at this early date, before Wedgwood had begun business on his own account. The very common Liverpool printed tiles (which seem to have been actually made at Barnes's factory), though they naturally have the charm of the contemporary styles of engraving— chinoiseries after Pillement and subjects from Bell's *Theatre* are very common—have little ceramic interest, unlike the early Liverpool printing on Staffordshire salt-glaze and cream-colour to be mentioned later. The printing is usually in black, or (more rarely and agreeably) in brick-red. It is of course in muffle-colour applied over the glaze. Among the later tiles are some in the Neo-Classical manner —designs of urns are typical—printed in black and washed over with a pleasant green enamel-colour.

Nothing has yet been said of the eighteenth-century productions of 'Lambeth', which undoubtedly continued to make delftware at least as late as 1775. The 'Merry

Man' and kindred armorial plates with their clean white enamel and sparing decoration are a noteworthy late seventeenth- and early eighteenth-century type already discussed as possibly the work of a Dutchman. The octagonal plates with masks, grotesques, and pendants are nearest to the Dutch; others with the inscription within a characteristically bold laurel wreath are more certainly English and later. Some blue-painted globular or pear-shaped drug-pots on high foot, with bluish enamel and names of drugs in darker blue, are hardly distinguishable from Delft, but their abundance in the finds in London excavations gives weight to their ascription to Lambeth. Other wares must have been made, and these probably included a large proportion of the big chargers now fashionably called Bristol, and some of the blue-and-white posset-pots are also probably Lambeth. But it seems certain that no distinctive new style was created, and the potters were content to follow the Dutch fashions. They doubtless also made many common wares, not thought worth preserving, such as the little jugs—pickle-jars or mustard-pots—with reeded neck and rough foliations in blue which occasionally come to light.

Dublin delft does not come within the scope of our title, and the period of its manufacture has not yet been settled; but it must be mentioned here as likely to be mistaken for Bristol or Liverpool. A very bright blue and a purple monochrome, and borders of feathery scroll-work, are features of the most numerous class, dateable to about 1750–60, which is sometimes marked with a harp or the name 'Dublin'; the initials 'N E' are also recorded. But a marked piece with the Sackville arms, in the Victoria and Albert Museum, bears the unexpectedly early date 1735, and is painted in a very pale blue.

A word should be said regarding the delftware attributed to Staffordshire. The belief that this was ever made was due in the first place to a statement of the untrustworthy Simeon Shaw, and confirmation has been sought in the name Lane Delph. This is due to a confusion: 'Delph' in the Staffordshire name and 'Delft' both take their origin from kindred words, meaning a place delved or dug out, and the former thus does not indicate a place where 'delftware' was manufactured. No considerable find of tin-enamelled ware has ever been made in excavations in the Potteries, and its whole technique is in fact foreign to the lead-glaze traditions of the Staffordshire industry.

Mortlake delft is also probably a myth, due to an error of the late Professor Church in stating that there is a marked punch-bowl at South Kensington. The bowl in question (which is unmarked) and a landscape tile-picture are said to have been removed from an old pottery at Mortlake, founded in 1752 by William Sanders; but both are apparently Dutch, and Sanders' 'white ware' was perhaps lead-glazed ware in Staffordshire style.

By the end of the eighteenth century tin-enamelled ware had altogether ceased to be made in England. The perfected 'cream-colour' of Wedgwood and his contemporaries in Staffordshire offered so many practical advantages over the other that its extinction was inevitable. The lead-glazed ware, moreover, was in some indefinable way more in harmony with the Neo-Classical taste. Few collectors, however, will fail to find the amiable incompetence of the delftware, even without its charming decoration, vastly more sympathetic than the hard efficiency of its supersessor.

PLATE V   *See pages* 55, 56, 65

(*a*) BUST OF CHARLES II. JOHN DWIGHT'S GREY STONEWARE
FULHAM, ABOUT 1680
Victoria and Albert Museum

(*b*) MUG. RED STONEWARE, PROBABLY
MADE BY THE BROTHERS ELERS
LATE 17TH CENTURY
Victoria and Albert Museum

(*c*) MUG. DWIGHT'S MARBLED
STONEWARE
FULHAM, LATE 17TH CENTURY
British Museum

CHAPTER IV

STONEWARE: DWIGHT AND ELERS, AND THE EARLY RESEARCHES AFTER THE SECRET OF PORCELAIN

MENTION has already been made of the extensive importation into England during the sixteenth century of the Rhenish stoneware jugs, and of some imitations made in this country in other materials. The trade evidently began at least as early as 1500, since the tall grey-white Siegburg jugs often found in London excavations can hardly be later than this; while an English inventory of 1509 refers to 'Kruges' which were almost certainly of Rhenish ware. But of the making of a true stoneware in England there is no sure evidence until the seventeenth century had well advanced. It is true that in the reign of Queen Elizabeth a William Simpson, petitioning for the sole right to import the German wares, undertook, so far 'as in him lieth', to 'draur to the making of such like pottes into some decayed town within the realm, wherebie manie a hundred poor men may be sett at work'. Again in 1626 a patent was actually granted to Thomas Rous and Abraham Cullen, and another in 1635 to Ramsey, Arnold, and Ayliffe, for the making of 'stone potts, juggs and bottells'. But none of their productions have been identified, and it has usually been supposed that they merely imported the Rhenish wares (the name Cullen is very like Cologne!). While it is easy to separate from the main body of imported German stoneware some classes with a title to

English origin—such as, for example, the so-called grey-beards or bellarmines (pear-shaped bottles with a bearded mask on the neck) which are so commonly found in England, or the globular jugs with English arms—one almost invariably finds, after all, that they have unquestionable correspondence with other specimens undoubtedly German. But it is indeed surprising that no one, immigrant or native, should have succeeded in making stoneware in England before 1671, when John Dwight of Fulham (*b.* 1637, *d.* 1703) took out his first patent, and there speaks definitely of his discovery of 'the mystery and invention of making . . . stoneware, vulgarly called *Cologne* ware . . . never before made in England'. Stoneware, it should be explained here, is pottery fired at a high temperature to the point of great hardness and vitrification. Though the latter property makes it impervious to liquids, it is as a rule glazed by a process quite peculiar to its manufacture: salt is thrown into the kiln when the fire is at its hottest, and this unites with the surface of the pot itself, making a thin film of very hard glaze. The obvious practical advantages of such a ware made it widely popular.

Dwight's stoneware is naturally of great interest, but is very rare. The brown-mottled bellarmines (a name given, by the way, long after the creation of the type, in derision of an unpopular cardinal) to be regarded as Fulham productions differ from the Rhenish only in such small particulars as the absence of a spiral string-mark on the foot, where the pot was cut off the wheel, and a slightly different character in the bearded mask and armorial reliefs, among which is found the double 'C' or 'C R' under a crown for Charles II. Well-authenticated specimens are at South Kensington and in other museums. Such bottles must have been made in great quantities, since Dwight secured an agreement in 1676 with the Glass-Sellers' Company to supply them with all the stoneware they needed, instead of the German. The bottles were probably never prized and so are seldom seen to-day; and they are in fact of little artistic importance. Whether Dwight made other kinds of stoneware precisely in German style is doubtful. Some blue-and-purple-coloured fragments found in a walled-up chamber on his pottery site are indistinguishable from undoubted Rhenish wares, and though their presence is unexplained, we must continue to regard the similar grey, blue, and purple jugs with English royal initials, 'W R', 'A R', 'G R', often claimed as Fulham, as of Westerwald origin like the rest of their kindred. On the other hand, there is very good reason for attributing to Dwight's factory some much finer wares than these. Some note-books of the potter's, which survived until the nineteenth century and were transcribed by Jewitt and Lady Charlotte Schreiber, contained recipes for all sorts of wares; and some brass stamps for applied reliefs, now in the British Museum, were found, it is said, on the site of the pottery. By these means have been identified various 'mouse-coloured', brown, and 'marbled' pear-shaped bottles, made of Dwight's stoneware, and some beautiful little jugs with globular body and cylindrical reeded neck, their grey substance indefinitely streaked and clouded with brown and black (Plate V, c), or splashed with brown and blue, or with double walls, the outer pierced with open-work sprays. The applied reliefs on some of these, of cranes, flowers, grotesque figures, etc., are interesting when they can be linked with the stamps or with Dwight's own notes (as when he mentions the use of blue for staining them), but are of little artistic merit in themselves. A curious decoration of birds and flower-sprays engraved deeply in the body after firing (as on a mug in the British Museum) is almost certainly glass-engravers' work done outside the factory. Especially noteworthy are some nearly white jugs of the same globular form as those mentioned above: these will be further discussed later on. But the most important of all Dwight's ware, in the history of English art, are the exceedingly rare figures, one of which bears an inscription unquestionably associating them with the Fulham potter. A recumbent half-length figure of his daughter is inscribed '*Lydia Dwight dyed March 3 1673*'; this, with another standing figure of a little girl with clasped hands, also believed to be Lydia Dwight, is in the Victoria and Albert Museum. Finer still perhaps in modelling are the small busts of *Charles II* (Plate V, A) and *James II*, both in the Victoria and Albert Museum, and the great life-sized head of *Prince Rupert* in the British Museum. A *Mars* at the latter museum, like a *Jupiter* at Liverpool and a superb *Neptune* at South Kensington, are of a brown colour, with the salt-glaze so thin as to be a mere gloss, in no way obscuring the clean sensitive modelling. The Dwight stoneware thus finished, though obviously suggested by bronze, may be said to approach perfection as a material for ceramic figure-modelling. Moreover these works are unlike most porcelain and other pottery figures in being not merely casts put together by a workman from a *maquette* made by the artist, but his actual unduplicated work; in the *Charles II* one may sense the very touch of his boldly used modelling tool. His identity has not yet been discovered, but it was suggested by Mr. S. K. Greenslade that the young Grinling Gibbons (*b.* 1648, *d.* 1721) was responsible for these figures, and several of his early monumental works (such as the Adam by the font in St. James's Church, Piccadilly) seem to support the attribution. It is disputed by Mrs. Esdaile, who argues that Gibbons was not a modeller but a carver. The technique of some of the Dwight figures, however, is distinctly a cutting away rather than the typical adding and pressing of the modeller. Most of the figures were in the collection, dispersed in 1871, of C. W. Reynolds, who had them, through a Thomas Baylis, from a descendant of Dwight himself, and not (as implied by Sir Arthur Church) from a find on the pottery site. With the acquisition of the *Charles II* by the Victoria and Albert Museum a year or two ago all the Reynolds figures (which numbered only seventeen) can now be accounted for, and only a few others have ever been found. (Some *Seasons* at South Kensington in a rather similar grey body with an opaque cream-coloured glaze or enamel are not Dwight's ware as is sometimes supposed, but are most likely productions of Coade's Artificial-Stone Works at Lambeth, where busts and figure-models, often very large, were made in cream, grey, and black materials approaching stoneware.)

That Dwight was not alone in this period in making stoneware in England is shown by the record of a lawsuit brought by him in 1693 in defence of his patent rights, which had been renewed in 1684. In this Thomas, Aaron, and Richard Wedgwood (three brothers) of Burslem, James Morley of Nottingham, and John and David Elers of Fulham were the principal defendants. Symon Wooltus of Southampton and Matthew Garner and Luke Talbot of Southwark were also cited. Of these, Morley's Nottingham stoneware is well known in inscribed and dated pieces closely resembling Fulham in form (such as a mug dated 1703 at South Kensington), but invariably brown in colour. An earlier posset-pot in the Lomax Collection is inscribed '*Samuel Watkinson and Sarah his wife major and majoress of Nottingham 1700*', and an advertisement sheet in the Ashmolean Museum, of about 1690–1700, shows several Fulham shapes as well as others, such as 'decantors' and 'flower-pots', not found in any other ware. The Burslem stoneware made by the Wedgwoods is vouched for not only by the lawsuit records but by references to 'brown stone', 'dipped white stoneware', and 'freckled' in Wedgwood's list of Burslem potters at work about 1710, already referred to in a previous chapter. Actual specimens remained unrecognised until lately, though fragments of brown 'capacity mugs' had often been found in local excavations. These last are cylindrical mugs of certified volume, impressed with the royal initials and often with the royal bust in relief taken apparently from a coin. They were made also at Fulham, in a grey ware. A thin and well-made glossy brown stoneware mug or jug in the British Museum (F 42), of the usual Dwight form with reeded neck, formerly called Nottingham, can now be identified as Staffordshire on the showing of the fragments; while some tall cups at South Kensington, in two instances not of true stoneware but 'freckled' in imitation of it, may also count as Staffordshire wares of this period. These are especially interesting as probably the 'Crouch ware', stated by Simeon Shaw to have been made before the typical white Staffordshire stoneware had been invented. (A later grey or drab ware with white reliefs, to be discussed in the next chapter, cannot possibly be Shaw's 'Crouch ware', though it is often so called.) The other chief defendants in the suit, the brothers Elers, rank among the most influential figures in the history of English pottery; but before their ascertained achievements are discussed in their bearing on subsequent developments, something must be said of the other and later English stonewares, so far as they took their own course, independent of the Staffordshire industry.

The typical Nottingham stoneware made by the Morley family is of various shades of a beautiful russet-brown colour, produced by a wash of ferruginous clay. It is thinly and delicately made, and at its best charmingly decorated with freely incised designs of formal flowers and inscriptions (Fig. 5), which were also done in darker brown or in 'resist' so as to appear of a lighter colour. Other pieces show rouletted or simple stamped patterns of circles, etc., bands roughened with little bits of applied clay, and (more rarely) moulded patterns and applied reliefs—which are

FIG. 5. NOTTINGHAM STONEWARE LOVING-CUP

individually of no great interest. The numerous inscribed dates (which began, as stated above, with a posset-pot of 1700) cease with one of 1799, and soon after this the manufacture apparently came to an end. Nottingham stoneware is one of the most distinctively English types of pottery. It was not uninfluenced by Staffordshire, as is shown by such forms as the puzzle-jugs with pierced necks and the vessels in the form of bears covered with shreds of clay for fur. It is indeed not impossible that some of the wares attributed to Nottingham may even be early

59

Staffordshire, and the name 'Crouch ware' be a corruption of Crich, a place in Derbyshire where a similar brown stoneware was made and whence possibly both the neighbouring manufactures for a time obtained some of their clay. Shaw actually said that his Crouch ware was so called from a Crouch clay, obtained from Derbyshire. The Nottingham tradition was taken up at several places in the Midlands and the North—at Belper near Derby, at Brampton and Chesterfield, and at Codnor Park and Denby, where the manufacture of excellent stoneware by Bourne and Co. continues to this day. The mid-eighteenth-century brown stoneware of Swinton in Yorkshire was apparently indistinguishable from Nottingham.

The later (eighteenth century) Fulham wares were mostly heavy grey cylindrical mugs, the tops dipped in rust brown, with applied reliefs of topers and of hunting-scenes with dogs and trees and houses, clumsy and rustic but vigorous in style. The reliefs of the second half of the century were often square in shape or in round-topped panels. The royal busts sometimes included were not always, it should be noted, those of the reigning sovereigns. The productions were obviously articles of common trade, and included also jugs and mugs made for inns (with their signs) or for proprietary mineral waters, with appropriate reliefs and inscriptions such as the '*Iron Pear tree water near Godstone Surry*' on a great jug in the British Museum. The inscriptions were in the early part of the century incised with a pointed instrument, but from about 1760 they were impressed with printers' types. These serviceable wares evidently supplied a wide market over the South of England; they were unpretentious, but often of noble form. The factory still exists but is now chiefly devoted to the making of filters and industrial wares. Stoneware of Fulham derivation was made in the late eighteenth and

PLATE VI

See pages 72, 73, 74

(*a*) FIGURE OF A HORSEMAN
EARTHENWARE
STAFFORDSHIRE, ABOUT 1740
Mr. Wallace Elliot's Collection

(*b*) FIGURE OF A LADY
EARTHENWARE
STAFFORDSHIRE, ABOUT 1740
Mr. Cecil Higgins' Collection

(*c*) TEAPOT. BLACK, WITH DECORATION IN WHITE CLAY
STAFFORDSHIRE, ABOUT 1740
Mr. Wallace Elliot's Collection

(*d*) TEAPOT. CLOUDED GREY GLAZE
STAFFORDSHIRE (WHIELDON TYPE), ABOUT 1750–55
Mr. Wallace Elliot's Collection

nineteenth centuries at Lambeth (Stephen Green's, James Stiff's, and Doulton's factories) and at Mortlake (Kishere's). The Bristol stoneware mugs for inns should also be mentioned, though of no great artistic importance.

John Philip and David Elers, whose work must now be considered, were silversmiths, of a family originally Saxon, and are believed to have come to England in the train of William of Orange, in or soon after 1688. In the Dwight lawsuit of 1693 it was stated that David Elers had learned the art of making stoneware at Cologne and had practised it for about three years at Fulham. Shortly after 1693, as we know from a contemporary report, the Elers had migrated to Staffordshire, and it is customary to attribute to them the introduction into that county of salt-glazing. But since the Wedgwoods of Burslem were also cited by Dwight as infringing his patent at a time when the Elers were still at Fulham, this theory would seem not to hold. Moreover no fragments of salt-glazed vessels have yet, as far as I am aware, been found on the Elers factory-site. This was at Bradwell Wood, a remote spot to the west of the valley which divides Newcastle-under-Lyme from the chief pottery towns of Burslem, Tunstall, Hanley, Longton, Fenton, and Stoke. In fact no good reason can be found for ascribing to the Elers any specimens of the comparatively rare late seventeenth-century stoneware in 'Cologne' style, and this is remarkable since in the lawsuit they admitted having made 'brown mugs' as well as 'red teapots'. Possibly the 'brown mugs' were not Cologne ware but akin to the red teapots, or it may be wondered whether they made (at Fulham only) some of the thin brown-glazed stoneware now attributed to Dwight. We cannot say. But whatever their brown ware may have been, it is clear that with the red teapots we begin a new stage in the history of English pottery, which calls for consideration at some length.

Besides his achievement in regard to the 'Cologne' wares Dwight deserves credit for research in another direction. In his patents of 1671 and 1684 he specified not only stoneware but also 'transparent earthenware commonly known by the names of porcelain and China and Persian ware. . . .' And the claim serves to remind us once more that this was the period of the vast importations from China which inspired so much of the delftware described in the previous chapter. Not only the demand for tea-table wares due to the introduction of the new beverage, but the problem of the porcelain material itself was naturally exciting the interest of potters and scientists throughout Europe at this time; soft-paste was already being made in France at Rouen, and perhaps at Saint-Cloud. There can be no doubt that Dwight hoped to make porcelain by the refinement of stoneware of the German type, and the 'white' globular mugs already mentioned, with their thin, very pale brown, and translucent body, must have seemed to him a veritable porcelain, though we know now that the Chinese material must be made in a quite different way. In any case these mugs, well represented by two in the Schreiber Collection with silver mounts dated 1682, must rank among the most important surviving pieces of English pottery. They are beautiful, alike in form and substance, and were shaped with a care and feeling amounting almost to reverence for a thrillingly new and fine material. Porcelain would also seem to have been in its maker's mind in the case of a tall cup now in the Victoria and Albert Museum, supposed to have been made by Francis Place (*d.* 1728), who experimented with pottery at York. This is the one specimen 'authenticated' as his, on the authority of Horace Walpole; it is in many respects similar to Dwight's ware, of grey stoneware veined with black and brown, and in shape, with its horizontal moulded ridge, is apparently a copy of a Chinese (Fukien, *blanc de Chine*) white cup. It is possible, however, that the Chinese cups were themselves copied from English wares of this shape (which may have been derived from silver), though it would be astonishing to find such experiments in porcelain manufacture copied so promptly in China. No other conclusion seems possible in the case of the *blanc de Chine* mugs of Fulham form, where a meaningless band below the handle was obviously copied uncomprehendingly from the detached roll on the English model. These have often been wrongly called Dwight's porcelain, just as the Fukien tall cups have been attributed to Place, or to a man named Clifton who is said (with very doubtful accuracy) to have made a fortune out of improvements on Place's methods.

The European search for the porcelain secret was sent away on a false trail by another circumstance. Besides the familiar white Chinese porcelain there was at the same time imported into Europe much unglazed red stoneware, made at Yi-hsing, near Soochow, by the Great Lake in China, which passed under the name 'red porcelain' and was believed to be merely a variety of the white. It was much sent with consignments of tea, and was supposed to be the best material for brewing it. Dwight was not alone in attempting to imitate it as part of his research, as a step towards the making of the white. Böttger at Meissen actually preceded his discovery of true porcelain by making the beautiful red stoneware associated with his name, while the potters of Delft, content to copy the external appearance of the blue-and-white in a soft tin-enamelled earthenware, made also the relatively soft imitation of Yi-hsing ware which is especially associated with the names of Arij de Milde and Jacob de Caluwe. In his notes Dwight repeatedly uses the word 'porcelaine', and this must not be taken too literally. But his reference to 'red porcelaine' leaves us in no doubt, and the mention of Staffordshire 'red clay' makes us wonder whether it was not through him that the brothers Elers, strangers to England, should have learned of the resources of that county. It is in fact recorded that John Chandler, one of Dwight's workmen, was enticed away by the Elers, and some arrangement between the two Fulham potters has often been suspected, so that we may well anticipate difficulty in separating the work of the two manufactures. And this is indeed what we find. Little silver-mounted red mugs in form like those of 1682, with the same peculiar roll below the handle, would at first sight seem to be unquestionable productions of John Dwight. But no case of exact correspondence between the applied reliefs in Chinese style, which usually decorate these mugs and tea-pots, and the Dwight brass stamps, has yet been found, while a fragment with a relief of plum-blossom, nearly but not exactly corresponding, was discovered by Mr. John Cook and Mr. H. W. Maxwell actually on the site of the Elers' factory in Staffordshire. It must be noted further that the Elers in their defence in the lawsuit asserted that Dwight had never produced porcelain under his patent, and most of the surviving red ware of late seventeenth-century date can be linked into a single class. All this may perhaps justify us in thinking that Dwight left it for the Elers to put his ideas on this subject into practice, with the help perhaps of his unfaithful workman.

The importance of the Elers' red ware has for long been admitted, but the extreme rarity of English speci-mens which can be of their time has not always been so clearly appreciated. Of twenty or more pieces figured as theirs in books on English pottery, not more than four can in my opinion be Elers ware. Specimens in the style of the familiar drab-and-white Staffordshire salt-glaze can be no earlier than about 1730, as I shall explain in dealing with the latter; that is to say of a date long after the Elers had left the district. Crabstock handles date from the middle of the eighteenth century and 'rose-engine-turned' (or basketwork) specimens again must date from the time of Josiah Wedgwood or later. The fantastic king and queen sometimes supposed to be William and Mary correspond in style with specimens referring to John Wilkes and 'No. 45' of his *North Briton*, of 1763. As regards the period of the Elers' stay, it is certain that one or both the brothers went to Staffordshire in 1693, since we have Dr. Martin Lister's report of them there in that year. In 1699 they are said to have come to the end of their clay, and in 1700 John Philip was in Dublin, where he had been set up as a china- and glass-merchant by Lady Barrington, and his son Paul was born there in the same year. There is no evidence that he ever returned to Staffordshire, and his brother David is supposed to have kept their shop in the Poultry, London. In 1699, too, Martin Lister again spoke of them as having worked (past tense) in Staffordshire and having been 'not long since' at Hammersmith. The date of their departure is usually given as 1710, but this rests solely on the word of the hopelessly inaccurate Simeon Shaw. We have thus less than seven years' authenticated work to account for, ending not later than 1700.

The group of red ware forming what it would be best to call the 'Dwight-Elers' class is for the most part of exceedingly delicate workmanship, thinly made (evidently turned on the lathe) in the Oriental manner in a fine-grained material varying in colour from a deep vermilion to a dark brownish red. Among the applied reliefs used for decoration the usual twiggy plum-blossom (Plate V, B) has been mentioned already and is often charmingly

5

placed. But the most original and attractive of all the reliefs are some *chinoiseries* in the style of the illustrations to John Ogilby's edition of Nieuhof's *Embassy to the Grand Tartar Cham* of 1669. These are moulded in countersunk relief, beautifully and rhythmically drawn; their recognition as Elers work is due to the genius of Mr. W. W. Winkworth. A teapot discovered by him and a little four-sided tea-jar (not a scent-bottle, as generally supposed) at South Kensington, formerly thought to be Meissen, show these *chinoiserie* reliefs; the teapot bears an imitation Chinese mark also found on another with characteristic plum-blossom, and these marks with some others are impressed all over a beautiful handleless tall cup in the British Museum. These 'Chinese' marks should be carefully distinguished from the more confused characters added as marks on some of the later red ware, and more especially from a mark 'I F' written Chinese fashion and sometimes misread as 'I E' for John Elers! These 'I F' wares are mid-eighteenth century or later (a kindred teapot in the Hanley Museum bears the impressed mark of the potter Myatt). Somewhat less accomplished but certainly of the Elers period are some teapots, cylindrical mugs with incurved top, and pear-shaped jugs bearing reliefs of rather bossy plum-blossom and of a 'merry-andrew' and a wyvern which come near to the Dwight stamps, but again do not correspond. Moulded, not plain reeded, bands and a rather light or bright-red body seem general in this subdivision; a teapot at South Kensington bears a mark of a stag in a circle which strongly recalls the Elers' supposed compatriots at Delft, who used a running fox, a hind, and a unicorn in the same way. In most cases the curve and form of the handles have a distinct seventeenth-century character. Rare white- and green-enamelled specimens are known (as in the Solon Collection) and are

generally thought to have been decorated in Holland or
Germany.

These charming pieces stand then as the probable
Elers ware, though Dwight may perhaps have made some
of them. We may note here the testimony of Dr. Martin
Lister, who as a scientist may well have known Dwight,
but did not mention him when he spoke of the red ware
'done in England, to a far greater perfection than in
China, we having as good materials . . . and far better
Artists in Pottery. But in this particular we are beholding
to two *Dutchmen* brothers who wrought in *Staffordshire.*'
It was the refinement of these little mugs and teapots (and
no doubt their high selling-price also) which first suggested to the Staffordshire potters the possibility of a
wider market. Their fertilising influence upon the local
slipwares produced in the two or three decades before
about 1760, in the so-called Astbury and Whieldon
pottery and the salt-glazed stoneware of Staffordshire, a
body of wares of great artistic importance. These will be
discussed in the next chapter; but it should be pointed
out here that there is no sure evidence that this result of
the Elers' incursion was immediate. Simeon Shaw's well-
known story of Astbury and Twyford taking service with
the Dutchmen and learning their secrets by pretending to
be half-witted can scarcely be accepted, since the first-
named was no more than twelve years old when J. P.
Elers left the district. It is more likely that their influence
on the Staffordshire pottery was due to a recollection and a
tradition of refinement taken up by some potter of character and enterprise, rather than to actual contact.

CHAPTER V

THE RISE OF STAFFORDSHIRE: ASTBURY, WHIELDON, AND AARON WOOD

WE have an interesting glimpse of the state of the Staffordshire potteries on the eve of their rise to national importance in the list drawn up by Josiah Wedgwood, from information gleaned from his older workmen, of the potters at work at Burslem about 1710–15. They were headed by his kinsman Dr. Thomas Wedgwood (*b.* 1655, *d.* 1717), who has already been referred to as a probable maker of slipware and as a rival of Dwight's in the previous century. This Dr. Thomas and his son, also 'Dr.' Thomas (*b.* 1695, *d.* 1737), stand as links between the old local craft and the coming new industry. There were three other Wedgwoods on the Burslem list, and we read there of makers of 'butter-pots', 'red dishes', 'black and mottled', 'cloudy', 'moulded' and 'dipped', 'brown stone', and other types easily recognised. 'Cloudy' and 'mottled' were either stoneware or red ware glazed with manganese with an effect such as was described by Dr. Plot in his *Natural History of Staffordshire* of 1686 as a 'motley colour'. They were not, as Church seemed inclined to suggest, the multi-coloured glazes familiar at a later date on the Whieldon ware. Slipware and brown and buff stoneware were thus still the chief products of the Burslem kilns, and these have been described in previous chapters. The spur to improvement was undoubtedly the awareness of porcelain and the example and memory of the brothers Elers. A

68

PLATE VII   *See pages* 75, 77, 98

(*a*) ' PEW-GROUP.' SALT-GLAZED STONEWARE
STAFFORDSHIRE, ABOUT 1740
British Museum

(*b*) FIGURE OF A SHEPHERD.
EARTHENWARE WITH COLOURED
GLAZES. STAFFORDSHIRE (RALPH
WOOD'S FACTORY), ABOUT 1770
Victoria and Albert Museum
(W. Sanders Fiske Gift)

(*c*) FIGURE OF A BIRD. EARTHEN-
WARE WITH COLOURED GLAZES
STAFFORDSHIRE (WHIELDON TYPE)
ABOUT 1755
Victoria and Albert Museum
(Schreiber Collection)

white ware like porcelain was the ideal aimed at, though a subconscious artistry allowed the potters for a time to be content with their much better and more original coloured wares. How soon a white ware began to be produced is a problem which is made none the easier by the wild but widely repeated statements of Simeon Shaw. Much turns on the career of John Astbury, who died in 1743 aged fifty-five. To him are ascribed by Shaw two innovations of far-reaching importance—in the use as a surface wash (parallel with the tin-enamel) of the non-plastic white Devonshire clay, and in the introduction of calcined flint into the body of his ware. The effect of the latter was to produce not only a lighter-coloured pottery, but one which was refractory enough to be fired to great hardness without collapsing, a quality of great value where the imitation of porcelain for tea-table wares was concerned. It should be mentioned that Wedgwood gave the credit for this calcined flint to Thomas Heath, who is supposed to have noticed its whiteness when using it to doctor his horse. According to Shaw flint was introduced about 1720, and we have some confirmation of this in a patent for grinding flints taken out by Thomas Benson in 1726. The first step in the desired technical advance was undoubtedly the invention or perfecting of the white stoneware now familiarly known as 'Staffordshire salt-glaze'. The 'dipped white' stoneware in Wedgwood's list was probably something like a cup in the Victoria and Albert Museum, formerly in Enoch Wood's collection, of a light buff colour with the top half dipped in ferruginous clay which has fired to a rich brown; Dr. Plot actually has a note to the effect that a yellow-firing clay, 'being the lightest they make any use of', was called white by the potters. The earliest white piece, and even this is really grey, is a little circular flask in the British Museum with the date

1724 incised and coloured brown. (An often-cited mug of 1701 at Stoke is actually German.) But the regular manufacture of the white stoneware did not begin until the 1730's. With more careful refinement of the clays used, thinner walled vessels became practicable, and the introduction of porous plaster moulds for casting was a revolutionary step in this direction, making possible a lightness of substance previously unattainable. Moulds of metal, alabaster, and fired clay ('pitcher') into which the clay could be pressed had long been in use when the porous mould, according to Shaw's account, was brought to Staffordshire from France by one Ralph Daniel shortly before 1750. But the earliest cast pieces (such as some of the Portobello teapots) are apparently no later than about 1740. In the casting process a liquid clay-mixture is poured into an assembled piece-mould which gradually absorbs water and so becomes lined with a layer of clay; after the residue has been poured away and the clay lining has dried somewhat, the mould may be detached. Vessels of all manner of rectangular and polygonal shapes, not available by the throwing process, can be quickly made in this way. Such thin-walled vessels could hardly have been fired with success in any body less refractory than the new flint-holding composition. Mr. William Burton has pointed out that the composition used for the salt-glaze when fired to a moderate temperature gave a cream-coloured ware, and this lighter body encouraged the potters to develop the lead-glazes; more delicate colours became worth while, and refined yellows, browns, and purples from iron and manganese, and green from copper, began to be used. Most important of all in this connection was the introduction of a fluid glaze-mixture into which the ware, previously fired to an absorbent 'biscuit', could be dipped, instead of being dusted with powdered galena on the raw body, by the method of the slipware potters. Liquid glazes are by Simeon Shaw put to the credit of Enoch Booth working for the potter Warburton of Cobridge, about 1750; but from the appearance of the wares and in view of the difficulty of galena-glazing such pieces as the thin and delicately-shaped early teapots, one would judge it to have been in use at least ten years before this.

These then were the technical improvements which made possible the sudden enormous expansion of the Staffordshire industry. They were inspired, as we have seen, by the brief incursion of the brothers Elers, whose work with a local clay proposed a standard previously unthought of and first suggested to the potters the imitation of porcelain, red and white. For a period of twenty years or so the resources of the slipware potters in the use of a pure clay technique were coupled with these innovations and brought into existence a novel range of ceramic wares having much of the vitality in design of the earlier types, with their warm and varied 'earthen' colour enriched by a new beauty of coloured glazes. It was an exciting new birth, lapsing too soon to the dull ordinariness of the perfected cream-colour.

Turning to the aesthetic side, we must admit at once that we do not know the names of the artists responsible for the new styles. Tradition associates the earliest wares employing the applied and stamped reliefs in the Elers manner (but under a lead-glaze) with John Astbury or his son Thomas; but it is certainly known, from excavations on the site of his pottery at Fenton Low, that Thomas Whieldon (*b.* 1719, *d.* 1795) also made the 'Astbury' type, and the typical pieces celebrating the victory of Portobello in 1739 show that none of it can be quite as early as is often supposed. Whieldon in fact seems to have made all the finer sorts of ware, and I think it is more than likely that they were due to his enterprise and inventive powers. He was at work as a master-potter by about 1740, and is said to have retired when the demand for his favourite wares had declined before the advance of the plain styles popularised by his former pupil and partner Josiah Wedgwood. In view of the traditions, we may perhaps believe that Astbury was the first to take up again the Elers method of impressing with metal stamps pads of applied clay; on the glazed wares it was usually white clay. Apart from these conjectures, and the personal achievement of Aaron Wood as modeller and 'block cutter', which will be discussed in due course, no certain ascriptions to individual potters and artists can be made in the following brief account of the principal types.

The great attraction of the lead-glazed ware is its colour, which was inherited from its predecessor the slip-ware, and this justifies us in dealing with it first. The earliest relief-decoration, which includes shields of arms and heraldic birds and beasts and formal foliage, is sometimes witty and amusingly contrived (as on the Portobello bowls and mugs of 1740 or so) but as often clumsy and ill-executed, with parts missing and the superfluous clay not properly removed round the stamped motives. Rosettes, formal flowers, and vine-leaves with grapes, linked by winding stems made of rolls of clay formed by hand and applied, are usually much better; the stems in fact are admirably strong and rhythmical and well placed. But the effect of the reliefs in general depends on the contrasts they give under the yellow-toned glaze with the warm reds, chamois buff, and rich browns and blacks of the ground colours (Plate VI, c). Touches of green glaze and the occasional use of red-brown clay for the reliefs enhanced this effect, while handles and spouts formed of white or coloured clay gave a similarly charming counterchange.

72

In one very characteristic class the glaze over a cream body was stained with blurred patches of manganese-brown of rich tone, giving the so-called tortoiseshell ware. A similar colour was dabbed on the delightful 'Astbury' figures, in which a very simple use of red-brown and white clays gave accent to the work of an untutored but gifted modeller (Plate VI, A and B). Little musicians (whole bands are known!) are most often met with, but the beautifully stylised horses and riders are perhaps the best pieces; all seem to be by a single hand, whose original notion it probably was to fashion the local material into such figure-models; they can hardly have been suggested by porcelain. They represent the very beginning of the Staffordshire manufacture of 'Image Toys', as they were called. A brilliant black glaze, due to iron and manganese, is often attributed to Whieldon (fragments with it were found at Fenton Low); it appears on some of the earliest teapots. It is also called 'Jackfield', but the black glaze actually made at that pottery in a somewhat later period is browner in tone and commonly decorated with unfired painting, gilding, and silvering, and not with reliefs. More subtle in technique are the 'agate' wares formed by mingling brown, white, and blue-stained clays in distant imitation of a veined or marbled natural stone. (The name 'solid agate' distinguishes it from the rather later ware with marbled glazes.) Perhaps the finest examples are those in which a bold and rhythmical or more or less symmetrical effect has been aimed at; the pieces with finer marbling generally have a prevailing blue-grey tone due to the tinting of the glaze by the cobalt in the blue-stained clay. Agate ware of course could not be thrown on the wheel, and in parts requiring manipulation (such as handles) the markings are generally blurred.

The forms of these early wares show no special ceramic

originality, though shapely enough, but were strongly influenced by the contemporary silverware, the simple grace of which they often share. Teapots were commonly of depressed globular form and coffee-pots pear-shaped, sometimes with three feet in silver style, moulded with masks. Knobs on the lids in the form of birds (not for the potter Daniel Bird!) were again probably taken from silver, but the popular lion knob was perhaps copied from some chance piece of Elers ware. Cups and saucers seem to have been seldom made, or at least seldom survive.

A second phase in the lead-glazed ware, dating from about 1750 onwards, is by custom more particularly associated with Whieldon's name, though it is certain that he made the earlier types as well. This phase is chiefly noteworthy for the development of the coloured glazes. Slate-blue and grey, purple, green, and yellow-brown were flooded on and clouded in the soft, generously applied glaze with a full-toned and harmonious effect. In some of the best pieces the grey and slate-blue alone sufficed (Plate VI, D). For the decoration the bits of clay stamped after application had now given place to reliefs previously moulded and stuck on with slip by a process known as 'sprigging'. The Chinese stems, vine-leaves and grapes, and some stylised rosette-like flowers done in this way were strong and vital in effect. Much of this 'Whieldon ware' was in forms with relief decoration produced by the casting process referred to above. Many of the beautiful plates and dishes show by their moulded basketwork borders with references to the 'King of Prussia' that they were made in 1756 or later, when the young Josiah Wedgwood was in partnership with Whieldon, and many must also date from the period of his independence (1759 onwards). The same incomparable glazes were applied with charming effect to grotesque figures moulded from the

Chinese and to figures of birds which show that the influence of Meissen porcelain was being felt even in Staffordshire, though they are in no sense copies (Plate VII, c).

The unglazed red ware of this period is of much less interest. It is surprising that the reliefs on this do not include any found on the glazed red ware particularly associated with Astbury's name, though on the other hand a large class, formerly called Elers ware and distinguished by stamped reliefs of linear scrolls and interlacements, may be linked with some early white salt-glaze. The stamped name 'ASTBURY' occurs, it is true, on red wares with rose-engine-turned 'basketwork', but this technique is believed to have been an introduction of Wedgwood's, of about 1760, and the potter in question was no doubt a younger member of the numerous Astbury family. One may wonder whether this stamp, and a black unglazed teapot at Hanley with a traditional ascription to Twyford, were perhaps the sources of Simeon Shaw's Elers-Astbury-Twyford legend! The crabstock handles and rococo scrolls of a great deal of the red ware show it to be of this later period. Artistically it lacks both the exquisite workmanship of the Elers ware and the interest of the Staffordshire glazes and bodies. Much of it was probably made by Josiah Wedgwood to meet a demand, though he more than once expressed his contempt for the material.

The strong original impulse behind the Staffordshire pottery of this 'Astbury-Whieldon' period is shown by its almost total neglect of painting on the earthenware body. It is true that there was in Staffordshire no tradition such as inspired the delftware potters, but a suitable light-coloured ground was already available, as a primitive 'blue-and-white' (or rather blue-painted cream-colour) bowl of

1743 in the British Museum proves. But the potters in general, as far as the lead-glazed ware was concerned, remained faithful to their applied reliefs and coloured bodies and glazes, all, it is to be noted, derived in essentials from the local slipware.

The white salt-glaze opened a new field, but even here one of the earliest types makes use of contrast of colour: this is the drab or greenish grey ware with white reliefs, including the characteristic linear interlacements already referred to. It is one of the most attractive classes, commonly showing several additional small points of interest. Twiggy handles with 'knots' deftly opened with a knife, neatly cut facets for thumb-rests, and many such devices, all give pleasure to the observer with an eye for what may be called clay quality. Excavations at Burslem have associated this class especially with the second Dr. Thomas Wedgwood, who died in 1737. The reliefs on this drab ware are found also on salt-glaze entirely white, showing that it is not a precursor but a contemporary of the latter, and that it is not as is often supposed the 'Crouch ware' referred to by Simeon Shaw and discussed in the previous chapter. It certainly dates from within a few years of the Portobello mugs of 1739–40.

The forms of the salt-glaze vessels and their applied relief-decoration follow much the same stages as in the lead-glazed ware already described. We have first the stamped reliefs; among these, besides the motives common on the 'Astbury' type, we find baskets of flowers, large rosettes (often gilt), dogs' heads, and heraldic wyverns accompanied in some cases by incising of hatched triangles and chevrons; these are followed by the sprigged reliefs which for some reason are less common, though Chinese plum-blossom for long remained a favourite motive. Agate ware, though seldom used for salt-glazed

76

PLATE VIII *See pages* 83, 102

(*a*) PUNCH-POT. SALT-GLAZED STONEWARE ENAMELLED IN COLOURS
STAFFORDSHIRE, ABOUT 1755–60
Mr. Wallace Elliot's Collection

(*b*) and (*c*) TEAPOTS. CREAM-COLOURED EARTHENWARE PAINTED IN RED
AND BLACK. STAFFORDSHIRE, ABOUT 1770–75
Victoria and Albert Museum

vessels, made a delightful medium for some little figures of cats and rabbits, with clean, controlled stripes and markings in white and brown enhanced by touches of deep brown and blue-stained clay pigment. These date from the 1740's and are contemporary with the most interesting of all the Staffordshire figures, the famous 'pew-groups' (Plate VII, A) representing seated ladies and gentlemen, generally rustic-looking and sometimes playing musical instruments; and there are rare specimens with Adam and Eve and a delightful Tree of Knowledge. These are capital instances of the potter's special art of modelling natural objects. Judged by an irrelevant standard which might require the forms to resemble 'nature', the pew-groups are crude and worthless; but their vitality is in fact all their own. Arms and legs were stylised in the direction of the handles customarily made for pots and have the same sort of life and spring; hair was rendered in quite unnatural strong coils; fingers were straight but very firm, and so on. One famous piece which passed at Mrs. Hemming's sale into the collection of Mr. Wallace Elliot 'represents' a woman, but is a bell-shaped vessel thrown on the wheel, with a delicious pair of arms, a spherical head, and other details stylised with the utmost sureness and humour. The correspondence of some details (such as masks) on the benches in the pew-groups with those on table-wares suggests that they all proceeded from the same inventive genius. We have every reason to believe them all to have been the work of Aaron Wood, who was born in 1717 and was apprenticed to Dr. Thomas Wedgwood in 1731. He became the most famous 'block-cutter' of the time, working for John Mitchell of Burslem, for Thomas Whieldon, and doubtless also on his own account. Block-making, it should be explained, involves the preparation first of all of intaglio moulds carved in alabaster or some other material; impressions from these are taken in clay and assembled to form a substantial model which was fired and salt-glazed and subsequently used for the preparation of porous plaster or other working moulds, from which the actual wares were made by casting or pressing. To Aaron Wood may be ascribed a very large proportion of the early white salt-glaze moulded relief-designs on table wares, which are marked by naïve in-

FIG. 6. STAFFORDSHIRE SALT-GLAZE TEAPOT

genuity and a fantastic humour. They show medleys of all manner of subjects—shields of arms, stag-hunts, grotesque figures, birds and animals, etc.—usually in panels, the raised borders round which conveniently mask the joins in the moulds (Fig. 6). Teapots were made in the form of houses, kneeling camels, and (important once more for dating) Admiral Vernon's victorious ship (Fig. 7). The taking in the West Indies of Portobello in 1739 and of Chagre in 1740 were repeatedly celebrated in

Staffordshire pottery, and the circumstance is especially valuable when (as here) typical pieces actually dated are rare. Moulding from shells appears early, as on a Chagre teapot otherwise decorated in the so-called scratch-blue technique (which forms a class by itself); it remained a favourite motive for some time and occurs on an extant

FIG. 7. STAFFORDSHIRE SALT-GLAZE TEAPOT

'block' dated 1749 and bearing the initials (perhaps as owner, not modeller) of Aaron Wood's brother Ralph. A little later perhaps are some fantastic pseudo-Chinese figures and plants recalling the Ogilby edition of Nieuhof's *Embassy* already referred to as used by Elers; these are found also on 'Whieldon ware' and recall a legend that Aaron Wood when engaged by that potter stipulated that he should work alone in a locked room, possibly for the

79

reason (as I conjecture) that he wished to conceal the printed sources from which he adapted his designs. However inspired, his earlier reliefs were thoroughly original and well accord with his son Enoch's account of his lively temperament. The later reliefs (about 1755 onwards) have less interest. Some scroll and basketwork patterns, occasionally in pierced open-work, were perhaps suggested by Meissen porcelain and were immensely popular. A 'block' for a spittoon with scallop shells and vines, in the British Museum, bears the incised signature of Aaron Wood, and another with basketwork, at South Kensington, is incised with the initials 'J B 1763'. Solon conjectured (but asserted almost as a fact) that this is the signature of J. Baddeley of the firm of R. and J. Baddeley of Shelton, and the statement in subsequent books that this type of design 'appears to have been most extensively manufactured by the Baddeleys' and so on, has no other foundation than this guess! Quite possibly the blocks were duplicated for different manufacturers and the initials put on them were owners' initials. A block for a sauceboat with this pattern is in the Museum at Etruria, and confirms the belief that salt-glaze of this sort was much made by Josiah Wedgwood, but a precisely similar model was used for a Longton Hall sauceboat. Some reliefs of fruit and flowers and a landscape design are found also on Worcester porcelain; both may have had a common origin in silver. But by this time the original native Staffordshire impulse was pretty well spent.

Some mention should be made at this point of the relatively insignificant 'scratch-blue' salt-glaze with decoration incised and filled with blue colour. The drawing —of sprays of flowers, birds, and inscriptions—is usually artless and weak, and without much merit. The 'scratch-blue' pieces form the majority of the dated salt-glaze, covering a period from 1748 to 1776, or if we include the 'scratch-brown' flask at the British Museum even going back to 1724, but the whole class tantalisingly differs in forms and treatment from the typical uncoloured wares described above and is thus useless for dating them; it was evidently the work of potters not engaged on the relief-decorated ware. Puzzle-jugs, bowls, and wide cylindrical mugs are usual. Also coloured with patches of blue are some mugs and jugs with the initials 'G R' stamped on a pad; though early-looking, these are amongst the latest salt-glaze, dating from the reign of George III. Some exactly similar jugs in lead-glazed earthenware are known with the impressed mark of Wedgwood.

Standing quite apart from everything previously made in Staffordshire is the salt-glazed ware enamelled in colours. This was again due to the fashion for porcelain, though in the result it bore little resemblance to it. As to its origin we have as usual Simeon Shaw's dubious account, ascribing it to two Dutchmen who settled at Hot Lane (Cobridge), and from whom, presumably, the first native enameller, in Shaw's account, one R. Daniel of Cobridge, learnt the art. It is interesting and a kind of confirmation that the earliest enamelling found on salt-glaze, dating from about 1745–50, is apparently from the hand of a Dutch decorator of Delft, who also painted Chinese and Meissen porcelain. (There are examples in the Schreiber Collection.) We know that salt-glaze had found a market in Holland, and we must suppose that Shaw's two Dutchmen decided to try their fortunes nearer the source of the new ware. The Delft work is distinguished among other things by the preponderance of a brownish red and a mannerism of horizontal dotted lines for water. The Dutch-Cobridge work is thought to be that in *famille rose* style, with figures and flowers in somewhat thick but delicately

81   6

applied 'dotted' or 'jewelled' enamels including an opaque
white. Both these styles are charming but not especially
English, whoever may have been responsible for them.
On the other hand, nothing could be more English and
unlike porcelain than the efforts to imitate it by a painter,
working about 1750–60, whom we may associate with a
typical great punch-pot in the Schreiber Collection. His
pink-and-blue sky was apparently copied from the Dutchmen, but his audacious freedom of style and his terrific
palette of green, turquoise, pink, and blue were altogether
a novelty. His trees show a characteristic feathery touch,
and his landscapes, with houses and smoking chimneys,
have a most engagingly childish quality. To this 'punch-
pot painter' are to be ascribed also the great flaunting roses
that appear in reserve on coloured grounds of a frantic
intensity. The green, opaque light blue, brown, crimson,
and inimitable turquoise grounds were often diapered
with ermine spots or a 'fish-roe pattern' of circles; handles
and spouts of a different colour gave startling contrasts,
without precedent in porcelain and obviously suggested
by a similar usage in the 'Astbury ware'. Such decoration
must rank as peasant art, untutored but immensely vital.
Enamel-painting has often been rightly deplored, as far
as delftware is concerned, as a finicking degenerate follower of the bold high-temperature painting; here it has
none of these bad qualities, but a primitive strength. The
identity of another hand brings in question the names of
two actual makers of porcelain. We know that William
Littler of Longton Hall produced porcelain between 1752
and 1760, and we have good reason to believe that
William Duesbury (who was in London from 1751 to
1753, and at Longton about 1754–56) was for a time
associated with him. Duesbury from 1756 onwards made
porcelain at Derby, but had been at first an independent

enameller whose London 'work-book' has survived and shows references to 'Stafartshire' wares. 'Swiming swans donn all over' is one entry which can only refer to some salt-glaze figures enamelled in thick brilliant red, turquoise, and purple. Certain salt-glaze teapots formed like overlapping cabbage-leaves and some figures copying Meissen closely resemble Longton Hall porcelain, and the enamelling on these links them with other coloured reliefs and with the painted work of another most gifted hand. This master painted Chinese subjects which are exceedingly loose and free in style but very sensitively drawn, and are further enriched by fantasies on the Chinese diaper borders with a fascinating counterchange of colour. His masterpiece is a large punch-pot in Mr. Wallace Elliot's collection (Plate VIII, A). Such a piece may have been done by one of Duesbury's Staffordshire painters; it is almost certainly too late for Duesbury himself. To Littler is also ascribed, largely on the authority of Simeon Shaw, a distinct class with a beautiful deep blue glaze, sometimes painted over in white enamel touched with black, sometimes poorly gilded. The dark blue ground on Littler's porcelain (which is better authenticated and will be described in the second part of this book) is of a quite different tone, but this may be due to the different recipient. The white painting moreover occurs on the porcelain. Lastly, some mention should be made of the transfer-printed salt-glaze. This belongs to a late phase (about 1760 onwards), and much of the actual ware was probably made by Josiah Wedgwood. The printing is Liverpool work done by Sadler and Green. The brick-red chiefly used, for fable subjects, pastorals in Watteau's manner, exotic birds, etc., gave a soft 'primitive' effect that puts this amongst the most agreeable transfer-printing on English pottery. Moulded borders painted over in turquoise were usual, and in rare instances several colours—such as red, purple, and black—were used for printing on a single piece, with a very pretty effect.

By 1760 the salt-glaze had begun to be superseded by the perfected cream-colour, which was in many ways more serviceable. In spite of the sensuous charm its delicate material has for us, it must be admitted that the salt-glazed ware was not only brittle, but actually too hard and its minutely pitted 'orange skin' surface too uneven for it to be pleasant in table use. Silver was worn away by it. By 1770 it was hardly being made at all for the wider market, and by 1787 its manufacture is said to have ceased altogether. But it had laid the foundations of the Staffordshire trade on the Continent, and the new cream-colour was everywhere accepted as an improved variety of the English '*Steingut*', '*grès d'Angleterre*', or '*Engels porselein*' already known in Germany, France, and Holland. The appearance of a Saint-Cloud porcelain form in a flower-pot in salt-glaze may well be taken as an indication of the enterprise of a Staffordshire traveller, who had brought home a sample of the porcelain his firm should set itself to copy and replace.

But, as I have said, these early Staffordshire potters created their own styles, whatever may have suggested them in the first instance. Down to the first establishment of Josiah Wedgwood as an independent potter in 1759, most of the characteristic Staffordshire productions had shown some visible kinship with the local slipware, even when, as in the case of the white salt-glaze and its enamelling, this kinship implied no more than a certain humour and peasant simplicity. With the advent of Wedgwood an educated taste supervened, though the native style survived for a time in a few types of ware to be described in a subsequent chapter. Chief among these are the early

Ralph Wood figures, which closely follow the Whieldon tradition. Consideration of these is deferred, since in date they are subsequent to the rise of the famous potter who wrought so great a change, for good or ill, in the whole Staffordshire industry.

CHAPTER VI

WEDGWOOD

IT is nowadays fashionable to decry the achievements of Josiah Wedgwood, and on the artistic side they have certainly been over-rated. But it must be remembered that, though born of a family of potters, he was first and foremost a business man, a gifted and determined organiser of industry, not an artist, and even his high standard of technical excellence was dictated chiefly by a regard for his commercial reputation. It was perhaps as a business man, again, that he put his trust in the coming vogue of the neo-Classical style, and the trend of events having proved him right it became his privilege to dictate the application of that style throughout Europe. But there was unfortunately a touch of self-righteousness and complacency about him, masking his self-interest in professions of public spirit, and we should like him better had he not so painstakingly sought the acquaintance of the rich and influential, though it was largely in this manner that he was enabled to raise the status of Staffordshire pottery to a point at which cream-coloured earthenware could take the place of porcelain on the tables of the great, and his vases and cameos be valued as highly as veritable works of antiquity. He was the first English potter to obtain a European reputation, and his influence made itself felt not only in the smaller European *faïenceries* but in such princely concerns as the Berlin and Fürstenberg porcelain-factories.

PLATE IX *See page* 89

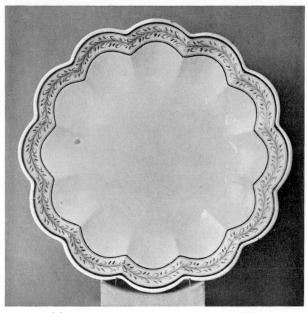

(*a*) DISH. CREAM-COLOURED EARTHENWARE
STAFFORDSHIRE (WEDGWOOD'S FACTORY), ABOUT 1775
Victoria and Albert Museum

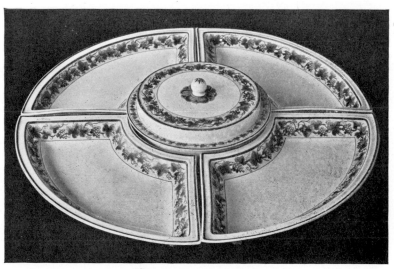

(*b*) SET OF SUPPER-TRAYS
STAFFORDSHIRE (WEDGWOOD'S FACTORY), ABOUT 1775
Victoria and Albert Museum

His actual achievement was a contribution to amenities rather than to art. His cream-coloured ware was not only cleaner and more durable in use than anything as cheap that had preceded it, but in its forms it showed a practical intelligence that gave attention for the first time to the fitness for their purpose of spouts and strainers, handles and lids, securing at once an economical lightness and a 'modern' efficiency. It was no mean accomplishment. His notions of art as embodied in his decorative wares were largely those of this age; it was an 'educated' taste, accepting what was fashionable, not a native sense of beauty or of traditional craftsmanship, and his productions move us less on that account. His ideal of a minute mechanical perfection was entirely consonant with the taste he showed for 'pure' and dry classical forms.

The facts of Wedgwood's career have so often been related that no more than a brief outline is called for here. He was born in 1730, thirteenth child of Thomas Wedgwood of the Churchyard Pottery at Burslem. At the age of nine he began work in the family pottery, and in 1744 he was apprenticed to his elder brother Thomas. In or about 1749 he joined (or succeeded) one Thomas Alders of Cliff Bank, Stoke, in partnership with a merchant named John Harrison, and in 1754 he became junior partner with Thomas Whieldon of Fenton, with whom he remained until 1758 or 1759. In the latter year he started work on his own account at Burslem, having (it is said) discovered a method of making a fine green glaze. In 1762 he met Thomas Bentley, a merchant of Liverpool, who drew his attention to the antique, then being popularised by Sir William Hamilton and the Comte de Caylus, and with whom as partner he began in 1768 to build a new factory, house, and village which he named Etruria (Greek vases being then called Etruscan). Bentley remained his partner in the matter of 'ornamental wares' only, until his death in 1780. The Burslem factory was not given up until 1771–73, when the workmen and plant were gradually transferred to Etruria. Wedgwood died in 1795, and the still-existing manufacture has remained in the hands of his descendants.

Wedgwood's Burslem work was at first in the styles described in the previous chapter. His improved green and yellow glazes enabled him to add some new types, among them the well-known vessels moulded in the form of cauliflowers and pine-apples and some plain green pieces decorated with gilding. Some moulded patterns of landscapes (attributed to a William Greatbach) are found with these glazes, and also in the salt-glazed wares which were evidently at first among his most numerous productions. Improving the cream-coloured body, he seems to have aimed at the complete elimination of painting and coloured glazes, and in 1763, after securing the patronage of Queen Charlotte, he named this ware ' Queen's Ware'. The shapes continued to be much inspired by silver—'feather-edging', beading, and above all pierced decoration, being adapted in this way. Pierced designs are sometimes erroneously thought to have been invented at Leeds, which in this matter as in many others merely took up and developed Wedgwood's innovation. William Wood, a son of Aaron Wood, was apparently employed in designing forms for the cream-coloured ware. When decoration was added it was often done outside the factory. Much ware was sent to the Liverpool transfer-printers, as an account for 1764 shows. Mrs. Warburton of Cobridge is recorded to have done some (unidentified) painting for Wedgwood, and in 1768 a decorating shop was opened by him in London, at first at Great Newport Street, afterwards at Chelsea. Here it was that in 1773 the famous 'Frog

Service' of cream-coloured ware was painted for the Empress Catherine of Russia; the whole decoration of laboriously painted English landscapes and classical leaf borders, with the exception of the 'crest' of a green frog (the service was for the Grenouille Palace), was in dark blackish purple. A few pieces are in commerce, though the bulk of the service was still at St. Petersburg when Dr. Williamson wrote his book on it. It stands as a landmark in the history of English ceramics, but in itself cannot, I feel, take a very high place as a work of art. Such elaborate painting, however, was quite exceptional. Slight borders of laurel, 'husk', anthemion, and other slight formal foliage became usual with the advance of the Classical mode (Plate IX). A technical improvement in the cream-colour was brought about by the introduction, at some time before 1775, of china-clay and china-stone in the body and glaze, and Wedgwood accordingly offered violent objection to the renewal in that year of Richard Champion's patent for these materials (see Part II under Bristol). Later still, bone-ash was added, but not apparently at first by Wedgwood. A little before 1780 Wedgwood introduced a modification of the cream-colour in the form of a fine white earthenware which he called 'pearl ware'. In this the yellow tone was counteracted by a touch of blue; it is not so pleasant in colour but was very suitable for decoration in blue, and made possible, in the hands of his imitators and successors, the immense development of blue-printed ware which took place at the end of the eighteenth and in the early part of the nineteenth centuries.

But Wedgwood's great ambition, from the time of his first meeting with Bentley, was to make decorative wares, 'vases' that should stand comparison with the ceramic art of antiquity. Already in his Burslem period the cream-coloured ware was made into carefully finished vases with engine-turning or gilding or with stripes of brown or other coloured slip. Coloured glazes or slips were used in marbled effects, and more elaborate work in the same style was done by a refinement of the 'solid agate' ware of his predecessors. The coloured clays were very skilfully disposed to imitate natural stones, and these 'onyx' and 'pebbled' vases have been considered among Wedgwood's greatest achievements. But though well-proportioned and graceful if judged by the Classical canon, and of course very well finished technically, they have little true ceramic interest. They are cold as stone. The same must be said of most of the subsequent achievements on which Wedgwood prided himself. The new materials introduced by him are often admirable in themselves; they are evidently the result of long and patient research, and have the distinction, almost a preciousness, that must needs belong to fire-won products of such great refinement. But in their use Wedgwood had no thought but to simulate the works of classical antiquity. At first Greek vases were his model, and since the merit attaching to these lies almost entirely in their quite inimitable painting, and not in their material or shapes, his copies were naturally a complete failure. For the rest his models were the classical engraved cameos in gem-stones or sculpture in marble, so that none of his work speaks of its origin in clay, even at second hand. Their interest lies in the restrained and graceful forms themselves, and in the serious naturalistic modelling inspired by the new mode, with its strange tincture of entirely unclassical sweetness and sentiment. Their high finish may be claimed as fine workmanship, and there is feeling in it though it owed nothing to the traditional potter's craftsmanship.

The first material that received Wedgwood's attention at the new Etruria factory (and even earlier) was the black-

PLATE X   *See pages* 92, 94

(*a*) VASE. GREEN AND WHITE JASPER WARE
STAFFORDSHIRE (WEDGWOOD'S FACTORY), ABOUT 1780–90
Victoria and Albert Museum

(*b*) PORTRAIT - RELIEF. BLUE
JASPER WARE : DAVID GARRICK
STAFFORDSHIRE (WEDGWOOD'S
FACTORY), ABOUT 1780
British Museum (Falcke Gift)

(*c*) PLAQUE. BLUE JASPER WARE
INFANT BACCHANAL
STAFFORDSHIRE (WEDGWOOD'S
FACTORY), ABOUT 1780
British Museum (Falcke Gift)

bodied ware that had occasionally been made in Staffordshire from the beginning of the industry's advancement.
From this he produced about 1767 his first specimens of
what he named 'black basaltes' ware or 'black porcelaine',
a very hard fine-grained stoneware which could be polished
on the lapidary's wheel. It was indeed so hard that a very
slight rubbing brought out a dull gloss. Some of the first
Etruria productions (of about 1769) were the rare 'bronze
Etruscan' vases of black basalt with lightly fired dull gilding, and the often enormous 'painted Etruscan' vases,
with copies of Greek vase-painting in matt-surfaced red
and white enamels on the black ground (thus reversing the
technique of the 'red-figure' vases). This painting was
probably done at the Chelsea workshop under Bentley's
supervision. More important works in black basalt were
the life-size library busts of classical and modern authors
made from 1770 onwards. Many vases were decorated in
relief with fluting and engine-turning. Among other
materials the local unglazed red ware, which Wedgwood
despised since it 'reminded him of the red teapots' he
had made at Fenton and Burslem, was renamed *rosso antico*
and used in the same styles as the basaltes, like the buff
or 'cane-coloured' ware made from a local marl. The
latter was sometimes painted with formal foliage, etc., in
blue and other coloured enamels. In all these wares it
was Wedgwood's ambition to produce a type of cameo
relief-decoration inspired by the engraved gems, and it
was a matter of untiring research with him to make a
material worthy of it. True porcelain as used in China and
Germany he seems to have thought of as tainted. He
thoroughly disliked the gaudy painted dolls of Meissen
and the rest, and there can be no doubt that he would have
approved of the words of his admiring biographer when
she spoke of Chinese porcelain as 'oriental barbarism in

art . . . in which truth was outraged and taste disregarded'. The delicious soft-pastes he doubtless despised as entirely unpractical. His search was thus for a new, fine-grained, hard material, beautiful in itself and capable of being moulded into the most delicate relief-work. This he found at length, towards 1775, after experiments with refined stoneware or semi-porcelain and a cream-coloured terra cotta, in a material made with a novel ingredient in the form of the baryta (barium sulphate) of Derbyshire. He called this 'jasper ware'. It was vitrified and slightly trans-lucent, and white in colour, but could be readily stained with metallic oxides to the familiar lavender-blue, pink-ish lilac, sage- and olive-greens, yellow, and a peculiarly velvety black. In 1777 a method of staining only the surface layer resulted in the more economical and usual 'jasper dip'. The notion of white reliefs applied to a coloured ground was doubtless suggested to Wedgwood by the cameos of antiquity in layered stone, as much as by the humbler white reliefs of his Staffordshire predecessors. With this material and the other wares described above he proceeded to make all sorts of small decorative articles never previously supplied by the potter—such as mounts for snuff-boxes and opera-glasses, beads and buttons, plaques for inlaying in furniture, as well as cameos and intaglios for seals, and more or less useful wares such as teapots. Wedgwood was in close touch with Boulton and Fothergill (later Boulton and Watt), the Birmingham metal-workers, and sent large numbers of jasper cameos for mounting in their cut-steel jewellery. Vases (Plate X, A) were not made until about 1780–85, but it is said that as many as two hundred and fifty models for vases proper, besides candlesticks, ewers, flower-holders, and the like, were made in Josiah's own lifetime. Some small figures in the round were made in white jasper, in the style of biscuit porcelain. In 1779 there were catalogued some seventeen hundred different subjects in the cameos and intaglios, which were apparently collected like antique gems, though, as Professor Church pointed out, no collector could possibly accept the relatively coarse-grained and lumpy jasper versions as adequate substitutes for the originals.

The reliefs—on basalt as well as jasper—at first offered difficulties in the matter of their application to a large curved surface, by the Staffordshire method of 'sprigging', and these were not overcome until about 1775. Difficulties due to unequal contraction also delayed the production of white reliefs on the coloured jasper; vases in bluc-and-white were in fact not made until after Bentley's death.

For models Wedgwood made constant use of the antique, employing James Tassie as early as 1769 to supply casts of gems and obtaining access to the Duke of Marlborough's famous collection. Coins and medals were also used. Wedgwood's accounts with various people (such as Grant and Hoskins, Mrs. Landre and John Flaxman, senr.) for the supply of casts of busts and other larger antique models have often been mistaken for evidence of original work. It was his practice to alter and adapt the antique models, toning down and sweetening their frank paganism and clothing their nudities to suit English taste, and in comparatively few cases is it possible to give the artist's name. Even where the work was original and contemporary it was often altered at Etruria and the modeller's name was suppressed. Signatures were never countenanced, and it is an ironical circumstance that one of the very few signed pieces is Hackwood's relief of Wedgwood himself. Perhaps the best and most enduringly valuable of the jasper reliefs are the heads of 'illustrious moderns' begun in 1774. Some of these were after existing waxes by the Gossets and others; but many were specially modelled by William Hackwood, John Flaxman, junr., J. C. Lochee, and Joachim Smith. In his Catalogue Wedgwood invited orders for original portrait-medallions in jasper, which were no doubt made by these modellers. Hackwood was Wedgwood's right-hand man in the modelling shop. He worked for the firm from 1769 to 1832 and had a share in the adapting of an immense number of classical reliefs, mostly supplied in a preliminary state by a small army of Italians working under Flaxman and Henry Webber in Rome. Hackwood was an accomplished craftsman and no mean modeller. His portrait reliefs of (amongst others) George III, Queen Charlotte, the Prince of Wales, David Garrick (Plate X, B), and of Wedgwood himself and his relative the Rev. W. Willet, are particularly good. Flaxman's portraits (Sir William Hamilton, Capt. Cook, etc. etc.) show a higher relief and are even better; his other work was much altered in the factory and is somewhat hard to identify. Some sentimental-classical reliefs of women and children (Plate X, c) are said to have been modelled by Lady Templetown, Lady Diana Beauclerk, and Miss Crewe, but it is probable that they did no more than supply sketches for the subjects attributed to them.

One famous work of Wedgwood's has yet to be mentioned. It was typical of his sterile revivalism that he should devote several years in an endeavour to reproduce with perfect accuracy a Roman work in coloured glass: the famous 'Barberini' or 'Portland Vase', of which fifty copies at the most seem to have been produced by him between 1786 and 1790.

Wedgwood was the first Staffordshire potter to adopt a regular factory mark, but it is inaccurate to assert that no other potter had previously used a labour-saving stamped mark. It is doubtful whether the 'Wedgwood' mark was used before the Wedgwood and Bentley period (1768–1780); an irregular early mark of the name with each letter separately stamped has been alleged, but apparently no piece so marked has ever been cited. It is also a mistake to suppose that 'Wedgwood' alone dates from 1780 or later, since the partnership with Bentley was for ornamental wares only, and useful wares made during the same period from about 1770 onwards were sometimes (but not always) marked 'Wedgwood'. To distinguish the wares of Josiah's own lifetime is a matter of some difficulty. Fineness of workmanship counts for much; but many pieces will always, in Church's quaint phrase, 'demand ocular comparisons by experienced connoisseurs'. For negative evidence may be mentioned a group of three letters side by side used as an impressed mark in addition to 'WEDGWOOD' from 1860 onwards (a key is given in Rathbone's Catalogue of the Etruria Museum); and the random toolmarks, stars, and 'commas' often in pairs, which belong to the early part of the nineteenth century, as does a mark with a letter forming part of the same stamp as the 'Wedgwood'. It should further be noted that porcelain with a printed mark in red dates from 1812 to 1816; 'WEDGWOOD & CO' is a mark of Ralph Wedgwood, a cousin of Josiah's, used at Ferrybridge in Yorkshire; and 'WEDGEWOOD' is that of W. Smith's mid-nineteenth-century factory at Stockton-on-Tees. It is also certain that foreign manufacturers occasionally forged the mark.

A few types sometimes said to have been introduced by the Wedgwood firm at the end of the eighteenth century (such as lustre-ware) are reserved for discussion in a later chapter dealing with the nineteenth century, to which their development properly belongs.

CHAPTER VII

THE CONTEMPORARIES OF WEDGWOOD: RALPH WOOD, THE LEEDS FACTORY, AND OTHERS

ENGLISH pottery after Wedgwood's rise to fame could hardly escape his powerful influence, and its history tends to become a record of imitations, most of which can receive but a bare mention here. The new markets opened up attracted a host of competitors, and potteries in many places where previously red earthenware alone had been made began to make cream-coloured ware in the hope of a share of the spoils. In Yorkshire, for example, where coal was abundant, Mr. Oxley Grabham in his thorough little monograph has noted no fewer than thirteen factories making Staffordshire types of ware in the latter part of the eighteenth and the early nineteenth centuries. Some of them marked their productions with a stamped name in the approved Wedgwood style, but most left them unmarked in the hope of securing their acceptance as the genuine Wedgwood article. In North Staffordshire, of course, the factories were more numerous still; everything combined to give them advantages. Not only had they abundant coal and clay and ready access by water to most parts of England, but, as Col. J. C. Wedgwood has pointed out, the absence of large estates facilitated the development of an industry carried on by a great number of individual potters, each working on his own small plot of land. In this way was built up the great Staffordshire trade in pots, which even now serves a world market.

In the styles adopted, porcelain alone offered an influence rivalling that of Wedgwood. The Worcester and Derby factories had won a considerable success in England, and in spite of the new Classical mode not every maker of cream-ware had the austerity to abandon painted decoration in porcelain style. Thus we find here and there enamel-painting that frankly copies at second hand the bouquets of flowers and pictorial work made popular by Sèvres, then the fashion-leading porcelain-factory. More notably we find, occasionally, painting derived indeed from porcelain but so stylised in peasant fashion (like the decoration on salt-glaze described in an earlier chapter) as to rank as genuinely original work. One potter alone seems to have had the will to resist the forces of the time and continue the Staffordshire tradition of coloured glazes: this was Ralph Wood of Burslem.

The Wood family altogether made a very notable contribution to Staffordshire ceramic history. The great part played by Aaron Wood in the early period, and his son William's smaller share in the making of the cream-colour, have already been mentioned. Aaron's brother Ralph (b. 1715, d. 1772) and the latter's son of the same name (b. 1748, d. 1795) were general potters who, besides making the current types of ware described in the two previous chapters, for at least fifteen years after the arrival of cream-colour continued the Whieldon style with slight modifications in a class of figures of great beauty and interest. These have a soft, translucent lead-glaze under which were laid green, yellow, brownish purple, grey, and a clear quiet blue in such a way that the colours were partly taken up by it; but the patches of colour tended to remain distinct, with the effect of painting, not flowing and blending as much as on Whieldon ware. This range of underglaze colours lent itself to delicious soft harmonies quite unlike anything previously done in England or else-where. Colour-glazed figures in the same technique had been made by the followers of Palissy two centuries earlier, but with a quite different effect. The models were for the most part not original, and were the work of a French-man, John Voyez. Many were adapted from figures by Cyfflé of Lunéville and other French sources; some were taken from the antique. A feature of most, evidence of a keen eye for glaze effect, is the reliance shown on rounded forms without deep hollows, with details sometimes lightly incised for accent. In expression they are commonly heavy-featured with full—even protruding—eyes and thick lips. The well-known *Vicar and Moses* is one of the best and most characteristic early models, and long remained popular. But the early 'Toby jugs' were perhaps Ralph Wood's most notable creation. Their humour has been called Hogarthian and English, but it is practically certain that they too were modelled by the foreigner Voyez, from a print with verses referring to 'Toby Philpot', published in 1761. These jugs remained popular in many variations for more than half a century. Space will not allow a separate description of each: for the 'King Hal', 'The Planter', 'The Gin Woman', 'The Thin Man', 'The Hearty Good Fellow', and the rest, the reader should consult Capt. Price's cata-logue and Mr. Read's book. The Ralph Wood figures are now admirably represented at South Kensington in the col-lection presented by the late W. Sanders Fiske (Plate VII, B).

The earliest of the Wood figures can hardly have been made before 1760, that is about ten years before the death of the elder Ralph. Towards 1780 the 'translucent colours' began to give place to enamelling over the glaze, with a great loss of charm, and this latter type of colouring was characteristic of the immense output of Enoch Wood (*b.* 1759, *d.* 1840), son of Aaron, nephew of Ralph the elder, and successor to the latter's son. Enoch Wood was himself a modeller; he began business on his own account in 1780 and took as partner from 1790 to 1818 one James Caldwell. His busts are perhaps his most noteworthy work: that of *John Wesley* was modelled by him from life in 1781. But very few of his productions are of serious artistic importance; only when some painter's native fancy was given rein (as in a naïvely coloured *Lucretia* at South Kensington, with pink and orange draperies), and the current Derby porcelain style forgotten, can we think of the Enoch Wood figures as in any way genuine things. Before the end of the eighteenth century he added actual porcelain—a rather greyish material—to his productions (which included also useful and decorative wares in jasper, basalt, and creamcolour), and the figures made in this often bear the same mould-numbers as those in earthenware. This circumstance alone is sufficient to disprove the still current contention that they were made at Lowestoft. It should be mentioned that the Ralph and Enoch Wood wares were commonly marked with the name of the firm, and a curious mark 'W(***)' may also be ascribed to Enoch. Some of the later Wood figures were of very large size (a *Mother and Child* and a *Fortitude* at South Kensington, the latter over 23 in. high, are good examples), and these are sometimes found with the mark 'Wedgwood'. This, it is believed, was added to figures made by the Woods for Josiah Wedgwood, to enable the latter to fulfil orders including this type of 'goods'; a bill for figures supplied in this way was published by Mr. Frank Falkner. Perhaps the best enamel-painted Staffordshire figures were not the Woods' but those of Neale of Hanley, which show very clean workmanship and bright definite colours, including a rich dark brown and a clear turquoise, with lively sprig patterns on the costumes.

99

A distinct type of decoration in underglaze high-temperature pigments appeared in Staffordshire towards the end of the eighteenth century and deserves a word or two. A rather dull blue-and-green and a thick brownish orange are conspicuous among the colours applied in blurred touches, notably over moulded reliefs. The type is usually associated with Pratt of Fenton, but it is certain that the so-called 'Pratt ware' was made by other Staffordshire potters as well as by those of Sunderland and other places in the North.

The Yorkshire potteries are an interesting group, centred on the great manufacture at Leeds (1774, at latest, onwards) with which for certain periods the factories at Swinton ('Rockingham') and the neighbouring Mexborough (Don Pottery) were united. Though black basalt, 'tortoise-shell', and 'blue-printed' were made at these places, it is on their plain cream-coloured 'Queen's Ware' that their reputation chiefly rests. Wedgwood's types were taken up and in many cases surpassed in a material of great refinement (Fig. 8). Pierced decoration is especially characteristic and of exceedingly delicate workmanship, but moulding was as common, and even figure-modelling was also used for the cruets and centre-pieces which were the finest achievements of Leeds in plain cream-colour. Independent coloured figures are less distinctive and closely resemble the later Wood models. Collectors are often at a loss to separate Leeds from Staffordshire, and this is not seldom an impossibility. The colour of Leeds is at times distinctively greenish or of a deep cream, but it undoubtedly varied a good deal. A close study of the contemporary illustrated Leeds catalogues (which were issued in several languages) will sometimes appear to settle the question in favour of Yorkshire; and it certainly seems that the Staffordshire cabbage-leaf spouts and scrolled handles were never used at Leeds. But the twisted handles with leaf terminations were not, as is often supposed, peculiar to the latter. Besides the plain Queen's ware, certain other types of Leeds are noteworthy: a glaze marbled with brown and grey slips, and a ware minutely speckled in remote imitation of granite, and

FIG. 8. VASE. LEEDS CREAM-COLOURED WARE

known by that name, were charmingly used in wide bands; and an opaque brown glaze, imitating the Chinese 'dead leaf' colour, was used to enclose panels on which were painted bouquets of flowers in enamels, in the style of the porcelain known as Batavian; this last, so far as English wares are concerned, is quite peculiar to Leeds. A coarser 'granite' ware, often with the brown particles left rough, was also made by Ralph Wood at Burslem.

The enamel-painting on certain classes of cream-colour resembling Leeds, of about 1760–80, is of great interest for its almost 'peasant' vigour and novelty. The most charming type, in my opinion, is that painted in red and black only, with full feathery scrolls enclosing inscriptions, such as 'God Speed the Plough' (Plate VIII, c) or a dedication. An original and very satisfying harmony is made by these colours with the deep cream ground. The class is disputed between the partisans of Leeds and Staffordshire. The same two colours are seen also in some flower-painting, much stylised, with lively spiky stems and club-shaped leaves (Plate VIII, B), and this is associated again with some very fantastic figure-painting with buildings rendered in the most summary way, in colours employing also green and a rose-purple which makes a charming discord with the red. Vertical bands of curious diaper-patterns employ the same palette of colours and show an able 'peasant' artist giving life to the dull classicism of the period. Other hands may be detected in more naturalistic but still free and vigorous flower-painting, among which some very pleasant green monochrome work is believed to have been done in the Leeds factory. Most of the types here discussed are in fact called Leeds in the trade, but, for the reasons given above, cannot be definitely assigned. Doubt may even be expressed as to whether the painting was done in the factories at all. It is known that several 'outside' decorators were at work in the period. Robinson and Rhodes of Leeds advertised enamelled Staffordshire stoneware in 1760 and may well have done this charming work in the rising time of the local manufacture. Again, we cannot point to any productions of the enamelling shop of Mrs. Warburton of Cobridge, who is known to have worked for Wedgwood; she was herself a notable manufacturer of cream-colour.

Finally, there is the not uncommon English cream-colour with enamelling known to have been done in Holland!

The more careful imitations of the porcelain-painting of flowers, exotic birds, figure-subjects, and the rest, are of less interest. Some of this is thought to be the work of one of the potteries at Liverpool, where delft was given up in favour of cream-colour towards the end of the eighteenth century, and where a factory called Herculaneum in emulation of Etruria was eventually started in 1793–94. Other specimens bear the Ferrybridge mark 'Wedgwood & Co'.

The transfer-printing on cream-coloured ware tended to follow the Liverpool (Sadler and Green) tradition; but a new and peculiarly Staffordshire style, especially associated with J. Aynsley of Lane End, shows black or red printing painted over in colours. 'Keep within Compass' and prize-fighting and convivial subjects are typical and sometimes signed. William Greatbach (who had been with Wedgwood) produced at Lane Delph some cream-colour similarly decorated. Some of his marked pieces are dated 1778. Thomas Radford, who engraved for him, also worked for the Cockpit Hill factory at Derby, and an 'R' in a circle surrounded by sun-rays is said to be his mark. Thomas Rothwell, an engraver who worked for Palmer at Hanley, and at Swansea, introduced at the latter place a novel style of engraved landscapes of no great merit. Underglaze blue printing in the style of Caughley porcelain is found on the 'pearl ware', but the fullest development of this branch did not take place until the nineteenth century.

The attribution of unmarked cream-colour must always be somewhat conjectural. Apart from the very numerous Staffordshire makers (among whom the Turners of Lane End, Elijah Mayer, Palmer and his successors Neale and

Wilson, all of Hanley, William Adams of Tunstall, and
Josiah Spode of Stoke, are believed to have equalled
Wedgwood's ware in quality), there were potteries making
it at Cockpit Hill in Derby (about 1751 to 1779), at
Temple Back in Bristol, where Ring engaged a Shelton
potter in 1785, at Swansea (the 'Cambrian Pottery' from
about 1765), where some of the white earthenware was
called 'opaque china'—a fashion followed elsewhere, and
from 1792 onwards at Ferrybridge, where a kinsman of
Josiah, Ralph Wedgwood, joined the firm to make it
'Wedgwood & Co' in 1796. At Castleford in Yorkshire,
founded in 1790, David Dunderdale tried to rival Leeds
and issued a similar illustrated catalogue of Queen's ware,
in several languages. At Liverpool so much Staffordshire
ware was printed that it is hard to distinguish the local
productions, which were undoubtedly numerous (Fig. 9);
much was intended for the American market. Farther
north several potteries at Southwick, Sunderland, and
Newcastle began making rough white earthenware with
transfer-printing before 1800, but the history of the group
belongs rather to the nineteenth century. Relatively little
of all this was marked and generalisations are hazardous;
but it may be said that Swansea was as a rule somewhat
low-fired and lacking in resonance; Bristol inclined to a
deep cream-colour or was else dead white, as was much of
the North Country ware. Shapes and patterns were freely
copied one from another and are no guide at all. Standing
a little apart from the rest is the deep brown-glazed earthenware introduced about 1788 at Swinton—the so-called
'Rockingham ware'. The pleasantly uneven colour of this
glaze, which was obtained from manganese and iron, is
still popular for teapots used in unfashionable circles and
has been made with equal success at many other factories.

Many of these potters also made stoneware in the

Wedgwood styles; most indeed made black basaltes. Turner imitated jasper in a semi-porcelain; his blue often has a distinctive slightly greenish tone. The blue jasper of William Adams, who had been with Wedgwood, was quite equal to his master's, but usually of a stronger tone approaching violet. Turner and Elijah Mayer both

FIG. 9. JUG. CREAM-COLOURED WARE WITH LIVERPOOL PRINTING

specialised in a fine-grained buff stoneware ('cane-colour') of excellent quality. Very few innovations appeared before the end of the century, but mention may be made here of the green and dark red-brown stonewares of Samuel Hollins of Shelton, of Turner's busts and vases and jugs with relief-decoration in a fine cream-coloured stoneware, of the half-glossy white teapots of squarish shape with blue enamel lines made at Castleford, and the busts in a similar or drab-coloured material of 'Herculaneum'. The two last, however, strictly belong to the nineteenth century, and an account of the later work of these and other industrial potteries will be found in Chapter XV.

PART II

ENGLISH PORCELAIN OF THE
EIGHTEENTH CENTURY

CHAPTER VIII

CHELSEA

TURNING from earthenware to porcelain we enter a
new world, a world of sheer amusement, where considerations of usefulness are irrelevant and seriousness an
impertinence. Porcelain can be turned to use, of course, but
its true genius is to charm and surprise, and it was the
happiest accident that on its rediscovery in Europe its
technique should have come to maturity precisely in the
period of the irresponsible and capricious *rococo* style. No
better medium could be imagined for this than the nervous
and plastic porcelain, and the hard-paste of Germany was
especially fit for its fantastic play. Soft-paste had to be
more substantial, and the early Saint-Cloud was aptly con-
stituted to embody the austere graces of the *Louis Quatorze*.
In the succeeding period the soft-pastes (to which the
English porcelains mainly belong), though not failing altogether to take up the forms of the new movement, relied
upon lively and fanciful painting rather than upon the
plastic extravagances of the Germans. But everywhere
porcelain was the product of a desire to please the eye
and hand; it was unpractical, amoral, even absurd, when
judged by the familiar puritan standard. It existed only for
the delight of a leisured class.

We must come then to a consideration of English as
of every other china of the great period unprejudiced
by notions of fitness or correctness, prepared only to take

pleasure in its sensuous charm and playful resources in decoration, modelled and painted.

Chelsea is here taken first among the English factories because it provides the earliest dated specimens. In the case of Bow we have an earlier written record, of a patent granted in 1744, but no Bow specimens of that date or anywhere near it are known for certain. Some 'goat-and-bee' jugs of Chelsea are actually dated 1745, and bear the factory name and the mark of an incised triangle which has given its title to the earliest period of Chelsea porcelain, covering the five years down to about 1750. It is believed that at this time Charles Gouyn, a French Huguenot and jeweller, and Nicholas Sprimont, a silversmith, now shown by Dr. Bellamy Gardner to have come from Liège, were partners in the manufacture. The porcelain material they made was a soft-paste of French type; that is to say, it was composed chiefly of a glassy compound of silica and alkali, called a 'frit', ground up and mixed with a white clay and a certain amount of lime or chalk. Such frit-porcelains were of an entirely artificial character. Lacking natural 'fat' clays, they were unplastic in the shaping. They were also unstable and likely to collapse in the firing, so that kiln losses were high, and they were on this account as a rule costly to produce. Gouyn is known to have been a Frenchman, but may not have been the 'arcanist'. A Thomas Briand, who showed some specimens of what was apparently a soft-paste of French type before the Royal Society in 1742–43, has sometimes been conjectured to have been the pottery-chemist concerned in the manufacture; but there is no proof of his association with it.

The triangle-marked Chelsea is a beautiful and fragile substance, glassy in texture and milk-white in colour, showing brighter flecks in its translucency when viewed by transmitted light. It is indeed so like glass at times that it has been mistaken for it; a specimen actually triangle-marked was included in the famous Alfred Trapnell Catalogue under the heading of 'Bristol glass'. Its interest is partly that attaching to *incunabula* of any kind. The forms were obviously close copies of silver; the goat-and-bee jugs themselves have a known original (they are little cream-jugs with the creatures named moulded in relief). Some cups in the form of folded strawberry-leaves come out especially well in porcelain and are charming. But besides the attraction of its material, this early work has aesthetic merit in some degree in its naïve decoration of flowers and insects in bright colours, scattered about to conceal flaws in the paste in the usual contemporary manner. They were doubtless suggested by Meissen, but are as a rule nothing like it, though a specimen occasion-ally shows the clear firm style of the latter in its earliest painting of European flowers. Figures were seldom made. A group of *Lovers* in the British Museum has been identified as Chelsea by a mark of a trident intersecting a crown, in blue, which occurs also (but very rarely) on pieces of unquestionable triangle type. Some exceedingly rare teapots in the form of grotesque Chinamen are also of the period; they are charming 'primitives', very well modelled, and somewhat resemble Saint-Cloud porcelain; but both were perhaps derived from Meissen.

Standing a little apart from the well-understood Chelsea, both earlier and later, are some rare figures, usually left unpainted, which form a much-debated class obvi-ously of the period shortly after 1750. These are associ-ated with a naïvely modelled *Girl in a Swing* at South Kensington, and include an exceedingly good *Hound*, a group of *Hercules and Omphale* (in the Schreiber Collection), and *Britannia mourning the death of Frederick Prince of Wales*, who died in 1751. Bevelled and champfered bases are a peculiar but not invariable feature of the class, which shows a somewhat greyish-toned paste, not unlike the mature Chelsea in its smooth close texture, but in chemical composition coming close to the triangle porcelain. Many theories have been put forward to account for these figures. They may have been Chelsea experiments towards a new paste, though 1751 is rather too late for this to be likely; or they may have been the work of some seceding Chelsea hands. A legend recorded by Simeon Shaw, about some Staffordshire-born workmen who left the factory because their services were not properly appreciated, may have had some foundation in fact. The links with Chelsea (for example, some of the 'toys' mentioned below) are unquestionable, but there are also unmistakeable differences, and the origin of the class for the present remains a mystery.

By 1750 at the latest the Chelsea factory had found its manager of genius in Nicholas Sprimont (Gouyn having apparently seceded or been sacked); its patron of taste in Sir Everard Fawkener, secretary to the Duke of Cumberland; and, if tradition is to be believed, in the interest of George II it obtained the nearest equivalent to royal favour ever enjoyed by an English factory. (In Germany by this date every royal prince and elector had, or dreamed of having, his own porcelain-factory.) For nearly twenty years onwards, with one or two intervals, porcelain of all kinds continued to be made at Chelsea, of a quality which at its best is unsurpassed by any other.

The new paste and glaze made under Sprimont's direction are so different from that marked with the triangle that many people have supposed that there were two distinct Chelsea manufactures; but wasters found on the known

PLATE XI

See pages 116, 117

(*a*) TEAPOT. PORCELAIN, PAINTED IN COLOURS
CHELSEA, ABOUT 1750
British Museum

(*b*) CUP AND SAUCER. PORCE-
LAIN, PAINTED IN COLOURS
CHELSEA, ABOUT 1755
Mr. Leigh Ashton's Collection

(*c*) DISH. PORCELAIN, PAINTED IN COLOURS. CHELSEA, ABOUT 1755
Mr. A. Stanley Johnson's Collection

site of Sprimont's factory (which was in Lawrence Street and Justice Walk) have included pieces of 'triangle' type and thus practically settled the matter. A tiny anchor in relief on an applied oval medallion was added as a mark on the new paste, which is of fascinating quality —smooth, of a cool white colour, with a surface texture only describable as 'firm' and 'solid', not 'watery' and seldom crazed. In substance, especially at first, it was often thick but never clumsy. This substantial character is in fact one of its charms; it is a quality shared with the best soft-pastes of France. When, towards 1753 or 1754, the raised-anchor mark began to give place to a tiny red-painted anchor, the paste underwent no essential change, but had become even smoother and less liable to blemishes. There was in fact an intermediate stage when the raised anchor was painted over in red. A technical peculiarity of both raised- and red-anchor pieces is the presence of three round spur-marks on the bases; and by transmitted light the paste shows round bright spots, often of considerable size, due to aggregations of the frit, which Mr. William Burton thinks was deliberately left coarse to help to give stability in the kiln. These Chelsea 'moons', as they are called, should be distinguished from the bright flecks, 'tears', and irregular spots in Bow, Derby, and Longton Hall. The sensuous attraction of this delicious Chelsea paste counts for much in the collector's enthusiasm. And rightly so. Porcelain is a precious material, wonderful in itself. Each make has its own particular charm in this respect (at least in the eighteenth century!), though it is tempting to say that none is quite so lovely as that of Chelsea in the period of five or six years after 1750.

In its styles of painting Chelsea could no more escape the influence of the Saxon porcelain than the manufacturers of earthenware could avoid copying Wedgwood later on. The vogue of Meissen was universal and its output immense. But if little of the Chelsea painting and modelling was novel in type, in colour and handling they have a manner entirely their own. One does not complain that English water-colourists after Girtin painted landscapes; they achieved originality in doing so, each in his own style, though the *genre* was not of their own invention. In the same way the Chelsea painters took up the little landscapes with figures, the slight Japanese designs, and the sprigs and bouquets of naturalistic flowers, types that had been invented as porcelain decoration at Meissen, and made of them something fresh and unmistakeably English. Some Meissen designs were actually copied, it is true. As evidence of this, apart from correspondence between surviving pieces, we have a record that a Meissen service belonging to Sir Charles Hanbury-Williams was lent to Sprimont at the latter's request in 1751. And that Meissen was constantly in mind is shown by the appeal made by Sprimont in a surviving manuscript, 'The Case of the Undertaker of the Chelsea Manufacture of Porcelain Ware', for heavier duties on the German porcelain. But most of the decoration was newly designed at Chelsea.

The forms in this middle period also show the German influence; but the simpler lobed, fluted, and leaf-shaped cups, plates, and dishes were generally preferred. There were also new borrowings from silver in the relief designs for plates with borders and edges 'nurl'd', 'wro't', and 'scollop'd', as they are called in the contemporary catalogues. Plain octagonal cups and saucers and bowls are typical raised-anchor forms. Large vases were seldom or never attempted.

Perhaps the commonest designs on the raised-anchor pieces are the versions of the so-called Kakiemon patterns, after the Japanese. These I am inclined to think were not directly copied but taken from Meissen examples. But in spite of this they show an admirable understanding of the Japanese art, in the delicate sparing touches of enamel-colour by which the designs are built up. Equally charming is the sense of rhythm with which the motives are placed, as in the flowing tails of the birds in one design, or their spiky accents in another. The wandering branches of plum-tree and the asymmetry of some figure-pieces are given the same delicate vitality that we find in Japanese art, but with a sort of English straightforwardness, and a new beauty of colour in which a soft purple appears besides the usual Kakiemon blue, red, yellow, green, and turquoise. These are red- as well as raised-anchor types and appear in the Sale Catalogues of 1755 and 1756, surviving copies of which were reprinted respectively by Mr. William King and R. W. Read. The factory had in 1754 initiated a custom of holding public sales by auction of its productions, and the catalogues where they survive are records of the greatest value. I shall have several occasions to quote their charming phrases. One Kakiemon pattern called 'Octogon plate, Hob in the Well' refers to a familiar Chinese subject, of the boy who saved the life of his companion by breaking the water-jar into which he had fallen; it was evidently renamed after a popular English play of the time.

Blue-and-white was never popular at Chelsea, but what is virtually the only pattern found, of Chinese birds and stylised bamboos, is so lovely in its soft tones and rhythmical design as to make us wonder at the rarity of its type. This pattern is usually marked with an underglaze blue anchor, as is an almost equally rare design in the 'brocaded Imari' taste, with much underglaze blue, red, and gold. This is infinitely better than its Japanese model.

Another very rare pattern was inspired by the Chinese *famille rose*, and shows an exquisitely sensitive touch; there is an example in Mr. Herbert Allen's collection on loan at South Kensington. These last three types belong to the red-anchor period, though the 'brocaded Imari' was repeated later.

Turning to the landscapes with little figures in the Meissen manner, we meet the work of the very gifted artist whom we know as the 'Fable painter', from the subjects of his most familiar work (Plate XI, A). His early painting in colours, with a warm brown usually conspicuous in the foreground, is free and spirited, and quite distinct from Meissen. An increasing delicacy is seen in his red-anchor work, which is often in soft crimson-purple monochrome or in cool fresh colours, luminous but low-toned. Feathery trees and beautiful aerial perspective with softly rendered distant hills are to be noted particularly (Plate XI, B). Exquisitely graceful tiny figures with minute heads stand about with outstretched arms among the grass-grown ruins so delicately painted on these little masterpieces. The great dishes of the Warren Hastings Service (there is one at South Kensington), with their fantastic beasts, are perhaps his most 'important' works. The scattered flowers and insects usually combined with these little landscapes are of the contemporary Meissen type, very sensitively painted but not strikingly original. They belong to the second stage of the evolution of the so-called *deutsche Blumen*. These were the European flowers introduced by Herold a little before 1740, by way of variation on the formal 'Indian' (or Oriental) flowers. The true Chelsea quality appears in some large tureens with these flowers in soft purplish-blue monochrome charmingly contrasted with the fresh yellow and green of the applied leaves and twig handles. These may be identified

PLATE XII

See pages 117, 120

(*a*) FIGURE OF A BEGGAR
PORCELAIN
CHELSEA, ABOUT 1755
*Dr. and Mrs. Bellamy
Gardner's Collection*

(*b*) FIGURE OF A LADY
PORCELAIN
CHELSEA, ABOUT 1755
Mr. Cecil Higgins' Collection

(*c*) DISH. PORCELAIN, PAINTED IN COLOURS. CHELSEA, ABOUT 1755
Dr. and Mrs. Bellamy Gardner's Collection

with the 'beautiful round tureens' of the 1755 catalogue 'with sprig handles and a dish to ditto enamelled with blue flowers'. They may be seen at South Kensington. Occasionally, as on a magnificent dish in the collection of Mr. A. Stanley Johnson, opulent bouquets were painted with the utmost delicacy and feeling (Plate XI, c). The lovely stiff 'specimen' flowers of the first Meissen stage sometimes appear alone on the raised-anchor pieces; and a little later, perhaps inspired by these, the Chelsea artists painted some beautiful and very distinctive botanical flowers (Plate XII, c), which Dr. Bellamy Gardner has traced to an interesting local source in some drawings in a book by Philip Miller of the Chelsea Physic Garden. These were doubtless the 'India plants' of the catalogues, and the 'Sir Hans Sloan's flowers' of a contemporary advertisement. I do not know a better specimen of these than the dish with a crown imperial at South Kensington. The aesthetics of such botanical flower-painting on porcelain are often disputed. Can such literal copies have any merit? it is asked, and are porcelain plates the proper place for them? The second question needs no answer in the *rococo* period, and to the first it may be replied that if the copies were indeed literal, little could be said in their favour; but there is a vast difference between the Chelsea pieces with their firm drawing and clean, bright, unnatural colours, with impossible blue-green or yellow-green leaves, all imbued with an artist's heightened sensibility, and the lax or laboured naturalism of Pegg, Absolon, or Pardoe in a later and more familiar class. Figure-painting on a larger scale than the mere *Staffage* of landscapes was rare. There are some beautiful plates with scenes of children in gardens, framed in *rococo* scrollwork, and the Meissen type with figures in border panels was also copied with a peculiarly naïve and childish touch.

Some Cupids, deftly painted in brick-red monochrome, anticipating a later style of Sèvres, may be noted as a charming rarity in this period. A saucer in the Victoria and Albert Museum, the gift of Mr. J. Rosen, is painted in colours with figures on a wharf, and may be by the same hand as these, but the type is exceedingly rare and I do not feel quite sure that it is not Derby work. But it has the red-anchor naïveté and delicacy of touch.

It was hardly to be expected that transfer-printing, though newly invented in 1753 at the neighbouring Battersea enamel-factory, would be welcomed at Chelsea. One very unusual specimen, however, is known—a raised-anchor saucer in the British Museum, printed with a pastoral scene with classical buildings and figures very much in the early Battersea style.

The figures made at this time are by far the best in English porcelain. A few rare white busts require mention first of all: the *Duke of Cumberland*, *Frederick Prince of Wales*, and a very large *George II* are the chief; Dr. Gardner has also a head of a charming baby boy in Fiammingo style. These are apparently never marked, though Franks declared that he had seen a Duke of Cumberland with the raised anchor. I think it possible that the sculptor Roubiliac had a hand in them. He was a friend of Sprimont, who stood godfather to his daughter in 1744; and the *George II* is distinctly like a signed marble by him at Windsor Castle. This question of Roubiliac's work at Chelsea is a difficult one: had so eminent a sculptor actually completed these models one would have expected some record or announcement of the fact. My own theory is that these and the other models claimed for him below were perhaps roughed out by him and finished by the regular factory modellers. It is precisely on royal portrait-busts like these, if on anything, that Roubiliac would have worked for his friend's factory, rather than on the mere adaptations (to be mentioned presently) which have been erroneously attributed to him.

Of the more usual coloured raised-anchor models, the figures of birds are by far the most important, and indeed form a class by themselves surpassing anything of the kind done elsewhere. The *genre* was again a Meissen invention, and a few instances are known of exact copies in Chelsea. But the majority were adapted, as Dr. Bellamy Gardner again has shown, from engravings by the Englishman George Edwards. They were thus not 'invented' or modelled from 'life', but their aesthetic merit is not diminished by this. Their spirited forms speak of a life that is their own, quite different from the equally authentic life of the Kaendler models in Meissen porcelain, with their queer anthropomorphism and harsh, almost satirical, humour. They strike their own note too in their fresh fantastic colour with its characteristic warm red brown and their rock-bases painted with curious 'moss' and applied leaves coloured a rich turquoise green. There is a fine series of these birds in the Schreiber Collection, where the grave *Hen Harrier* and the lively crested birds, now identified as the Guan and the Touraco, will attract particular notice. Of human figures, several, such as the *Hurdy Gurdy Players*, standing and seated, are exact copies from Meissen. The famous *Nurse* after Palissy first appears as early as this, as well as in red-anchor. The colouring of all these shares much the same palette as the raised-anchor birds. Some Callot *Dwarfs* are also typical, and a tall figure of the *Doctor*, from the Italian comedy, in the collection of Lady Ludlow, with a letter in his pocket inscribed 'Memoire disabella 1750', is interesting for its date. A white figure known as a *Gardener's Companion*, in Dr. Bellamy Gardner's collection, is a monumental affair and stands quite by itself; it has been suggested that Roubiliac had a hand in it.

The change to red-anchor is most clearly marked in the figures. The colours became softer, with delicate clear yellows and pale mauves, and an inimitable light vermilion red, set off by a fine black. All were sparingly used, giving full play to the soft white of the porcelain itself. The sprigs of flowers on the costumes are of exceptional delicacy, quite independent of Meissen models, and the applied flowers on the bases are carefully painted, with a ring of dots for stamens, unlike those on any other English figures. The modelling is both subtle and broad, sensitive to the play of light on the glaze, but never fidgety and often purposely indefinite. Some of the models were cribs from Meissen, but most were original work by one anonymous artist. I have always liked especially a vigorous *Chinaman pulling his beard* that was in Mr. Alfred Hutton's collection, and the sparingly coloured *Beggar* (Plate XII, A) like the *Carpenter* at South Kensington is an epitome of all the red-anchor virtues. The exquisite crinoline lady figured in Plate XII, B is a perfect example of the red-anchor sentiment as well as of its charm in colour and modelling. The great *Maypole group* in Lord and Lady Fisher's collection must also be mentioned as the largest assemblage of the period, and the *Virgin and Child* (the 'exceeding fine figure of a Madonna and Child with a cross in it's hand', of the 1755 catalogue) for its subject, which is rare in English porcelain. The most ambitious of all are a set of figures allegorical of the *Senses*—a man with an eagle for *Sight*, a woman with a tortoise for *Touch*, and so on. These are exceptionally large, approaching a foot in height, too large, as some people think, for the toy-like quality proper to porcelain figures. They have been thought to be the work of Roubiliac and show something of his style. More proper to porcelain, and indeed one of the most delightful amusements of the *rococo*, are the tureens and dishes in the form of birds and animals, which needless to say were also a Meissen invention. Red-anchor small figures of birds are rarer than those of the earlier period, and these tureens were presumably made instead. Mr. Cecil Higgins has the best collection of these master-pieces of the red-anchor maturity; they show the same quick modelling as the raised-anchor birds, together with the delicate fanciful colouring and lovely perfection of material one expects in this period. A big and somewhat unpromising *Swan* tureen at South Kensington reserved a surprise for the guest, in the exquisite bouquets of flowers painted on the flange and only to be seen when the 'lid' is lifted. Of the same order of perfection is the 'very fine tureen in the form of a RABBIT BIG AS LIFE' of the 1755 catalogue, now in the Schreiber Collection. Some smaller dishes in the form of melons, cauliflowers, figs, and bundles of asparagus show the same qualities. Such trivial use of natural forms will of course come under the ban of the doctrinaire puritan. Disliking their high spirits, he will readily find a reason for condemning them. But reason plays a strictly subordinate part in the *rococo* aesthetics, and a general delight in these childish fancies is attested by their wide popularity in the faience of the period—in Strasburg and Marseilles, for example—as well as in por-celain. It is one of the contradictions of *rococo* that, while indulging in a riot of abstract scrollwork, it should have run also to naturalistic forms such as these tureens and the painted flowers already mentioned. All perhaps had a common origin in a love of surprise.

Chelsea is the only English porcelain with a European reputation, and this rests almost entirely on a class of objects not mentioned hitherto: the snuff-boxes, seals, and the like, collectively known as 'toys'. Such *Galantereien* were made at most of the German factories and were again a Meissen invention. They formed a very considerable part of the Chelsea productions, and in 1754 a sale was devoted exclusively to them. No copy of the catalogue has ever been traced. The announcement ran: '. . . Porcelain Toys, consisting of Snuff-boxes, Smelling-Bottles, Etwees and Trinkets for Watches (mounted in Gold and unmounted) in various beautiful Shapes, of an elegant Design and curiously painted in Enamel. . . . A large parcel of Porcelain Hafts for table and Dessert knives and Forks.' The *rococo* fancy had full play in these. Tiny figures and groups of birds, bunches of sweet-smelling flowers, and Cupid in many disguises are among the subjects which speak for themselves. In others the amorous allusion was emphasised by an inscription in French that was misspelt, as it would appear, by being ignorantly copied from somebody's handwriting, presumably Sprimont's own. Only in this way, for example, could 'L'ESPERANCE' have been copied as 'L'ESPERANUE' or 'JE VOUS CHARMERAY' as 'JE VOUS CHARMEIAY'. Among the inscriptions we find 'TROMPERIE D'AMOUR' on Europa and the Bull, 'MUNI POUR VOUS RESISTER' on a figure of a soldier; 'PEINE PERDU' is on a boy trying to rouse a pig, and the exquisite bouquets are inscribed 'POINT DE ROSES SANS EPINES'. There is a sentimental but never sickly fragrance about these 'toys'. They are mocking but never cruel or savage in their satire as Kaendler's often are. Their simplicity and sentiment are of a kind we are tempted to claim as specially English. But in spite of this they have enjoyed a European reputation, as I have said. They were included in the sale in 1756 of the stock of Laumas and Rolyat 'late of Lisbon'; Lady Charlotte Schreiber bought some of hers at Granada and Valencia, and also at Hamburg, The Hague, Rotterdam,

Hamburg, and Frankfort, and the finest existing private collection known to me is that of Herr Otto Blohm of Hamburg. The miniature figures (such as Lord Fisher's *Gardener* and *Sportsman*) show the same delightful modelling, which even the tiny seals are contrived to show—the little people looking up with a sort of childlike wonder and happiness. The 'toys' began to be made in the raised-anchor period, showing links with the birds on the one hand and on the other with the disputed '*Girl in the Swing*' class of figures; they continued to be made until the end of Sprimont's proprietorship in 1769, and also, probably in diminishing numbers, until the closing of the factory in 1784. They thus belong in part to a period known from the mark as 'gold-anchor', which must now be considered. The earlier boxes sometimes have lids of enamel made at the Battersea factory (1753–56), where a closely similar style of flower-painting has suggested a common hand. But the style in both was copied from Meissen.

It seems that work at Chelsea stopped in 1757 and no sales were held in that or the following year. Sprimont was said to be ill and Sir Everard Fawkener was in financial difficulties. The latter died in 1758, and in 1759 Sprimont apparently became sole proprietor and sales began again, but with a different auctioneer, and continued until 1761, when Sprimont's illness was again mentioned. In 1762, though no sale was held, some work was evidently done, since a vase in the British Museum is recorded as made and presented in that year; in 1763 the famous Mecklenburg-Strelitz service was made and another sale held. Some porcelain apparently continued to be made as late as 1768, when the auctioneer Burnsall spoke of porcelain 'even still brought from that noble manufactory', but there was apparently no great activity. By 1763 Sprimont is said to have made a fortune out of the factory. This may have been partly due to his adoption of a less extravagant paste for the porcelain. A notable change in it was the inclusion of the ash of calcined bones, and a thicker, more glassy glaze was brought into use. The former change may have been due to a workman who had been employed in the interval at Bow, where it had been included in the paste since 1748. It made the ware more stable in the kiln. The new glaze was liable to craze and inclined to have a greenish tone where it pooled in the hollows of the figures and gathered in drops round the base of plates and dishes. But it was not always (or, perhaps, not at first) so thick, and some gold-anchor-marked pieces resemble red-anchor, while some still marked in red have the thick glaze. It is probable that the red mark was for a time used after the resumption of work, and the gold-anchor something of an ⚓ afterthought following the general free use of gilding. The practice of grinding the foot of plates, etc., level, already usual in the earlier period, was now made imperative by the gathering of drops of glaze.

This change of material was accompanied by a very marked change of taste in the modelling and decoration. What we call the 'gold-anchor style' contains some strangely compounded elements from Meissen and Vincennes, but it is a distinct and individual style, nevertheless, and full of character. We are so much in the dark as regards the *personnel* of the factory, early and late, that it is idle to make conjectures as to the authorship of the style. Perhaps it was Sprimont's personal taste unfettered by any notions of Fawkener's, or possibly one unnamed director of painting and modelling was succeeded by another. We do not know. The change can hardly have been due to the movement of fashion, since gold-anchor is more extravagantly *rococo* than its predecessor, and the contemporary movement in France towards *Louis Seize*

PLATE XIII   *See pages* 126, 127, 128

(*a*) TWO FIGURES OF MASQUERADERS. PORCELAIN. CHELSEA, ABOUT 1760

Mr. R. W. E. Cecil's Collection

(*b*) VASE. PORCELAIN, PAINTED
IN COLOURS
CHELSEA, ABOUT 1765

Victoria and Albert Museum

(*c*) TEAPOT. PORCELAIN, PAINTED IN COLOURS
AND IN GILDING ON A 'MAZARIN' BLUE GROUND
CHELSEA, ABOUT 1765

Victoria and Albert Museum

was scarcely felt at all. An awareness of the rise of Vincennes and Sèvres is of course obvious and important. The change was certainly not due to Roubiliac, who would never have modelled pastorals after Boucher, for example, and the impressed 'R' on some gold-anchor figures is not his initial but that of an unknown workman or 'repairer' who put the specimen together. In figure-modelling the genesis of the gold-anchor style may be found in Kaendler's figures of the 1750's, which show the same regal pose and magnificent gestures. Much of the charming simplicity of the early style was now lost, it is true, and extravagant *bocages* (or formal trees) were added to the figures, not always to their advantage, while the costumes were smothered in brocaded patterns in colours and gilding. The bases, which had been simple mounds, were now enriched with gilt *rococo* scrolling and finally developed into elaborate pedestals. A larger scale also became usual. One model, *Una and the Lion*, in fact exceeds two feet in height. Others of course are still quite small, but share the general qualities of sumptuousness and largeness of movement and bearing. A few rare *Family Groups* may be considered intermediate in style. As regards the relative merits of the two styles, I do not think that an informed taste for porcelain, familiar with the masterpieces of Germany and France, will ever prefer the elaboration of the famous *Music Lesson*, for example, to the exquisite subtlety of the best red-anchor figures. But the fashion for red-anchor prevailing at the present time is (as usual) unintelligent in contemning gold-anchor wholesale as 'vulgar'. The best of the later figures, with their noble outline, fine rhythm and poise, have precious qualities also, and their colouring is harmonious and splendid. The *Reaper* and *Masked Actor* in the Schreiber Collection, and the *Shepherd* and *Shepherdess* lately given to the Victoria and

Albert Museum by Mr. W. A. J. Flörsheim, admirably represent their virtues; Mr. R. W. M. Walker's *Apollo* and *Nine Muses*, lent to the same museum, are even more monumental in style, though still true to porcelain. The set of eight *Masqueraders* in Mr. Robert Cecil's collection (Plate XIII, A) show the gold-anchor rhythms at their most varied, and are perhaps the best of all. A great *Pietà* group is quite exceptional, and of a model which is found also in Tournay porcelain, where it has been ascribed to a modeller named Gauron. An artist of this name is recorded at Chelsea, but at a later date (1773). He may of course have worked there earlier without being recorded, and it is possible that he had a hand in the creation of the gold-anchor style in figures.

Vases now began to be made in increasing numbers, often in the wildest *rococo* forms, their 'handles' contorted into a riot of scrollwork. They have unquestionable rhythmic vitality. In their decoration, too, we find the boldest use of the coloured grounds for which Chelsea is famous. These were the 'new Colours . . . found this year [1759] by Mr. Sprimont, at very large expence, incredible Labour, and close Application'. The unaccountably named 'Mazareen-' or mazarin-blue was undoubtedly inspired by the *gros bleu* of Vincennes: it is an uneven dark colour of the utmost richness. I like it best decorated only with gilt birds and flowers, as on two typical vases in the Jones Collection at South Kensington, or on the marvellous tea-service sold from the Viscountess Harcourt Collection. The famous claret ground, which was an entirely unsuccessful attempt to copy the *rose Pompadour* of Vincennes, varies greatly in quality. At its best it is a beautiful rich crimson, but it is sometimes only a dull pink. A lovely turquoise and a clear yellow were also copied from Vincennes. The painted decoration on the vases was apparently

often the work of experienced miniaturists, among whom
John Donaldson was, according to tradition, included.
The classical figure-subjects in the style of Boucher
may well be by his hand. The famous 'Dudley vases' in
the Bearsted Collection are usually cited as the classics of
this style, but there are several of not inferior quality at
South Kensington—in the Jones Collection and elsewhere. Sumptuous bird-painting after Hondecoeter and
landscapes thought to be by Boreman (afterwards famous
at Derby) are new types of subject on these vases. Better
than any of these, in my opinion, are the unpretentious
little Teniers subjects (Plate XIII, B) simply and firmly
drawn by an artist who, in another style, painted what is
perhaps the most deservedly famous of all Chelsea china—
the claret-ground tea- and coffee-service bequeathed to
the Victoria and Albert Museum by Miss Emily Thomson
of Dover. Many other styles of painting on the vases, too
numerous to be detailed here—cupids, allegories, and the
rest—all seem to have been inspired by Vincennes and
Sèvres.

Foremost among the table-wares must be placed the
Thomson service just mentioned. In this the forms, which
are in the most gracious and lively *rococo* style, the rich
crimson ground-colour, the incomparable soft gilding, and
the free, delicate, and unlaboured painting of Chinese
figures, with their exquisitely rendered draperies, may be
felt to reach perfection in their kind. The actual service
is doubtless that sold at Christie's in 1770 as a 'very
curious and matchless tea and coffee equipage, crimson
and gold, most inimitably enamelled in figures from the
designs of Watteau'. Nothing like this was ever created at
Sèvres, which otherwise inspired most of the table-wares
of the period. The 'exotic birds'—pheasant-like creatures
—of the French factory were boldly simplified and sprawl

magnificently across plates and dishes. More naturalistic birds are rarer. The famous Mecklenburg-Strelitz service, made in 1763 as a present from George III and Queen Charlotte to the latter's brother, and so undiscriminatingly disparaged by Horace Walpole, has mazarin-blue panels and painted garlands of small flowers on the border, enclosing exotic birds of the less flaunting kind. These are seen on the teapot figured in Plate XIII, c, which also shows the beautiful gilt designs on the mazarin-blue. The influence of Meissen, where the factory had been for the period of the Seven Years' War in the hands of the Prussians, is here almost extinct, though the forms of some plates with rich moulded patterns of *rococo* scrolls may have been inspired by it. The flowers, however, have now departed from the Meissen type, and have a looser, more opulent look, and in one not very attractive decoration are reserved on a gold ground. A charming type of landscape, originally of Meissen derivation, but copied at Vincennes, is in black washed over with green; a river scene apparently suggested by the Thames at Chelsea is painted on a plate in the Schreiber Collection.

The tradition of taste and delicacy of workmanship set up by these gold-anchor table-wares gives them an historical importance quite apart from their intrinsic merits. For they were the inspiration of the more numerous services produced at the Derby factory, and indeed at Chelsea itself, under the management of William Duesbury in the subsequent period. Sprimont sold out in 1769 to move 'farther into the country', and in the following year the Chelsea concern was bought by Duesbury and Heath. It was run by Duesbury until he closed it in 1784, in association with his Derby factory, which dictated the style of the numerous figures made thenceforward. But the table-wares of 'Chelsea-Derby' have much of the Chelsea dis-

PLATE XIV   *See pages* 132, 140, 143

(*a*) GROUP. WHITE PORCELAIN. BOW, ABOUT 1750
Mr. Wallace Elliot's Collection

(*b*) VASE. PORCELAIN, PAINTED
IN COLOURS
BOW, ABOUT 1755
Victoria and Albert Museum

(*c*) PLATE. PORCELAIN, PAINTED
IN COLOURS
BOW, ABOUT 1765
Mr. Leigh Ashton's Collection

tinction. In them and in the subsequent productions of Derby itself the rigours of Wedgwood's cosmopolitan neo-Classical were tempered by a genial quality that is entirely English. They retain a sweetness of colour and a measured grace even into the nineteenth century, and take rank as the most distinguished and national English porcelain ever made for table use. In spite of this Chelsea tradition, I propose to reserve 'Chelsea-Derby' for further consideration under the heading of Derby. The 'matchless art' of Nicholas Sprimont must be kept distinct, as the only English porcelain fully worthy of comparison with the best Continental wares.

CHAPTER IX

BOW AND LOWESTOFT

THE porcelain of Bow (strictly Stratford-le-Bow) in the east of London was the invention of Thomas Frye, an Irish mezzotint-engraver, who as early as 1744 took out a patent for making 'a certain material whereby a ware might be made of the same nature or kind, and equal to, if not exceeding in goodness and beauty, China or Porcelain ware'. In this patent he specified a clay brought from America, 'called by the natives unaker'. One Edward Heylyn of Bristol was also concerned with this patent, and the 'unaker' was discussed in a letter of 1745 by William Cookworthy of Plymouth and Bristol, who was later on the maker of the first English true porcelain. It was perhaps due to Cookworthy that the clay was sent to England. But nothing is known for certain of the porcelain made under this early patent. The later and accepted Bow china has a very distinct character, and no specimens resembling it and of so early a date have yet been recognised. Mr. William Burton was even of the opinion that no sort of porcelain could have been made with the materials specified. Perhaps Frye was unsuccessful with them and continued to experiment until he reached the formula patented by him alone in 1748, in which the characteristic ingredient was the white ash of calcined bones, referred to as 'animal substances of the Calcareous kind. . . .' Bone-ash had long been known as a possible ingredient in porcelain: it was proposed in a work of

1649, cited by Professor Ernst Zimmermann, and was in common use in milk-white glass (German, *Beinglas*), but Bow was the first factory to put it to practical use in porcelain-making, and its ultimate adoption in the standard English commercial china gives Frye's innovation some historical importance. Bone-ash in the paste has a further interest to the collector in the opportunity it gives him of applying (if he cares to) a chemical test devised by Dr. H. J. Plenderleith to prove its presence or absence, and so being helped in identifying the make of the piece.

For eleven years after the date of this second patent, that is until 1759, Frye remained manager at Bow, and during this period the factory was evidently very prosperous, owing much, it is believed, to Frye's taste, though the porcelain bears no trace of his personal style as an artist. In the following decade it declined both artistically and commercially, and in 1763 John Crowther, one of the owners, became bankrupt, his partner Weatherby having died in the previous year. The subsequent history of the factory is obscure, but there is good reason for Mr. Frank Hurlbutt's conjecture that William Duesbury of Derby aided or acquired the factory after Crowther's bankruptcy, and there is a tradition that some of the moulds were eventually, about 1776, removed to Derby.

One aspect of Bow history on which precise information is still lacking is the extent to which 'outside enamellers' were employed. In the following account I shall describe some work possibly by Duesbury and Giles, two of these independents; but another enameller of whom nothing whatever is known is Richard Dyer of Lambeth, who is mentioned in some miscellaneous papers of the Bow manager, one Bowcocke, preserved at the British Museum.

The Bow porcelain material of the fine period is of somewhat varying quality, but at its best of singular beauty. The white and enamel-painted pieces are of a creamy or yellowish tone, with a smooth glaze of almost waxen surface-texture. The glaze is easily scratched and commonly shows an iridescent surface, due it is believed to excess of lead. An almost invariable feature is the appearance of small tearings or partings in the paste; little pieces were torn out in the process of throwing on account of its unplastic 'shortness'—a defect shared with many soft-pastes. (That of Sèvres could not be thrown at all without the admixture of a liberal proportion of soft soap!) The Bow paste is actually quite soft to the file and readily discolours or stains, especially at the foot and rim. By transmitted light it shows a warm creamy translucency, with lighter flecks.

The originality and charm of its decoration lie chiefly in its colour and in the naïve simplification of its borrowed subjects. The typical Bow colouring at its best is of joyous freshness, rich in piquant discords. A very strong crimson-purple, a vivid translucent emerald green, and an opaque light blue are the characteristic elements in it.

Figures were evidently made in large numbers from the beginning. Typical of the earliest at present identified, dating from a couple of years or so after about 1750, are some *Muses* with queer heads and receding chins, charmingly modelled but without any great accomplishment. Their paste and glaze are somewhat primitive and sometimes have a greenish tone. A group of *Lovers with a bird-cage*; *Charity*, with a small child; and the exceedingly beautiful groups of the *Fortune-Teller* (in the British Museum) and *Lady and page* (Plate XIV, A) are perhaps the masterpieces of this class, most of which seem to be original, or at all events copied from engravings and not from Meissen. The painting of these figures raises the interesting question, one of the most controversial in the study of English porcelain, of the part played in early Bow by William Duesbury, who has already been referred to several times as an enameller of salt-glaze and proprietor of the Derby porcelain-factory. Duesbury was for a time an independent decorator in London. His work-book for 1751–53, which has lately been published in a valuable facsimile and transcription by Mrs. Donald MacAlister, shows him to have worked upon or sold 'Bogh', 'Stafartshire', 'Darby', and 'Chelsey' figures. I believe that a good deal of this work was in oil-paint or some other unfired pigment, not in enamel, and that this has in the course of time been damaged and eventually cleaned away altogether, leaving the figures in the white condition in which they abound to-day. Traces of this unfired pigment may sometimes be detected. The 'true enamel' decoration also done by Duesbury may best be identified by its recurrence on porcelain of different makes. On Bow we find some curious sprigs on the costumes of figures of the *Muses* family, and also a strong heavy red and a yellowish green, which may be signs of Duesbury's work in enamel. Besides the *Muses* a pair of figures in the Schreiber Collection of an *Actor and actress in Turkish costume* may be cited as probably painted by him. A pair of the famous figures of the actor *Woodward* as 'The Fine Gentleman' and *Kitty Clive* as 'The Fine Lady', in Garrick's farce *Lethe*, in Mr. McEuen's collection show another of conjectured Duesbury style: the latter is actually mentioned in his workbook. In fact a great many of the Bow figures of the first period come in question as possible examples of Duesbury's enamelling.

Some figures of this earliest Bow class bear incised 'planet-marks' like those here reproduced; on others an impressed mark 'T' or 'To' occurs, and this has been thought

133

to be that of a 'repairer' or modeller named Tebo (Thibaud), whose activities are often the subject of dispute. The mark is found also on the rather later Bow figures copied from Meissen, on some original Bow masterpieces to be mentioned shortly, and on porcelain from other factories (Worcester, Plymouth, and Bristol); while 'Mr. Tebo' himself is recorded as working in 1775 for Wedgwood, who had a very poor opinion of his ability. If we may pass the pure conjecture which associates this mark with this recorded person, then I think we may regard Tebo as both 'repairer' and modeller. In the porcelain of large factories (such as Meissen) marks stamped and incised in the paste of figures are not usually those of the modellers who designed them, but of the workmen who put them together. In such an establishment as Bow, however, the 'repairer' may well have done some modelling, and these original early figures are quite likely to have been Tebo's own creations. Some phrases used by Wedgwood about his work could quite well be applied to the *Muses'* heads, which are by no means neo-Classical; and the curious Anglo-French inscriptions incised on some of the pedestals—'Eraton for the Love', 'Polimnie', and so on—also suggest the Frenchman whom 'Tebo' is supposed to have been. But it must be emphasised that the 'T^o' mark is not always a sign of his original work.

To the middle and later 1750's may be ascribed the figures and groups showing the maturity of the Bow style. They were very often adaptations of Meissen models, but assembled with perfect understanding, with characteristically simplified heads vivaciously inclined, and bodies turned on the hips in a charming exaggeration of Kaendler's manner. The Italian Comedy figures— *Pierrot, Harlequin, Columbine,* the *Doctor,* etc.—from the Kaendler-Reinicke series of 1743–44, are particularly good in pose and movement. In colouring they are most lovely, with the strong rose-purple, opaque light blue, emerald green, and a pale yellow very conspicuous and effective on the beautiful creamy ground. A typical early-middle-period model is the *Sportsman* bequeathed by Colonel Croft Lyons to the Victoria and Albert Museum, where in the Schreiber Collection and the Broderip Gift practically every type is represented. The *Air* and *Apollo* are somewhat later, and especially delicious in colour. The famous so-called *Cooks*, carrying dishes of food, sometimes marked with a 'repairer's' impressed 'B', are almost certainly not the work in any capacity of John Bacon, R.A. (*b.* 1740, *d.* 1799), though they are commonly attributed to him; he is recorded in a very doubtful-sounding text as having been apprenticed to a china-maker named Crispe 'of Bow Churchyard'. Bacon's work at Bow (if indeed the Bow factory was meant by this) has not been identified; an unusually large *Flora*, after a classical original, is much more likely to be his, but there is no proof of this. Technical peculiarities of the Bow figures of the 1750's are a square hole at the back, probably for an ormolu mount supporting modelled porcelain flowers, and their heavy weight, which amongst other features distinguishes them from contemporary Derby. Figures to be ascribed to the latter do, however, sometimes (though rarely) show the square hole at the back. Towards 1760 a four-footed *rococo*-scrolled pedestal picked out in rose-purple became usual in place of the plain low mound bases. These pedestals are seen in what are perhaps the masterpieces of Bow modelling—the figures of *General Wolfe* and the *Marquis of Granby* made from engravings soon after the victories of Quebec and Minden in 1759. They usually have the 'Tᵒ' mark, and if they were Tebo's own work they are certainly his best.

135

In the later figures the fresh colour that was the great merit of the middle period was entirely lost, and the paste itself became grey or bluish toned. A dull underglaze blue was substituted for the beautiful enamel, the scrolled bases were picked out in pink and dull turquoise, and pretentious brocades took the place of plain colours. The

FIG. 10. BOW PORCELAIN FIGURE

modelling too was much less good, though some artless little people posing as the godlike creatures of gold-anchor Chelsea are amusing: a *Turkish Dancer* (with a very small head, Fig. 10) is typical. The mark of an anchor and a dagger in red appears on many of the later figures, and was perhaps suggested by a Chelsea workman engaged during the closed-time of the rival factory; the dagger is sometimes thought to have been taken from the arms of the city of London. Besides the red mark, underglaze blue letters, dots, and a crescent also appear, and the last-mentioned has sometimes led to the erroneous identification of Bow figures as Worcester.

A note of admiration should be uttered in praise of some of the Bow birds, made in the middle period. Their merits are quite different from those of the similar Chelsea figures; they are entirely fanciful in colouring, and there is no great range of models. But the painting of a pair of *Tawny Owls* in the Schreiber Collection, for example, is at once so fantastic and so delicate as to put them in the front rank of all English porcelain; the feathers are rendered in loose touches of clean red, purple, and warm chocolate brown, while on the bases are applied leaves of the inimitable emerald-green colour already mentioned as so characteristic of the Bow palette. Some *Cocks* and *Hens* are almost equally good, but the *Partridges* on the other hand are dully naturalistic.

The Bow vases with plastic work are very artless productions and were perhaps due to the rather limited inventive powers of 'Mr. Tebo'. Elaborate frills and masks with applied leaves and flowers and the usual rich colour combine to make them rather fearsome objects of a mixed appeal. One guesses Tebo to have prided himself upon his leaves, flowers, and shells (these last doubtless cast after nature), and it is likely, I think, that the sweetmeat dishes made up of tiers of shells and the salt-cellars of similar form found in Bow, Plymouth, and Worcester, were made by him alone.

Table-wares were undoubtedly the great stand-by at Bow. They are neither as varied in style nor as accomplished in workmanship as those of Chelsea, but they were probably more serviceable in use and survive in considerable quantity. The paste varies with the period, as noted above. It should be mentioned further that the grey later porcelain is often only slightly translucent and shows a dusky reddish tone by transmitted light. As the best pieces are never marked, a note on one or two character- istic forms will be useful for purposes of identification. Perhaps the commonest object is an ogee- or bell-shaped mug, which has a handle with a heart-shaped lower ter- mination: this is a Bow peculiarity. Another type of handle, on cups, sticks into the body in a horizontal line at the lower end. Among plates a common form has a thick convex base hollowed below, without a foot-ring; this is a Delft shape (copied from the Chinese), one of several instances of Dutch influence to be noted in Bow.

In decoration the table-wares tended to follow Far Eastern models rather than Meissen. One of the common- est early types copied the *blanc de Chine* of Fukien pro- vince, with sprays of plum-blossom in relief; this shows the paste to advantage. The Chinese *famille rose* was copied in a way that reveals no consciousness of a Meissen inter- mediary. On some famous inkstands inscribed with the name of the factory—'*Made at New Canton*'—and dated 1750 and 1751, are little sprays of plum-blossom with jewel-like touches of pink, white, and yellow, which even recall the Dutch enamellers' decoration on the Stafford- shire salt-glaze. Other versions of the Chinese themes are bolder, with flaunting, large, rose-pink peonies, and the rich Bow green always conspicuous. Some early vases often marked with an 'R' incised are painted with a variant of the *famille rose* decoration but with more subdued colour and rather stringy drawing; the same mark is found on vases painted in underglaze blue and enamel red in a style probably suggested by the 'brocaded Imari' of Japan. A tall beaker given to the Victoria and Albert Museum by Mr. Leigh Ashton stands almost in a class by itself, with the Chinese trees and rocks very freely drawn in the purest

red, green, blue, and an exceedingly rich plum-purple,
boldly put on with a colour-effect unmatched for splendour
even in Bow. A small narrow-necked vase in Mr. Wallace
Elliot's collection shows similar decoration, but I do not
know of another example. Perhaps the most numerous of
all Bow table-wares are those with the Kakiemon designs,
especially the so-called partridge (or quail) pattern, which
was done in quantity in every shape and form. There is
something free and sympathetic about the Bow versions of
these, and most people will prefer them to the tighter,
more carefully finished Worcester renderings of the same
pattern. The Bow red, notably, is richer and warmer than
that of Worcester. On an immense 'partridge pattern'
service belonging to the Duke of Northumberland is
a piece marked with a bow and arrow, the only instance
known to me of a Bow mark which has often been thought
apocryphal. The other Kakiemons are less common on
table-wares than on vases and show a wide range of accomplishment. A large elongated-egg-shaped vase in the Croft
Lyons Bequest at South Kensington is as delicately painted
as Chelsea, but with a Bow warmth. Some armorial mugs
and plates show the same delicacy. A famous bowl was
given to the British Museum in 1790 by a Thomas Craft,
who said he had painted it at Bow thirty years before, 'in
the old Japan taste . . . much esteemed by the then Duke
of Argyle. . . .' This bears a free fantasia on the Kakiemon
themes, with phoenixes and garlands added, in a style
seen also on some plates in the Schreiber Collection and
elsewhere.

Much of the European flower-painting on Bow porcelain is recognisably by one hand, this time inspired by
Meissen, but always very individual. His light blue,
emerald green, soft violet-purple, and peculiar yellow
combine in a gentle and unemphatic dissonance that is

exceedingly beautiful. One vase in Mr. Broderip's Gift at South Kensington has a sprawling bouquet of these flowers on one side, and on the other an equally characteristic spray of purple roses with vivid green leaves (Plate XIV, B). This vase is marked with a script 'B' in underglaze blue, which occurs also on other Bow wares; but I think it unlikely that it stands for 'Bow'. More exact but less personal copies of the Meissen flowers are sometimes found, and some full-toned fruit-painting which is not uncommon is so like that on some Chelsea that one suspects the very same hand, doubtless a migrant thrown out of employment by the closing of Sprimont's factory in 1757–58. A pattern of applied leaves favoured for plates and dishes also seems to have been exactly copied from Chelsea.

Transfer-printing is not very common on Bow porcelain, though the process had been invented and used on Battersea enamels from 1753 onwards, by Frye's fellow-mezzotinter John Brooks. I think it very probable that no use was made of it until the closing of the enamel-factory in 1756, when it would seem that two of the engravers, Simon-François Ravenet and Robert Hancock, moved thence to Bow. The latter stayed less than a year before going on to Worcester, where he remained for nearly twenty years. Ravenet, the greatest master of engraving for transfer-printing, virtually never signed his work, but some Bow plates with a delightful interior after Chardin are precisely in his style. Hancock's work is only occasionally signed; but some groups of sheep, pastorals with shepherds, and little landscapes, are recognisably in his style. All these are usually in manganese-purple, rather blurred on account of the soft glaze. A plate in the British Museum, with the well-known 'L'Amour' subject in the beautiful light brick-red also favoured for printing at Bow, actually bears Hancock's signature. It is very characteristic of the factory that it brought together its borrowed motives in naïve combinations suggesting the assimilations of peasant art. Here on this plate we find the European printed subject very effectively surrounded by a Kakiemon border. Again, on a teapot in the Schreiber Collection with a purple-brown print of Frederick the Great, 'The Prussian Hero' (which by the way confirms our dating of the Bow prints to 1756), we find also a spray of flowers in Chinese *famille rose* style, and applied leaves in the Meissen manner, coloured bright green. One curious class of *chinoiseries* on Bow china has the outlines printed in pale brown, rather in the Battersea style, and these are coloured over in the vivid green, pink, and yellow Bow enamels. Nothing like this is found on any other English porcelain of the period, though the style was much revived in the 1820's and 1830's. The Bow prints are charming primitives with their soft purple and red; they are seldom or never in a true black, and I think this last must have been perfected by Hancock after his arrival at Worcester, where the factory later on became very proud of its 'jet enamel'.

Painting in underglaze blue was done in quantity, early and late, and was always directly inspired by the Chinese (Meissen had had relatively little success with it). At Bow it has an engaging freedom, even a wildness. We may distinguish broadly two periods: the earlier of these shows, characteristically, a very vivid colour; the later a blue still rich and full-toned but darker. In both is noticeable a quality suggesting a crumbling of the pigment, actually due in part to its imperfect grinding, which has left some grains larger than others. This produces a liveliness and 'sparkle' that are naturally lacking in work done with modern machine-ground colours. Also contributing to the special Bow quality is the tendency of the blue to run in the soft glaze, and to this may be due also the bluish tone pervading the glaze itself, though it is possible that the latter was deliberately tinted with a touch of blue in the endeavour to make it more like the Chinese; or the blue-colour used for the painting may have 'flown' or volatilised in the kiln, as it sometimes does. Apart from these general indications and a mention of the occasional early use as marks of incised planet-signs (which as stated occur on early figures) and a script 'G' in blue, little help can be given towards the identification of the Bow blue-and-white. It is fantastic in style, and usually shows much amusing detail in the Chinese manner. In some of the rather later pieces we find Kakiemon motives and borders painted in blue, adapted in the familiar Bow way. One much-disputed class is that painted in reserves on a powdered blue ground. The plates are usually of the Bow form described above and the blue of the familiar later quality. Yet these are often claimed wholesale for Worcester, Lowestoft, or Caughley, where powdered blue pieces were certainly made, but were of a decidedly different quality. For the rest I can only recommend a study of the collection at South Kensington, where typical pieces are now set apart and show the peculiar colour and fantasy very clearly. It should be noted that printing in underglaze blue was apparently never done at Bow.

The Bow table-wares in polychrome after about 1760–1765 show the same sort of falling away as the figures. The beauty of colour has gone. Gold-anchor Chelsea and Worcester now supplied the models, and we find dull copies of such things as the mazarin-blue and birds of the former and the scale-blue of the latter. Fantastic but ugly rococo vases with powdered blue ground belong to this period and are sometimes painted with exotic birds by

the same hand as some Worcester, Longton Hall, and
Plymouth pieces, suggesting that they were perhaps done
in the workshop of an independent decorator, such as
James Giles of Cockspur Street, whose work will be discussed under the heading of Worcester. It is a remarkable
fact that Thomas Craft, in presenting his bowl to the
British Museum, stated that it was fired for him by
'Mr. Gyles'. This theory, it should be noted, involves the
supposition that the anchor-and-dagger mark commonly
found on later Bow was at least sometimes added by Giles.
Is it too wild a suggestion that if Duesbury aided the
factory after Crowther's bankruptcy in 1763 he would
have arranged that, for economy's sake, the wares should
be decorated by Giles, whom he is certainly known to have
aided at a later date? This would account for the new
palette of colours used on the later figures, as already
described, and also for the remarkable circumstance that
a pair of plates sold from the E. W. Stanyforth Collection
in March 1931, marked with both the blue square mark
of Worcester and the anchor and dagger in gold, were
painted with 'dishevelled birds' of precisely the kind most
convincingly associated with Giles.

The *rococo* vases are occasionally found painted with
very sympathetic but very unprofessional 'Watteau
figures', as on a great tureen and stand presented to the
Victoria and Albert Museum by Messrs. Stoner and
Evans. The same hand is familiar on many other Bow
pieces of this period, among the best being some lovely
dishes with lake scenes in a polychrome dominated by a
warm brown and several shades of green (Plate XIV, c).
Other ambitious *rococo* subjects with scrollwork and figures
after Nilson, etc., were also done. These all show a certain
degree of accomplishment, though one rejoices also in the
survival of something of the Bow naïveté—a quality

which may almost be said to distinguish the entire work of the factory, in all its periods. For Bow is indeed a kind of peasant porcelain. It can hardly have supplied an actual peasant market, but its qualities were such as appealed to an 'uneducated' sense of beauty rather than to 'taste'. An entirely unacademic love of bright colours, an ability to compose them regardless of the rules, and a probably unintended simplification of its sophisticated models— these are amongst the characteristics of peasant art found also in Bow porcelain.

The productions of the small factory at Lowestoft on the Suffolk coast (started 1757, closed soon after 1800), which was virtually an offshoot of Bow, are even better entitled to be called peasant porcelain. A bone-ash paste akin in composition to that of Bow was used under the direction of one Robert Browne, who is said to have taken employment at Bow with the deliberate intention of learning the secret. But the latter had passed its great time before Lowestoft was in going order, so that, except perhaps in the blue-and-white, we find little overlap in styles, and it was Worcester of the 1760's or its Chinese models which inspired the decoration of the unpretentious table-wares which were the chief productions. Little else was made. The figures formerly ascribed to Lowestoft are now known to be Staffordshire.

The coloured Lowestoft was limited to a few types. The chief of these shows artlessly painted Chinese figures in gardens and pavilions, no doubt copied from Worcester or from the so-called Mandarin porcelain much exported from China in this period: borders of pink diaper are characteristic of both originals and copies. A somewhat brownish red is usual on the Lowestoft, seen notably in the horizontal dashes indicating the ground. Gilding appears only on the more pretentious pieces in Worcester style. The flower-painting also copied Worcester or Meissen. One excellent painter, with a soft fluent touch, had a fondness for charming juxtapositions of pink and red; other styles are harder. These two principal types make up the bulk of the polychrome Lowestoft. More interesting and rarer are the 'occasional' pieces with inscriptions and dates, lately studied in great detail by Mr. A. J. B. Kiddell. The Norwich Museum, thanks to the devotion of Colonel Bulwer and his friends, now possesses a fine collection of these little masterpieces. Local views, inn signs, a ploughing or a cricket match (Plate XIX, A), ships, or mere names, all indicate sufficiently well the class of patron for which the factory catered. The painting is no more skilful or correct in the academic sense than the decoration already described, but shows an attractive, almost childish, simplicity. In the last period, towards the close of the century, stars and dots and narrow borders surrounding little sprig patterns, sometimes in monochrome, replaced the earlier Chinese and Meissen motives. The Staffordshire 'New Hall' wares are often similar to these but can be distinguished by their harder paste. Much of the painting in red and blue was scarcely more than a gay medley of colour, though some of the fantasies on the Chinese peonies and rocks are delightfully rhythmical and spontaneous. The bulk of the abundant blue-and-white is very like Worcester at a first glance, with similar patterns moulded after silver on jugs, tea-caddies, and the like, but the usual childish Lowestoft touch is soon detected and an examination of the paste can leave no room for doubt. But the collector is often more seriously puzzled to distinguish Lowestoft from the later Bow. The blue-and-white of the former can as a rule be recognised by a darker, more inky, blue (though the 'occasional pieces' sometimes show a richer colour), and the paste is generally softer

10

and lighter in substance and even more liable to discoloration. It has an almost toylike quality. The numerals which sometimes appear as marks on both makes are in the case of Lowestoft generally written inside the foot-ring, and a feature of the Lowestoft powdered blue is the shapelessness of the panels. The Bow painting in general is broader and stronger, with a more robust fancy. The Lowestoft artists seem to have amused themselves with their borders, which are often made up of childish and fanciful variations on the Chinese cell-diapers. Wherever a 'peculiar' border of this kind is seen on a doubtful piece it may be put down with fair certainty to Lowestoft. Printing over the glaze was never done, but underglaze blue transfers follow the Worcester style with the difference that the engraving was far less accomplished, with many broken lines and a woefully naïve style of hatching for shade. One or two *rococo* patterns in Pillement's style are very charming nevertheless. In spite of all shortcomings there is an unpretentiousness about this Lowestoft china which engages our sympathy where more efficient productions might repel us by their very assurance.

CHAPTER X

LONGTON HALL

WE have seen in the first part of this book how greatly the Staffordshire potters were influenced by the vogue of porcelain, and that by 1750—the rising time of Chelsea and Bow—the local manufacture of earthenware and stoneware led by Thomas Whieldon was already a considerable one. It would be surprising, therefore, if attempts were not made in the district to produce a veritable porcelain. True hard-paste in the Chinese and Meissen manner could scarcely have been hoped for, and something of the order of Chelsea or Bow must have been constantly in mind. We have already referred, in connection with a mysterious class of figures, to the legend of some Staffordshire workmen seceding from Chelsea, and this suggests the manner by which the two recorded early Staffordshire manufacturers of porcelain must have obtained their knowledge. That no great results were obtained in this branch of pottery—and there is even a gap of twenty years or more after their failure—until the introduction of Spode's bone-china at the end of the century, is doubtless to be explained by the precarious and unprofitable character of the soft-paste and its total foreignness to the local traditions. The Staffordshire potter was (and is) notoriously conservative and averse to speculative undertakings.

We have a record in the *Travels* of Dr. Pococke that in 1750 he visited Newcastle-under-Lyme and saw there

147

a potter 'from Limehouse' 'who seemed to promise to make the best china-ware', but had difficulties in firing it, and who also made 'statues of elephants, lyons, birds, etc.', apparently in salt-glaze. This porcelain has lately been identified by Mrs. Donald MacAlister on the ground of its exact correspondence in models and some details, such as the applied flowers, with salt-glazed ware. It consists of rather crude white figures (formerly called Bow) of pheasants, cranes, horses, cows, and other animals, a bagpiper and a little *Ceres*. One of the best models is a recumbent and very benevolent-looking lion. (There is a specimen in the Schreiber Collection.) They generally have a thick greenish-toned glaze which smothers the modelling in such a way that they have been named the 'snow-man family'. It may be remarked in passing that the porcelain of Limehouse in East London, which should bear some resemblance to this or to that made at Lowdin's Glasshouse, Bristol (see p. 173), has not yet been identified, though from advertisements which have been found by Mr. A. J. B. Kiddell and Dr. Bellamy Gardner it seems that blue-and-white was certainly made there. Researches by Mrs. MacAlister have shown that the Limehouse potter was probably either a William Tams or a William Ball, perhaps financed by a Rev. John Middleton, all apparently Staffordshire men.

Whether this obscure Newcastle manufacture had any connection with the later and relatively better known Longton Hall factory conducted by William Littler is not quite certain. Longton Hall is close to Newcastle-under-Lyme, and in one advertisement (of 1754) is actually referred to as 'near Newcastle in Staffordshire'. We also know from entries in William Duesbury's workbook that he had dealings with Littler and had enamelled 'Stafartshire' figures in 1751, just before the beginning

PLATE XV   *See pages* 154, 161, 166

(*a*) GROUP. PORCELAIN. DERBY, ABOUT 1765
Victoria and Albert Museum (Schreiber Collection)

(*b*) FIGURE. PORCELAIN
LONGTON HALL, ABOUT 1755
Mr. and Mrs. Donald MacAlister's Collection

(*c*) FIGURE. PORCELAIN
DERBY, ABOUT 1775
Mr. A. H. S. Bunford's Collection

of the advertisements from which most of our meagre knowledge of Longton Hall is obtained. We know that Littler made salt-glaze, and it is of course possible that the entries refer to this material, but it is equally possible that the 'snow-man' porcelain was in question and that the white figures surviving once bore Duesbury's unfired painting. We have seen that the porcelain corresponds with some pieces of salt-glaze, and it is significant that the latter are precisely of the type which most often bears unquestionable Duesbury enamelling.[1]

The Longton factory is briefly referred to by Simeon Shaw (who as usual gives a wrong date for it—1765), and his account was taken over by Ward in his *History of Stoke on Trent.* The facts about Littler's venture were first put down by J. E. Nightingale from a study of the advertisements in Aris's *Birmingham Gazette*, the *Manchester Mercury*, and the London *Public Advertiser*, between 1752 and 1758. The earliest of these referred to 'Porcelain or China Ware', though the second (1754) spoke of the 'first produce of the Factory . . . of useful Porcelain or China Ware'. The advertisements of 1757 and 1758 are worth quoting in full in the absence of any other contemporary evidence about the productions. In the *Public Advertiser* was announced 'new and curious Porcelain or China . . . of the LONGTON HALL MANUFACTORY consisting of Tureens, Covers and Dishes, large Cups and Covers, Jars and Beakers, with beautiful Sprigs of Flowers, open-work'd Fruit Baskets and Plates, Variety of Services for Deserts, Tea and Coffee Equipages, Sauce Boats, leaf Basons and Plates, Melons, Colliflowers,

---

[1] Whilst this was in the press, a sweetmeat dish with a 'snow-man' figure and painting by a Longton Hall hand has been acquired by Mr. Wallace Elliot, and seems to prove the connection here conjectured. It will be discussed in a forthcoming volume of the *Trans. English Ceramic Circle.*

elegant Epargnes, and other ornamental and useful Porcelain, both white and enamell'd'. The advertisement of 1758 in Aris's *Birmingham Gazette* spoke of 'services of Dishes and Plates, Tea and Coffee Equipages, and great Variety of Services for Deserts, Beautiful Essence Pots, Images, Flowers, Vases, etc. with fine Blue and White Ribb'd, Fluted and Octagonal Chocolate Cups and Saucers, Tea Sets etc.' Whether the manufacture came to an end in that year is doubtful. Perhaps Littler sold out to someone else. Duesbury was working as an enameller at Longton in 1756, and there is a tradition in his family that he owned the Longton Hall factory: it is perhaps significant that in 1758, precisely at the time of cessation of the Longton advertisements, Derby announced an increase of staff. On the other hand, in September 1760 a sale took place at Salisbury of the Longton Hall stock, 'as the partnership is dissolved'. This may indicate that a new firm continued Littler's factory until this date and produced a distinct class of later porcelain attributable to Longton Hall.

The several links with Staffordshire pottery that by a somewhat complicated chain of argument enable us to identify Longton Hall porcelain are set out in full in my *Old English Porcelain*. It is remarkable that so little other evidence can be produced in support of the attribution. But the class so attributed is coherent, and a rare mark which occurs on the earlier pieces may be convincingly read as standing for 'Littler Longton'. Why it was not used on the other wares is obscure. Perhaps indeed it was hoped to pass them off as Chelsea, or even as Meissen.

The earliest specimens are some plates, dishes, sauceboats, etc., with wide, uneven blue borders or grounds with reserved panels, probably intended to imitate the *gros bleu* of Vincennes. This was not imitated at Chelsea until about 1758, though in use at the French factory from 1749 onwards. The Staffordshire connection with France (see p. 84) may account for this, and for the mark and flowers mentioned below. The blue is commonly compared with that of 'Littler's' salt-glaze; it is really quite different in tone, but that does not exclude the possibility that both were made by the same potter. We find the same white enamel-painting on both. The reserved panels on the blue ground are very often found blank and the pieces are supposed to be unfinished; but I believe that they were decorated in unfired colours which have since been cleaned away. This work may well have been Duesbury's. Traces of unfired gilding of poor quality often remain. The material of these early pieces is a soft creamy-white and very translucent porcelain. The class is of slight artistic importance but valuable historically as often bearing the mark attributed to Littler —a device apparently of crossed L's with a tail of dots, imitating that of Vincennes. It occurs on a blue-ground butter-dish in the British Museum, which is painted also with flowers in enamel colours and so helps us to identify the remaining, unmarked, Longton Hall productions.

These have a character of their own, though no doubt the Meissen-Chelsea styles were aimed at throughout. Among the shapes we find jugs, equally broad at mouth and foot, of a form which is peculiarly English and Staffordshire; fruit- and leaf-shaped dishes and tureens which take up the Meissen notion and 'degrade' it to the level of peasant pottery; and *rococo* vases with modelled and applied flowers (probably the 'essence pots' of the advertisements), which in their artless desire to outdo in abundance their Meissen originals achieve a wild surprise that is half amusement. The great prickly vase in the Schreiber Col-

almost apply to leaf-dishes; but in view of that word it appears to refer to the custom by which porcelain figures were grouped on the tables at the conclusion of a banquet, together with sweetmeat dishes and the like. The 'Flowers' in the phrase quoted would in that case be flowers modelled in the round, in the fashion set notably by Vincennes (though originated at Meissen), such as rarely survive to-day. I do not know any Longton Hall flowers of this kind, but some white Derby roses are fixed in their original ormolu 'branches' on a group of birds from that factory, in the Victoria and Albert Museum. 'Branches', 'nozzells', and 'flowers' of this kind described as Staffordshire appear in Duesbury's work-book for 1751–53. They can hardly have been of salt-glaze. The main body of the presumed Longton Hall figures show common characteristics in a rather grey heavy paste, a lumpy, doughy treatment of the *rococo* scrolled bases, and colouring which includes a thick paint-like red, a harsh dry crimson, and the yellowish green seen also on the useful wares. In some cases patches of underglaze blue recall the early useful wares. The models are sometimes after Meissen, but as often apparently original. A 'Dr. Mills' is cited by Shaw as Littler's modeller and may have been responsible for these figures, which are often seated in curious postures, half turned to right or left (Plate XV, B). A small but very characteristic feature is the delicate outlining of eye-lashes and marking of nostrils in touches of red. The heads are as a rule care-fully modelled. A *Seated Musician* and a *Market Woman selling butter* are good examples with a touch of the racy Staffordshire character, and the masterpiece is perhaps the large *Britannia*, in the Schreiber Collection and in the British Museum. A few later figures show profuse gilding of good quality, markedly different from the sparing touches occasionally seen before. These were obviously inspired by gold-anchor Chelsea and should therefore date from after 1758. Chemical analysis reveals some interesting details about these and the earlier Longton porcelain. What we may call the early period apparently differs from the middle period in the use of a small quantity of bone-ash—perhaps suggested by a London workman. The middle period, of the Chelsea style, is notable for an abundance of lead oxide (doubtless due to flint glass in the frit), which gives the porcelain its characteristic weight; the latest figures, as we may regard them, show that a little soapstone was included in the paste, which is otherwise closely similar to that of the preceding period. This suggests a Worcester hand, and we may wonder if Richard Holdship, who sold his Worcester shares in 1759 and afterwards offered a soapstone formula to Derby, was not perhaps responsible for this addition. With characteristic Staffordshire caution it was used, like the bone-ash, in a small quantity only. Typical late models are the *America* in the Schreiber Collection (formerly called Bow) and a pair of figures of a *Man* and *Woman seated on a mound*. A fine equestrian figure of *Ferdinand, Duke of Brunswick* in Mr. Wallace Elliot's collection probably dates from about 1759–60, in view of his rise to fame after Minden, and thus belongs to this latest class. A remarkable fact about the Longton models is their recurrence in Plymouth porcelain, and this has been thought to be due to the purchase of the moulds by William Cookworthy, when they were sold at Salisbury in September 1760.

Mention should be made here of a rectangular tea-jar in the Hanley Museum described in a note accompanying it as given by Enoch Wood, who had it from a William Fletcher, who in turn remembered its being made by Littler about fifty-five years previously. The porcelain bears no resemblance to that described above and is very similar to some Liverpool, under which heading its class will be further described. Enoch Wood's testimony is not altogether trustworthy in view of his association with Simeon Shaw, and one suspects the same kind of error as that noted in connection with a Wrotham pot on p. 20.

PLATE XVI   *See page* 169

(*a*) PLATE. PORCELAIN, PAINTED IN COLOURS. DERBY, ABOUT 1790
Victoria and Albert Museum (Schreiber Collection)

(*b*) CUP AND SAUCER. PORCELAIN
PAINTED IN COLOURS
PROBABLY BY ASKEW
DERBY, ABOUT 1775
Mr. A. H. S. Bunford's Collection

(*c*) POT AND COVER. PORCELAIN
PAINTED IN COLOURS
PROBABLY BY ROBERT BREWER
DERBY, ABOUT 1790–1800
Mr. Wallace Elliot's Collection

CHAPTER XI

DERBY

THE Derby porcelain-factory was one of the longest-lived in England, and its output was so various as to defy generalisation. A charge of provincialism is commonly brought against it, but so far as this implies an untutored or unacademic style it is pointless: Staffordshire pottery before Wedgwood was entirely unfashionable in its taste, yet ranks among the best English ceramic ware. The epithet could perhaps be applied with some justice to the very numerous Derby figures, most of which merely aped and wearily maintained an obsolete London fashion. But the table-wares of the last thirty years of the eighteenth century are a very different matter, employing as they do an exquisite material unlike any other, creating their own style, and in spite of the restriction of the neo-Classical mode, making something living and truly English out of the dull stock motives of the time. To the collector, the earliest Derby also has the interest of *incunabula* and is indeed a comparatively recent discovery. Until Mr. Bernard Rackham pointed them out eight or nine years ago, the productions of the factory in its first period were unrecognised, and even now are commonly misdescribed as Bow and Chelsea.

The belief that porcelain was made at Derby before 1750 rests on tradition only and has little likelihood. The earliest evidence consists of three cream-jugs, with the incised date 1750 and the letter 'D' in two cases, and in the other the word 'Derby'. These jugs, two of which are in the Victoria and Albert and British Museums, have been thought to be the first productions of a new manufacture, inscribed in emulation of the goat-and-bee jugs of Chelsea. But they are so utterly unlike anything else surviving, in their dull pinkish-white colour, that they are practically useless as evidence. Their genuineness has even been doubted. There is good reason, however, to believe that a Huguenot named Andrew Planché was already making porcelain in Derby in 1751, and 'Darby' and 'Darbishire figars' were certainly decorated by William Duesbury in London in 1753. It is thought that these first things were made at the Cockpit Hill factory in the town, owned by John Heath and three partners, the history of which has lately been written by Mr. F. Williamson, and the appearance together of these names—Planché, Duesbury, and Heath—in a draft agreement, dated as for 1st January 1756 but apparently never executed, marks the beginning of a new phase in the history of Derby china. It seems that this proposed partnership was the occasion of the taking of new premises in the Nottingham Road, Derby, after which the Cockpit Hill works were turned over to the making of earthenwares. Nothing is heard of Planché in Derby after this year, though he may have stayed on. William Duesbury, who was described in the draft as 'enamellor of Longton', had in the previous year borrowed money from his father in order, as it would seem, to provide capital for this venture, which was to prove a tremendous success. As we have seen in previous chapters, Duesbury and Heath acquired the Chelsea factory in 1770 and may also have obtained control of those at Longton Hall and Bow. William Duesbury became sole proprietor on the failure of Heath, who was a banker, in 1779, and died in 1786. He was succeeded by his son William Duesbury

II, who in 1795 took into partnership a miniature-painter named Michael Kean, and died in 1796. Kean married his widow in 1798 and remained in virtual possession of the factory until 1811. Its later history will be given in the chapter on nineteenth-century wares (p. 218).

We do not know what chemist or 'arcanist' was responsible for the early Derby pastes. They were apparently attempts to copy the red-anchor Chelsea, but were as a rule unsatisfyingly light in substance and seldom so smooth and fine-grained as their model. Some of the earliest pieces (among the best of all) are creamy in colour, but we are constantly finding evidence that this tone was not liked in the eighteenth century, and a rather crude blueing of the glaze was doubtless intended to counteract it. This spoils much of the early Derby china so far as its actual material is concerned. The absence of a factory-mark in use before 1770 probably indicates a wish to palm off the wares as genuine Chelsea or Meissen productions.

From the start Derby evidently set much store by figures. The earliest seem to be some with white or creamy-coloured glaze commonly showing a dry edge at the foot where the glaze stops short; a funnel-shaped hole under the base is also common. The models include as master-pieces a series of Chinese groups, of which there are specimens in the Schreiber Collection and the British Museum. These, if they were original work, imply the presence of a gifted modeller; but others such as the *Florentine Boars*, some *putti* as *Seasons*, and a group of *Boys milking a Goat* (in Mr. Herbert Allen's collection), seem to have been cast from bronzes. These are the presumed Planché models. The recurrence of some of them, such as a *Dancing Man* with his arm raised, and his companion, in later Derby seems to be evidence of continuity. The coloured versions of these figures may be those enamelled in London by Duesbury, and the more common white ones may once have had his unfired colouring. The enamels are similar to those on the Bow figures attributed to him, with a strong red, bright blue, streaky pink, and a rather dull or dirty yellow conspicuous among them. Purple was often used for painting fur and hair, and the general effect is sometimes rather smeared. A charming group of birds in white, at South Kensington, with its original ormolu 'branch' and separate porcelain flowers, has its coloured counterpart in Mr. Herbert Allen's collection.

The next class is more like Meissen, as we might expect from the advertisements which appeared in 1756 and in 1757, when 'the Derby or Second Dresden' was announced. The figures are noticeably light in weight and often have the strongly blued glaze already mentioned. Their slight or pale colouring again suggests a consciousness of red-anchor Chelsea. In general they are the liveliest of all Derby figures and the numerous *Dancers* naturally come first to mind, but the *Lovers with a Clown* after Meissen, in the Schreiber Collection, is very typical of the figures of this period. They sometimes come very close to Longton Hall. A superb group of *Lovers* in Lord Fisher's collection was figured by Mr. William King as Derby, though in the opinion of other good judges it is held to be Longton. I incline to accept the former attribution, in view of the form of the pedestal and the curious rounded heads, which anticipate the next and most numerous Derby class.

Both the classes described above have only lately been identified as Derby, having been generally mistaken for Bow. The very numerous Derby figures of the 1760's were similarly classified in error as gold-anchor Chelsea, on which their style was obviously modelled, until Mr. Bernard Rackham, looking about for the unidentified and certainly numerous productions of Derby prior to 1770, noted them as a distinct subdivision amongst the un-marked Chelsea and observed a link with the later and well-ascertained Derby pieces in three or four dark un-glazed patches on the bases, left by the pads of clay on which the figures rested during their glaze-firing. The patches sometimes occur on the light-weight figures just described, and they are very constant in this third period. A dirty greenish turquoise is an easily recognised colour rarely absent from the costumes or bases of this 'patch family' (as they are familiarly called), while the heads are usually painted in a distinctive way, with bright red cheeks. Their dating is confirmed by a typical specimen formerly in the Leverhulme Collection, which bears the inscription 'George Holmes did this figer 1765', and a *Bag-piper* in Mr. Wallace Elliot's collection has a cryptic incised mark 'W D Co', probably for 'William Duesbury & Co.', which may perhaps be taken as confirmation of Mr. Rackham's discovery. In modelling they lack the gold-anchor nobility, though obviously aping it, and have instead a stiff and doll-like quality which is by no means neces-sarily a fault in a porcelain figure and is here in an amusing gawkiness raised almost to the point of becoming a posi-tive merit. Their rounded heads and peculiar noses are quite distinct from Chelsea. A pair of *Minuet Dancers* (illus-trated in many books as Chelsea) and a group of *Hurdy Gurdy Players* after Carle Vanloo (Plate XVA), all in the Schreiber Collection, are typical. Some *Miltons*, *Britannias*, and *Shakespeares*, long afterwards popular in Derby por-celain and Staffordshire earthenware, represent a purely English contribution to the stock of models. In the figures of birds and animals the Derby stiffness gives an effect of insensitive hardness to which their strong colouring con-tributes. *Bocages* are common on the figures and groups.

No useful wares or vases of the Planché period are known (apart from the problematical cream-jugs), and those of 1756 to 1770 are not at all common. Their paste is at a first glance not unlike Chelsea, but lighter in weight and without the fineness of grain and 'firmness' of the latter. The wares are attractive for their painting, which is chiefly by two hands whose work is also commonly seen on the costumes and pedestals of the figures. One man painted flowers with thread-like stalks; a red flower with some petals merely outlined is usually included in his bouquets. His work is seen on the light-weight figures of 1756–60 as well as later. The other artist painted birds, flowers (rarely), figures in landscapes, and (very notably) large moths. In colour a red inclining a little towards brown, hard to describe but easily recognised, and several shades of often brownish green, besides the 'dirty turquoise' of the figures, are all distinctive. The forms and decoration are a mixture of the red- and gold-anchor styles, and rarely original or especially fine. Perhaps the best results of the gold-anchor inspiration are some vases with 'mazarin'-blue ground (for long and still often miscalled Longton Hall!) and panels with river landscapes with little figures, or cupids in red monochrome, or other figure-subjects in colour. These are rather rough and rustic-looking, but the painting has character and a charming freedom. Some painting of Chinese figures is somewhat like Worcester, and a specimen of this sort formerly in the Hignett Collection is dated 1756. Painting of Kakie-mon flowers and 'banded hedges' in crimson mono-chrome, particularly on sauceboats, is another type, often miscalled Bow. There is a very good representative series of the early Derby coloured table-wares in the Schreiber Collection at South Kensington.

Painting in underglaze blue was no more popular at

Derby than at Chelsea, perhaps because the soft Derby glaze was not very suitable for it. Some Chinese landscapes in a rather dark blue, on sauceboats, plates, and dishes with openwork borders and flowers at the intersections, are almost the only early examples. (These are sometimes called Chelsea in error.) Later on in the Chelsea-Derby period some large covered bowls and stands show under-glaze blue, and some vases, spoon- or asparagus-trays, dishes, and covered sugar-bowls, are painted in an intense violet blue, again with Chinese landscape subjects. Some of these date from the 1780's and bear an unexplained incised mark, 'N'.

Printing over the glaze is believed to have been done on very rare occasions at the instance of Richard Holdship of Worcester, who came to Derby in 1764, offering to teach the printing process and at the same time proposing to Duesbury a porcelain formula which seems to have resulted in the tentative use of soapstone in the Derby paste about this time. But printed specimens are exceedingly rare, though the Derby (Cockpit Hill) cream-colour was apparently more often decorated in this manner. The rebus mark of an anchor and the word 'Derby', and in one instance a sun-face, are included in the prints ascribed to Holdship.

In 1770 the Chelsea concern was bought by Duesbury and Heath and for fourteen years worked in association with Derby. This period is usually called 'Chelsea-Derby', though lovers of the London factory, anxious as far as possible to preserve the integrity of its work, have insisted that it should be Derby, or at least 'Derby-Chelsea'. There is no doubt which partner was predominant. We do not know how the work was divided between the two places, but I think it is certain that the figures, with the possible exception of some few gold-anchor models still in demand, were all made at Derby; the Chelsea-Derby style is here clearly in the Derby tradition. Vases and table-wares, and particularly toys (now degraded to 'double-doves' at a shilling! and so on), continued to be made at Chelsea, as some surviving accounts prove. I think we may take it that most if not all of the wares with the so-called Chelsea-Derby mark—a 'D' intersecting an anchor in gold —were made at Chelsea. It is tempting to con-jecture that the introduction of a blue or purple mark of a crowned 'D' about 1780 indicated the resumption of this part of the manufacture at Derby. There are obvious anomalies among the marks: gold anchors (sometimes crowned) and red anchors are found on pieces certainly dating from after 1770, and on one service of 'hop trellis' pattern the 'D' and the anchor are painted side by side in gold. A fine bowl in the Schreiber Collection marked with a gold anchor, painted with coopers at work and bearing the arms of the Coopers' Company, is actually dated 1779, and another in the collection of Mr. R. W. M. Walker depicts Chelsea and Battersea churches, and is evidence of the London work at about this time. A rare mark of this period, on a service with the arms of the Duke of Hamilton, is 'DUESBURY LONDON' in a rectangle in puce; this service was perhaps decorated outside the factory (as was not unusual with armorial work) to Duesbury's order; the colours somewhat resemble those we ascribe to the enameller Giles, whose work will be further discussed under the heading of Worcester.

The Chelsea-Derby figures have rather a mass-produced look. Their colouring has a sameness in its constant use of pale yellowish green and brown for the bases, and in the pink flesh tones. A rich chocolate brown is a notable new colour, however, and the dirty turquoise of the earlier 'patch family' clears to a fine bluish tone, doubtless due to Chelsea experience now made available at Derby. The models have in general a sentimental air, and the influence of Falconet and Sèvres is apparent. The note of ecstatic sentiment of the period is struck by the phrases of an advertisement of 1772, which I cannot forbear to quote: 'A Display of Elegance and Taste reigns almost uninterrupted through the Articles that comprize this Sale. The Ornaments are a continued Variety of antique, select and peculiar Forms and Shapes, aetherial Colours and elaborate Decorations that alternately rise with increasing Beauty, and which distinguish Genius (British) not less conspicuous or meritorious than the Saxon or Gallic. Human Actions lively and naturally represented in many expressive and agreeable Characters; the Figures graceful, the Attitudes just, the Drapery loose and flowing, and finished with a nicety incredible; nor does the Table want its Requisites and Embellishments in all its various Occasions; the several Apparatus are contrived and adapted with much Skill, and painted and adorned with a luxuriant Fancy. Emulous to excell and happy to please, no Labour, no Expence have been spared; a chearful and vigorous Perseverance in the arduous Task has, it is humbly presumed, brought this Porcelain to a Degree of Perfection that merits public Attention.' Classical and sentimental motives were mingled as in the contemporary Wedgwood ware, but the sentiment generally prevailed. The famous 'Pensent-ils au raisin?' the Cupids as Discretion, etc., on architectural pedestals, with busts of Rousseau and Pope, and a Triton (after Wedgwood's classical model), all represented in the Schreiber Collection, may be cited as typical (but by no means the best) models in the new fashions, which may be classified as English Louis Seize. They maintained their hold until the end of the century. Livelier models in the Kaendler tradition were of course made occasionally, but there was a constant tendency to change the passionate amorous shepherds and shepherdesses of Meissen into smirking children or melancholy adolescents in the manner of Falconet. The charming figure shown in Plate XV, c is of an earlier model, known in the 'light-weight' paste of the previous period. One feature to be noted on the coloured figures is the delicacy of the painted sprigs on the costumes, which often show a revival of the early Meissen 'Indian flowers'.

Following the Sèvres fashion, Derby was the first English factory to take up the use of biscuit for figure-models. The vogue of this material marks the decline of the art of porcelain figure-modelling, since its avowed aim is to simulate the appearance of marble or stone, and the special opportunities of glaze and colour are renounced. If it were the merit of a porcelain figure to have the sharp precision of a carving in ivory or marble this would perhaps have been a technical advance, but the charm of porcelain is quite a different matter, and the seriousness of the new mode and its embodiment in the cold and literal biscuit are regrettable signs of the end of the great age of porcelain. This use of unglazed porcelain for figures was a notion of J. J. Bachelier of Vincennes and Sèvres, who claimed to have introduced it as early as 1751; but this was in a document prepared in self-defence long afterwards, during the Revolution, and there are no actual surviving specimens that can be of so early a date. At Derby it was made in 1771, or possibly a little earlier. One of the first and most important works in it were 'three grouped pieces' representing the *Royal Family* after Zoffany's painting, of which H.M. Queen Mary has the only known complete set. George III alone is in the British Museum, on an enamelled pedestal, and bears the Chelsea-Derby mark, showing probably that the decoration was done in London. It was stated by Haslem (a painter in the factory in its last period and its first historian) that the finest Derby biscuit was made by Michael Kean, and that the typical groups of *Bacchantes adorning Pan*, *Virgins awaking Cupid*, and *Virgins distressing Cupid*, were modelled by one J. J. Spangler (or Spengler) who came to the factory from Zurich in 1790. But these models appear in catalogues of sales in 1778 and 1782, and enamelled versions show the typical Chelsea-Derby colouring, so that a mistake seems probable. Some models, however, may be ascribed to Spangler with fair certainty on the authority of an old factory list. (It should be mentioned in passing that the incised numbers on Derby figures of about 1770 and later are mould-numbers corresponding to a factory list which was published in part by Haslem.) The *Belisarius and his daughter* was after Cyfflé of Lunéville and, like a *Russian Shepherd* group, shows Spangler as a competent modeller, who however generally preferred to adapt rather than invent. Pierre Stephan worked for the factory from 1770 to 1795 and made a series of Admirals, a set of the *Elements*, and doubtless much else not easily identifiable. To W. J. Coffee is ascribed on Haslem's authority a charming large *Shepherd* adapted from an antique Adonis by adding clothes to it. J. C. F. Rossi modelled an *Aesculapius* and other classical figures.

The vases of the Chelsea-Derby period were mostly made at Chelsea and were often painted by artists such as Richard Askew and Zachariah Boreman who are known to have worked there. The English landscapes on one in the Jones Collection at South Kensington are in the style of the latter. In form the wares commonly show the exaggerated slenderness and sweetness that mark the English notion of Classical as expounded by Wedgwood. Striped patterns and swags were popular as usual, and many vases have no pictorial painting but were merely decorated with reliefs picked out with gilding and coloured bands, for which the clear turquoise and an intense blue copied from the Sèvres *bleu de roi* were especially popular. This bright blue is sometimes called the 'Derby blue' and is a striking feature of the colouring of the later useful wares.

The Chelsea-Derby and Derby table-wares of the last thirty years of the eighteenth century represent, as I have said, one of the most notable achievements in English ceramic art. They are William Duesbury's title to fame. I do not know of any porcelain material at once so perfect technically and so charmingly sympathetic as the Derby of this period. Though as a rule thinly potted it is never meagre, but has much of the generous depth and ease of gold-anchor Chelsea. It is of slightly warm tone or milk-white in colour, with a liquid shining glaze, oil-like rather than watery, that provides a perfect ground for the thick soft gilding and sparing decoration in colours. On such a material the most frigid of Classical motives would take on an attractive warmth. But as it happens the Derby Classical was never very severe. The shapes were almost as plain and practical as Wedgwood's, but with a touch of the Dresden fancy in 'T'-shaped handles and flower-shaped knobs. The decorations in a description would seem thin and unpromising. A design of pendent 'husks' in black and grey, for example, sounds rather forbidding, but is actually charged with a sort of colour and feeling that are most attractive to a modern eye, and very English. Rendered in rose-pink and clear green, the compound stripes become almost too sweet, especially when alternating with very delicately painted garlands of small flowers. The pleasant fancy shown in combinations of colour in these stripes is not least of the merits of the

168

Chelsea-Derby patterns. The flower- and fruit-painting is decidedly mannered, but shows feeling in its delicate touches and clean fresh colour. Edward Withers was the best flower-painter of the period. The turquoise and intense 'Derby blue' already mentioned should be noted among the particular resources in colour. Some of the designs continued the gold-anchor Chelsea manner and employed the famous 'claret colour'; others were taken straight from Sèvres, with 'mignonette' garlands, 'hop-trellis', medallion-heads, and *œil de perdrix* grounds. Cupids in crimson monochrome or in colours were copied from the same source, but the rather ugly little people in this manner attributed to Askew still have an English charm (Plate XVI, B). Pictorial painting was out of fashion for a time, but came in again in the last ten or fifteen years of the century. To Askew are ascribed the popular 'classical' figure-pieces in the style of Angelica Kauffmann, painted in miniature style, and Boreman's Derbyshire scenes (Plate XVI, A) represent the type of hill- and river-landscape practised doubtless by other painters, including the brothers Brewer, who were water-colourists and drawing-masters, employed for a time at the factory. Thanks to the recent researches of Major W. H. Tapp, we are able to identify as John Brewer's some rather dull landscapes and bird-pieces, while the novel camp-scenes and shipping subjects (Plate XVI, c) were apparently done by his brother Robert. The famous name of William Billingsley is associated with some overrated naturalistic flower-painting. Much ingenuity has lately been spent in the identification of the work of these and various other hands, on the basis of some surviving pattern-books now at the Worcester Works Museum, and with the help of the numbers supposed to have been used by the painters and gilders. But the results are in my opinion unconvincing and often

contradictory. It is certain that the painters did not con-
fine themselves each to a single type of work. The landscapists painted figures also, and the flower-painters did
landscapes on occasion. Billingsley achieved another sort
of fame on account of his own porcelain, which was a
Derby body improved so as to be more like Sèvres, and
we know that during his chequered career after leaving
the parent factory he painted landscapes, classical figures,
and even a portrait of a racehorse, besides the soft limp
flowers for which he is famous. The early Pinxton made
by him for a few years after 1796 has many of the Derby
virtues: the little landscapes in particular have the same
English quality. But the fawn and yellow coloured grounds
favoured tend to cover up the porcelain in a sinful way of
which Derby was seldom guilty. A beautiful yellow and
a pale pink ground were popular at the latter factory, but
in general we can approve of the respect shown for the
beautiful white material, evidence of a still-living art of
porcelain, scarcely to survive the turn of the century. A
miniature-like and jewelled style of painting was the
fashion in the last ten years or so of the eighteenth century
and into the *Empire* period, and Derby porcelain was no
exception to the rule; but it is seldom that we find this
English ware falling into the errors of taste—the tawdri-
ness and smothering of the white china—of which even
Sèvres and Vienna, the fashion-leading factories, were as
often as not guilty. With this small triumph we propose
to leave the Derby factory for the present. Its further
history belongs to that of nineteenth-century English
ceramic art and will be touched on in a later chapter (pp.
218, 231). It should be added here that the customary mark on Derby china, from about 1785
onwards, was a crowned 'D' with crossed batons
and six dots; this was painted in puce, purple, crimson,

or blue until about 1810, when red began to be used for it. It was incised on biscuit figures, and there accompanied by the mould-numbers and the marks of 'repairers'.

The productions of a short-lived factory at Wirksworth in Derbyshire, which is recorded to have come to an end in 1777, have never been satisfactorily identified, and are presumably confused with those of Derby or Liverpool or some other factory. The discovery of wasters on the site is evidence that porcelain was actually made.

CHAPTER XII

WORCESTER
AND ITS OFFSHOOTS AT CAUGHLEY
AND LIVERPOOL

WE meet a new tradition, both technical and artistic, in the porcelain of these three factories. Undoubted connections of one kind or another link the London factories with Staffordshire, Derby, and Lowestoft, and with each other, but Worcester stands apart. Technically the difference is due to a new porcelain formula, one quite peculiar to England, invented or suggested, as I am inclined to believe, by the Quaker chemist of Plymouth, William Cookworthy, whose final achievement will be described in the next chapter. Cookworthy's researches into the materials of true porcelain, helped by the published *Letters* from China of Père d'Entrecolles, began as early as 1745, and in the course of these he is almost certain to have examined the possibilities of the Cornish soapstone which became the characteristic Worcester ingredient. It was the 'slippery stone' (*hua shih*) described by the Jesuit father. The manufacture of this soapstone porcelain began at Bristol, and Cookworthy was in fact referred to as the 'first inventor of the Bristol china works' in a letter of Sarah Champion's written in 1764, that is, long before the transfer to Bristol of his better-known hard-paste manufacture. I find that the late W. J. Pountney also regarded Cookworthy as a probable discoverer of the soapstone formula, and a further possible link is the common use of alchemical signs on the earliest 'Bristol or Worcester' porcelain. These might have been suggested by an apothecary, such as Cookworthy. But there is no positive proof or evidence of all this. It is presumption only.

The Bristol works which were the short-lived precursor of Worcester were conducted in a glasshouse called Lowdin's and were visited in 1750 by Dr. Richard Pococke, who recorded the fact in his *Travels*, mentioning the use of 'soapy rock' from the Lizard; the works were said to have been 'lately established' and a potter from Limehouse was employed. In 1751 the 'Worcester Tonquin Manufacture' was started in Warmstry House in that city by a company of fifteen gentlemen pledged 'to discover for the benefit of themselves and the other subscribers the real true and full art' of making porcelain. Among these promoters was Dr. John Wall (*b.* 1708, *d.* 1776), whose name has become associated with the first and most important period of the factory. The secret was apparently known to Wall as well as to the manager William Davis and to two workmen named John Lyes and Robert Podmore, who were to receive special payments 'the better to engage their fidelity'; the last-named, however, ran away and founded the Liverpool manufacture five years later. The Bristol works were closed in 1752 and advertised as now 'united with the Worcester Porcelain Company'.

Worcester enjoyed great commercial success in the 'Dr. Wall period', which is usually brought down to the death in 1783 of the manager Davis, seven years after that of John Wall himself. It was then bought by its London agent Thomas Flight for his sons Joseph and John, while Robert Chamberlain seceded to found a rival factory in

173

the city, the earliest productions of which are virtually unknown. (It was perhaps at first a decorating establishment only.) In 1792 Martin Barr was taken into partnership, making the firm 'Flight and Barr', and began the experiments with bone-ash which link up with Staffordshire and take us into the nineteenth century and a new era. The later history of Worcester is given under that heading on p. 217.

The first productions of Worcester are naturally hard to separate from those of Lowdin's Bristol. There exist some sauceboats, moulded after silver originals and painted in blue in Chinese style, and some standing figures of a *Chinaman*, which bear an impressed mark 'Bristol' or 'Bristoll' in relief and are plausibly regarded as made at Lowdin's glasshouse. Since the discovery of these it has been the custom to attribute vaguely to 'Bristol (Lowdin's) or early Worcester' a great body of pieces more or less resembling these sauceboats. But it is becoming more and more apparent that most of them must be early Worcester. Those bearing transfer-prints, for example, cannot, as I now believe, be earlier than 1756. It is, however, a singular coincidence that Dr. Pococke particularly mentioned 'beautiful white sauceboats adorned with reliefs of festoons which sell for sixteen shillings a pair' of a type which actually form a very large proportion of the surviving pieces of this 'Bristol or Worcester' class. The marked sauceboats are painted with undistinguished little Chinese landscapes with figures in blue, the only exceptions being some with rather artless copies of the Meissen flowers and an outlining of the reliefs, in colours; but on these the raised 'Bristol' mark has been painted over with a green leaf as if to conceal it. It is believed that these sauceboats were made from the Bristol moulds at Worcester, where they would naturally wish to obliterate the mark automatically produced by the moulds. It is obvious from this that the separate recognition of the pieces actually made at Bristol is almost impossible in view of the continuous history of the two factories. The marked figures of *Chinamen* were cast from a Fukien model and have no interest but their rarity and the curious touches of underglaze manganese purple which some of them bear. This decoration 'carries' some 'Bristol or Worcester' shell-shaped pickle-trays, and apart from these examples is extremely unusual on English porcelain, the Longton Hall *Pug-dogs* being almost the only other instance.

In general this earliest Worcester, as I propose to call the whole class, is somewhat monotonously confined to a few types, moulding from silver being a favourite decoration in all. This is perhaps to be accounted for by the presence among the original Worcester subscribers of a silversmith named Samuel Bradley. The facetted forms of some vases and little bottles are charming and well suited to porcelain, as are the raised scroll- and flower-enclosed panels which were filled with little paintings, generally inspired by the Chinese, or with prints. The blue painting is sometimes delicately done, but it was all of one type. That in colours is better, and again mostly by one or two easily recognisable hands. The most prolific of these worked with an unusually fine brush, giving an airy delicacy and rhythm to his graceful Chinese figures, birds, and landscapes (Plate XVII, B). The palette of colours was undistinguished, including red, green, and yellow of good quality, and a warm brown which was sparingly used in a manner quite distinct from the similar colour of the contemporary raised- and red-anchor Chelsea. Another hand is obviously the same as that of an enameller of the opaque white Bristol glass, and since the only painter's name recorded for the latter is that of Michael Edkins, it has become usual to attribute this porcelain-painting to him and to call these pieces Lowdin's Bristol. But there are equally good reasons (such as some of the shapes) for thinking that they are Worcester, and I do not feel convinced that they are by the same hand as the glass with bird-painting 'authenticated' by Edkins' grandson, or the delftware doubtfully attributed to him and mentioned in a previous chapter. *Chinoiseries*, including an acrobat-subject often repeated, and birds on rocks with spiky sprays of foliage, are the chief subjects by this painter, who had a mannerism of dotting the green-painted ground in a peculiar way, recalling some Dutch enamelling on Staffordshire salt-glaze. This early polychrome-ware is remarkable for its pleasant creamy-toned ground, which is totally unlike the later Worcester. One recalls Dr. Pococke's remark that the Lowdin's porcelain had a 'yellow cast'. As I have already remarked, the ideal porcelain of the eighteenth century was cold or even bluish in tone, like the imported Chinese wares, and there is little doubt that this creamy-toned porcelain, so pleasing in our eyes, was not then regarded with favour. It became the unfailing practice of the Worcester people to add a little cobalt to the paste and glaze to counteract the yellowish tone, and the resulting greyish colour (and greenish tone by transmitted light) is characteristic of Worcester porcelain to the end of the eighteenth century.

Before passing on to the well-established Worcester types, a word must be said about some mugs and jugs of much-disputed origin. These bear an incised or knife-cut mark of a saltire cross, sometimes also an incised stroke near the foot-ring, and are on that account known as the 'scratched cross family'. The typical shapes are a cylindrical mug spreading at the base and a

PLATE XVII   *See pages* 175, 178, 180

(*a*) SAUCER
PORCELAIN, PRINTED IN
BROWNISH BLACK
WORCESTER, ABOUT 1756
Mr. H. W. Hughes' Collection

(*b*) SAUCE-BOAT
PORCELAIN, PAINTED IN COLOURS
BRISTOL (LOWDIN'S) OR WORCESTER
ABOUT 1750–55
Victoria and Albert Museum

(*c*) JUG. PORCELAIN, PAINTED IN COLOURS. WORCESTER, ABOUT 1760
Victoria and Albert Museum (Tolson Bequest)

pear-shaped jug; there is often an incipient crack inside the vessel over against the place where the handle is attached. These pieces have been claimed as Bow on the evidence of a waster, but their porcelain material and decoration (usually in the Chinese style) are unlike the accepted Bow and very like Worcester, and Dr. H. E. Rhodes has called attention to two examples which seem to confirm the West of England view: one of these is dated 1754, the other has Worcester associations, and both resemble Worcester in style. Some painted marks like alchemical signs in several cases actually correspond with those found on accepted Worcester. It seems therefore likely that the class was made at Worcester from a special formula indicated by the incised mark. That the factory was willing to try out new pastes in this way is evident from a letter of Richard Champion in which he proposed to ask a Worcester friend to fire for him some specimens made from some American clay he had received. This was in 1765, but it is not impossible that Cookworthy or another made a similar request at an earlier date. The masterpiece of 'scratch-cross' is a jug marked with an 'L' (unexplained) in the Schreiber Collection; this has very charmingly painted figures.

By 1755 the composition of the Worcester body seems to have been finally decided upon, and remained constant for nearly fifty years. It was more serviceable in use than the London porcelains and would stand hot water without cracking. The glaze was hard, thin, and even—'close-fitting' is Mr. Rackham's apt description—and very seldom crazed. It was brushed thinly over the foot, and a line bare of glaze just within the foot-ring is often taken as a proof of Worcester origin. It was perhaps due to the soapstone in it that the Worcester body could be worked much thinner than its contemporaries, and a clean sharp-edged 'crispness' (Mr. Hobson's word!) is characteristic of the cups and saucers and dishes of the early period. Misshapen pieces are rare, and foot-rings practically never required to be ground to level. The silver forms continued in favour for some time; one form of jug, moulded in relief with 'cabbage leaves', remained popular for at least twenty years and was much copied at Caughley and Lowestoft. A long-popular low-relief pattern on a small leaf-dish, of a spray of rose-leaves and buds, was introduced probably before 1760 and was eventually named 'the blind Earl's pattern', after an Earl of Coventry who lost his sight in 1780. Towards 1760 plainer forms without extravagances of any sort began to be preferred: bell-shaped mugs and plain globular teapots are typical. Even when more showy painting came into favour the plain forms were not abandoned.

At the beginning of the essential Worcester types of decoration may be placed some versions of the Meissen landscapes with little figures probably dating from about 1755 or earlier. In these the country has become recognisably England, and the painter's touch, if not very correct, is free and sensitive: a beautiful pear-shaped jug on three feet (of course copied from silver), in the Schreiber Collection, is an early masterpiece of this kind. Flowers, again derived from Meissen, show the same touch. A little later we meet a development of this work notably in some mugs, of which one in the Frank Lloyd Collection, dated 1759, is inscribed to Dr. Wall's guardian, Lord Sandys. The figures have now taken a larger scale and the hill- and river-landscapes are beautifully rendered; their cool clean colour and perfectly simple direct handling make them the Worcester counterpart of the fable-painting of Chelsea. A great jug with the arms of Bawtrip (Plate XVII, c), bequeathed to the Victoria and Albert Museum by Mr. Legh Tolson, is another masterpiece by this unnamed artist. Two similar large jugs in the Worcester Corporation Museum are dated 1757 and confirm the range of date. Birds flying and on trees (especially owls) were a favourite motive of this painter, and his flower-pieces have a kind of softness and delicacy all their own. Exceptionally fine painting of this kind was put on many armorial mugs and jugs of the period, sometimes in a cool purple monochrome, with a most sensitive touch shown in the *rococo* mantling and scrollwork. The types referred to in this paragraph in my opinion represent Worcester at its highest level of artistic achievement.

Blue-and-white remained the commercial stand-by and figured largely in the firm's advertisements. The painted subjects were anglicised Chinese showing a full appreciation of the decorative possibilities of pendent foliage and spiky bamboos. On the huge hexagonal vases the painting often rose to the height of admirably rhythmical compositions of birds and flowering branches. Most of it is pleasant and workmanlike if not very exciting. The powdered blue with panels has a characteristic neatness. A blue of indigo tone remained usual throughout the Wall period.

Chinoiseries in enamel colours were of several types. The most attractive of all (Plate XVIII, B) depicts Chinese figures, rendered in clean, sure brush-strokes in colours which include a fine sharp red and black, setting off an intense turquoise blue; these date from about 1760. Others are painted in black or purple monochrome very fantastically, apparently inspired by the Chinese painting in black of European subjects; some crimson landscapes in panels reserved on a yellow ground are also a remarkable innovation. More exact copies of Far-Eastern types include some rare versions of a *famille verte* subject and the more numerous Kakiemon designs, especially the

179

'partridge pattern' which remained a stock decoration into the nineteenth century.

The rather uninspiring art of transfer-printing has always been regarded as a Worcester speciality. Some charming work was done there in the Wall period, and the signature of Robert Hancock, the most famous and prolific engraver for porcelain, appears on many pieces. The date of the earliest Worcester (or even Bristol) printing and its connection with Hancock have often been discussed, not without heat. It is, I think, now proved that the process was the invention of the Irish engraver John Brooks, and was first practised in 1753 at Stephen Theodore Janssen's Battersea enamel-factory, where Simon-François Ravenet was the principal engraver. It is my belief that Hancock (who was born in Staffordshire in 1730) worked under Ravenet at Battersea; and that at its closing in 1756 he went to Bow for a few months and then left for Worcester. Mr. H. W. Hughes, who in face of the most determined opposition has for long affirmed his belief that Hancock worked at Battersea, has pointed out some little prints in the British Museum, after drawings by L. P. Boitard, with Hancock's signature as engraver, which include several characteristic Battersea subjects and also some others appearing on early Worcester (Plate XVII, A), such as 'The Fortune-Teller' and the boy teaching a girl to play the flute. These delicious little 'primitives' had been thought to be Lowdin prints and their ascription to Hancock seemed doubtful. It now appears (unless we imagine that Hancock while still at Battersea sold and sent engraved plates to Worcester) that they must date from 1756 or later. Their appearance on Worcester at the same time as such finished work as the portraits of Frederick the Great, 'The Tea Party', and 'L'Amour', may be explained by his having taken *all* his engraved plates, early and late, with him

to Worcester. I think that Hancock's first concern at
Worcester must have been to perfect a method of making
prints in a true black (these are never found on Battersea
and seldom, if ever, on Bow), and that the experimental look
of the little squirrels, the ships, and the subjects after
Boitard, is due to the imperfect mastery of this. The research involved the discovery of a suitable black enamel
pigment and the determination of the depth of engraved
line necessary to hold the right amount of pigment for a
clean result. It should perhaps be explained that the plate
was first etched with needle and acid and the lines were
subsequently engraved with the burin to the required
depth. After the plate had been inked, and the surface
wiped clean in the usual way, an impression was taken on
paper and this was laid on the surface of the porcelain to
which the pigment was transferred by rubbing. Delicate
adjustments were necessary in transferring to a curved
surface. Other experiments were doubtless made by
Hancock in this period. As far as the relative merits of the
various styles of printing are concerned, I confess I prefer
the prints in colours, such as those in brick-red and purple
on Bow porcelain, to those in the perfected, unvarying, and
uninteresting later black, however clean and precise these
may be, and above all I prefer the imperfect little early
prints, with their almost tremulously careful linear quality,
to the assured pictorial perfection of Hancock's later
work. The charming sentiment of these early subjects
may indeed be Boitard's contribution, and it is probable
that Hancock owed much to him. Hancock's successor
at Worcester was James Ross, whose signature is found on
prints closely following his in style.

Apart from Hancock's initials and signature in full the
initials 'R H' in monogram with an anchor occur on some
of the prints. These are usually thought to be the marks of

Richard Holdship, a shareholder in the Company who was apparently concerned with the printing department. Some well-known verses referred to his authorship of a portrait of Frederick, while others made the reply:

> Hancock, my friend, don't grieve tho' Holdship has the praise,
> 'Tis yours to execute, 'tis his to wear the bays.

This suggests that Holdship had added his mark (an anchor for 'hold-ship') to Hancock's work. It seems that the former left Worcester in 1759 or 1760, after selling his shares, eventually going to Derby, where in 1764 he offered among other things to teach the process of printing in blue. The dates are important evidence of the introduction of underglaze blue printing, which was first practised at Worcester about this time and continued in use for many years; few pieces, however, can be dated as early as 1759. The Worcester work in this was, as usual, neat and workmanlike, but calls for little comment. Flowers were the usual subjects. One very popular design including a formal pine-cone (or strawberry!) was copied not only at Caughley and Lowestoft in transfer-printing but in laborious painting copied line for line on Chinese porcelain. Underglaze blue printing was much developed at Caughley, a rival factory not far away to which Hancock went on leaving Worcester in 1774, when he was bought out for £900. At least he was claimed in an advertisement of 1775, though there seems some doubt as to the work actually done by him at Caughley; a copper-plate with some of his engravings, published by Jewitt, has, however, the marks of the Caughley factory. The latter was founded by Thomas Turner, who is said to have been a pupil of Hancock's. Before its productions are discussed a description must be given of the later porcelain of the Wall period, which has a character very distinct from what had gone before, and if the evidence of the market counts for anything, is the most important of all Worcester porcelain.

The change that came over the Worcester styles soon after 1765 is put down with good reason to the migration of some artists, whose names are unknown, from the Chelsea factory, which about this time began to lessen its activity. The new manner naturally shows also an awareness of Sèvres, then at the height of its achievement. Coloured grounds especially were inspired in this way. The Chelsea claret-colour was continued at Worcester probably from the recipe of a Chelsea artist, but the earlier blue grounds were different, being not stained glazes of the *gros bleu* or Chelsea 'mazarin' type, but powdered blues. They were sometimes painted over with a reticulation of darker lines, or a similar effect was produced by wiping out, giving a more or less indefinite pattern of overlapping scales. This famous 'scale blue' ground, as it is called, counts as a Worcester invention, though it was probably suggested in the first place by the Meissen and Berlin *Mosaik* patterns. Pink scale, yellow scale, and more rarely brick-red scale are also known, the last-named being also done in outline only. In 1769 a sale announcement promised a whole range of new colours, some of which, such as the 'Purple' and 'Scarlet', can hardly be identified. The 'sky blue' (the *bleu céleste* of later advertisements) is a fine clear turquoise; while the immensely popular 'apple green' of the present-day market must be the colour more appropriately called 'pea green' in the contemporary advertisements.

The first use of factory marks on Worcester belongs to this period. A crescent, said to be taken from the arms of Warmstry, is the commonest mark; it was copied on Caughley, Bow, and Lowestoft. A 'W' of various forms and the 'fretted square', an imitation Chinese seal-character rather like the Union Jack, appear as a rule on the finer wares. A version of the crossed swords with '9' is also not uncommon. Besides these, all sorts of imitation Chinese marks and alchemists' signs had been used, probably as painters' marks, from the start, the commonest being a version of the character for jade, resembling 'T F' in monogram. This was at one time thought to be a Bow mark, for Thomas Frye, and does in fact occur on Bow porcelain, but in a slightly different form and much more rarely.

The Worcester porcelain of this period undoubtedly made a great fashionable success, but of its aesthetic merits it is more difficult to speak with confidence. I have never been moved by it to such admiration as I feel for the slightest piece of raised- or red-anchor Chelsea of even moderate quality. Its splendour has always seemed to me a heartless affair. Its material is unexciting, without the sensuous charm one finds in early Bow and in almost all Chelsea, and there is usually a note of slick assurance about the painting that is distinctly repellent; but it must be granted that this is a fault from which even Sèvres is seldom free in its later period. One cannot banish the thought that Worcester had from the start a strictly commercial intention, allowing little room for the unregulated fancy; nothing but a desire for profit would account for the dishing up of ten-year-old Chelsea fashions and belated *rococo* in the 1770's and 1780's. One recalls with misgiving the mid-Victorian boast of R. W. Binns, part-proprietor and first historian of the factory, that 'the finest productions and the most prosperous results' are always in perfect 'accord': 'finest' may perhaps pass, but 'most original' would certainly never do. But the new policy evidently paid, perhaps because the manufacturers had so correctly judged the conservative English taste.

Judged by the appropriate standard, this decorative porcelain ranks as first-rate work. It is never slipshod or defective, and a high level of skill is reached in all its processes. The profusely added gilding indeed will stand comparison with that of Chelsea or Sèvres. The forms remained plain, as I have said, the only exceptions to the rule of 'English good sense' in this matter being some large vases with frills, masks, and applied flowers, and some openwork baskets, which bear the familiar 'T⁰' mark of the presumed 'Mr. Tebo', who apparently came to Worcester about 1770. It was evidently he too who persuaded the factory to make the sweetmeat dishes in the form of shells which he had made at Bow and Plymouth, and the rare Worcester figures also bear his mark. These were apparently a brief venture, not certainly lasting longer than the period 1769–71, and four models only have been identified, by Mr. William King —a *Gardener* and a *Turk* and their female companions. Though not original in style, they are very well finished, as one expects Worcester productions to be, and this need not imply a long period of manufacture, since Tebo's experience would have sufficed.

The painting offers an interesting study in the identification, or rather grouping, of the pieces as by several recognisable hands. One of these is thought to be the Chelsea painter of the sprawling 'exotic birds': he shows a similar confident style, painting with a full brush and in clean colour, birds, fruits, and flowers. Another artist had been at Plymouth, where he is supposed to have been the 'Mons. Soqui' of a written record; his birds are strongly coloured, with thick stippling and faintly indicated trees; he was imitated by another artist, whose trees look like billowy clouds. Others (Plate XVIII, c) have different mannerisms, discussed at length in my *Old English Porcelain*. One figure-painter deserving mention may have been the Chelsea artist who painted the Thomson tea-service in gold-anchor Chelsea; he certainly adopted the same style, but I have never felt quite sure that he was the same person. The most elaborate figure-painting on all Worcester china is that of the well-known miniaturist John Donaldson, also a Chelsea painter, and some of it bears his signature. He is said to have painted vases 'sent to him in London'. His work at Worcester is, I think, rather laboured and dull. The flower-painting is often decorative in the Sèvres manner and clean in colour, but conventional and lifeless. The Worcester gilt lace-work is very elaborate and fine, and owes much of its quality to the thick soft gold employed, which is equal to the best on the later Chelsea. This quality of the gold may provide a means of distinguishing from the factory productions the work of James Giles of Cockspur Street, an outside decorator of Worcester porcelain whose activities have already been mentioned several times in the course of these pages. Giles's workshop was in Kentish Town, where there had been a short-lived porcelain factory, whose history was brought to light by Mr. A. J. Toppin; its productions have not been identified.

Giles advertised in 1768, as 'China and Enamel Painter' and 'Proprietor of the Worcester Porcelaine Warehouse', that he had 'a great Variety of White Goods by him' and that patrons could have pieces 'painted to any pattern they shall chuse'. He was promptly disclaimed by the factory; but in the following year he is recorded as the purchaser at the Worcester sale of services of 'jet-enamelled', that is to say, transfer-printed, ware. It has therefore been generally accepted that Giles was

responsible for the not uncommon specimens of printed
Worcester painted over in enamel colours, or with
enamelling added on the moulded borders. Some painting of exotic birds in the factory style, but with curiously
wild dishevelled plumage, also stands apart, and may
have been done in his workshop. Birds by this same hand
are found on Plymouth and Longton Hall porcelain as
well as Worcester, and can be linked with some added decoration on Chinese porcelain which is on general grounds
more likely to have been done at an outside decorator's
rather than in a factory. Landscapes in green and black
monochrome on Chinese and Worcester porcelain in the
Meissen-Vincennes-Chelsea style may also be Giles's
studio-work. In all these types the gilding is inferior to
the usual Worcester, being thinner and more easily rubbed
away, and as a rule not so well painted. A simple toothed
border is especially common, and this brings in the hand
of a painter named Jeffrey Hamet O'Neale, whose in-
correct but very charming figure, animal, and landscape
subjects are found on the Chinese porcelain (again with
the toothed gilt border), and on Worcester, where it is
sometimes signed with his initials. O'Neale's horses are
very individual fairy-tale creatures and his figures elegant
but over-slender, with curious spiky hands. A tufty tree
with crossed branches and red-brown rocks in the foreground are fairly constant mannerisms, but not absolutely peculiar to his work. I think we may conjecture some
at least of O'Neale's work to have been done as 'outside
decoration' for Giles. Against this view may be mentioned
that we find also on Chinese porcelain exotic birds by the
supposed Chelsea hand referred to above, but again with
the poor un-Worcesterish gilding. It is not unreasonable,
I think, to explain this by supposing the painter to have
worked for Giles in London for a time, before moving to

Worcester. The London factory enamellers, like Craft of Bow, would be well acquainted with 'Mr. Gyles'. The same sort of gilding in un-Worcesterish patterns is found on two beautiful armorial teapots undoubtedly of Worcester porcelain, bequeathed to the Victoria and Albert Museum by Mr. Legh Tolson, which bear also flower-painting by an unfamiliar hand. The same painter was, I think, responsible for the flowers and shield on a service of Chinese porcelain with the arms of Hayes of London, which is often turning up and being misdescribed as wholly Chinese work. As I have remarked in connection with Derby, armorial china painted to order is especially likely to have been done by an enameller like Giles. All this is of course conjectural, but the mystery and un-doubted quantity of Giles's work make it a matter of interest to the collector.

Towards the end of the Wall period some new types of decoration were introduced with the blue ground. One of these in its typical form has narrow wreaths of husk pattern in dull turquoise (a characteristic colour of the time) and black, enclosing landscapes with rather hard clouds or heaps of (often-spotted) fruit in strong colours, also rather hard in treatment. Some landscapes in this style are very like O'Neale's work and may have been done by him at the factory or even sent to him in London, as in the case of Donaldson. An exceptionally charming touch in landscape, as sensitive as that of the early period but rather more assured, is seen on a rare service of plates in Mr. Alfred Hutton's collection, with large central medallions on a white ground, painted with windmills, churches, trees, etc.

A very large and characteristic class not yet mentioned is formed by the 'Worcester Japans'. Some of these were fairly close adaptations of the 'brocaded Imari', with chrysanthemum discs and fan-shaped diapered panels. A long-popular design in the Japanese style, known as Queen's pattern, has vertical or spirally curved panels alternately red on white and white on blue with gilding. (This was copied at Derby and Lowestoft.) But the most original and splendid of all the Japan patterns are seen on the great hexagonal vases with very free fantasies on the Kakiemon and Chinese themes mainly in red, green, and gold, often associated with elaborate diapers and borders with passages of green fish-roe diaper and *bleu céleste*. These are really admirable inventions, with the birds and monsters and tufted plants ordered into rhythmical designs of an amazing complexity and intricate movement. 'Fine old rich dragon pattern' is an apt contemporary description for one of these (Plate XVIII, A).

Literal copies of Sèvres were only to be expected: the 'hop trellis' and 'mignonette' patterns, mainly in green and gold with tiny red dots, were as popular here as at Derby. The *bleu de roi* was used in an effective way in plain broad stripes with no other decoration but gold flowers, and the lovely gilding used as the sole decoration on some services makes a reposeful contrast with the more showy styles.

Little of exciting artistic importance was invented at Worcester in the 'Flight' and 'Flight and Barr' periods, and such new styles as are found were shared with the rival factory at Caughley and may have been invented there. But specimens are often ascribed to the latter in error when they happen not to bear the Worcester marks, which were the names of the proprietors written in blue. In the Flight and Barr period an incised 'B' is said to mark a paste containing bone-ash, tentatively introduced by Martin Barr at about the same time that Spode was also experimenting towards the standard English china body.

The pottery at Caughley (pronounced Calf-ley) in Shropshire was started about 1750, but porcelain was not made there until after 1772, when the premises passed into the hands of Thomas Turner, who had been in the service of the Worcester factory. In 1799 the works were bought by John Rose, a former apprentice of Turner's and proprietor of the Coalport factory on the opposite bank of the Severn. For some years Rose continued to make porcelain in biscuit at Caughley, but finally closed it in 1814.

The Caughley porcelain was known as 'Salopian', which is one of the marks; others were a 'C', an 'S', C S 希 numerals disguised to look like Chinese characters, and forgeries of the crescents of Worcester and (quite unaccountably) of the rampant lion of Frankenthal, printed or stencilled. The porcelain material contains soapstone and resembles Worcester except that it is generally whiter and not so green by transmitted light, probably because it was not so much blued. Forms were plain as dictated by the neo-Classical style, and fluted shapes in table-wares are especially characteristic of both Flight's Worcester and Caughley.

It requires some experience to distinguish the earlier blue-printed and -painted wares from those of Worcester. The blue is sometimes pale and 'misty', sometimes intenser and of a violet tone. But many designs were the same on both. There is indeed a tradition that Worcester sent wares up the Severn to be printed at Caughley; but this does not seem very probable, in view of Hancock's defection. Two famous blue-printed patterns supposed to have been designed for Turner by the young Thomas Minton are the 'Willow-Pattern' (both subject and legend are, I believe, purely European inventions) and the so-called 'Broseley Blue dragon'; Caughley porcelain examples of the latter are very rare, however, and the earthenware usually attributed to the factory, which some-times bears it, is more probably Staffordshire. The Salopian blue-painting includes a novelty, probably rather late, in some European landscapes with ruins on a large scale naturalistically treated; but otherwise it was mostly cribbed from Worcester and Chantilly, whose sprigs (like ears of corn) and mark were copied. An openwork basket formerly in the Sheldon Collection, bearing the 'T°' mark of the presumed 'Mr. Tebo', was also marked 'C', but was otherwise like Worcester. One formal floral design in radial panels in blue with gilding, known as 'Queen Charlotte's pattern' or 'The Royal Lily', was chosen on a visit by the King and Queen to Worcester in 1788, but seems to be commoner on Salopian than on Worcester.

The more pretentious Salopian shares with Flight's a style of dark blue and gilt striped patterns, with severe borders of circles and ovals in the same colours. A famous service in this style made at Flight's in 1792 for the Duke of Clarence is painted with allegorical figures in grey monochrome (Plate XIX, c). Some flower-painting in black or dark brown shows a Caughley peculiarity in the crowd-ing of the bouquets into a compact mass. The gilding on much Salopian is of a hard bright character, somewhat arbitrarily placed over the blue, and was, I believe, added at the London workshop of Baxter, father of a painter well known in a later period. A water-colour by the latter, done in 1810, depicting the interior of his father's studio, shows a bill on the wall headed '*Coalport White China*', and I think it probable that Baxter had earlier dealings with Turner and Rose. Some pieces shown on the painters' table seem to be blue-and-white ready for gilding to be added to them. The same sort of gilding, similarly placed, is seen on Chinese blue-and-white of the period, and this is obviously likely to be 'outside decorator's' work. Moreover, a jug in the Schreiber Collection has the underglaze blue 'S' of Salopian barred over with this gilding as though to conceal it.

The simpler Caughley polychrome ware resembles Lowestoft in being a somewhat crude imitation of the Worcester with Chinese figures and flowers, the latter being sometimes in red and blue only. A feature not absolutely peculiar to Caughley of this kind, but very common on it, is an impressed circle in the middle of the base. In spite of Hancock's advertised help, no overglaze black printing is known on Caughley.

The early Liverpool porcelain ranks as an offshoot of Worcester, both on account of its origin and in view of the styles of decoration adopted. It is for the most part of no artistic importance; it is merely Worcester spoilt. But something must be said about it by way of helping the collector to identify it, for it is very common and various and never bears a factory mark. It is in most cases hopeless to try and assign it to particular factories, though perhaps when we know the result of Mr. Entwistle's researches some light will be thrown on the several factory styles. Much of the porcelain was exported to America. The manufacture began in 1756, with the engagement by Richard Chaffers of Robert Podmore, the Worcester 'arcanist', and was continued by Philip Christian, Seth Pennington, William Reid and Co., Samuel Gilbody, and Zachariah Barnes; while John Sadler and Guy Green began their flourishing 'Printed Ware Manufactory' also in 1756, perhaps here again inspired by someone from Worcester. Not all the porcelain with their signed prints is Liverpool, however, since some mugs so decorated are believed to be Longton Hall, as I have explained. Besides the signatures of Sadler and Green, those of engravers named Evans and

PLATE XVIII   *See pages* 179, 186, 189

(*a*) DISH. PORCELAIN, PAINTED IN COLOURS. WORCESTER, ABOUT 1765–70
Mr. Herbert Allen's Collection

(*b*) TEAPOT. PORCELAIN, PAINTED
IN COLOURS
WORCESTER, ABOUT 1760
Victoria and Albert Museum

(*c*) VASE. PORCELAIN, PAINTED
IN COLOURS AND IN GILDING
ON A BLUE GROUND
WORCESTER, ABOUT 1775
British Museum, Frank Lloyd Collection

Billinge also occur. The printing was discussed on pp. 50 and 83.

The typical Liverpool porcelain is grey, with darker bluish-toned pools under the foot often full of black specks and bubbles; handles are often skimpy, or in the case of the wares moulded after silver (of singularly graceless form) often show a grooved edge, and end at the rim in a bifurcation like a snake's mouth biting it. A moulded pattern of palm-columns flanking painted panels below which are cabbage leaves is particularly common. The foot-ring of cups, bowls, etc., is usually not bluntly tri-angular, but cut back, almost undercut; the base of cylindrical mugs is usually flat and unglazed. (*Glazed* flat bases are sometimes found in Lowestoft mugs.)

The best Liverpool porcelain is that of Chaffers and Christian, which is clean and hard, with designs in red and blue and well-painted *chinoiseries*. A typical bell-shaped mug with grooved foot in Mr. Wallace Elliot's collection is painted with a curious picture of a Chinese *sampan*. It is clearly a soapstone porcelain like Worcester, and Chaffers, like the latter, claimed that it would stand boiling water. Another type, obviously inspired by Worcester and at one time mistaken for it, but also often miscalled Longton Hall (because of the blue), is distinguished by wide under-glaze blue borders crudely 'marbled' with gilding. The flower-painting on these and other pieces from the same factory (including the palm-column teapots) is often re-markable for its emphatic black outlining, but is free in style and sometimes very good; the exotic birds are stiff and mechanical and the figure-painting very laboured, though in one case formerly ascribed to Dr. Wall! Some jugs and a bowl at South Kensington are typical. Chinese figure-subjects closely copy Worcester, but are given away by the glaze: one type shows a curious blood-red in its colouring; very artless borders of scrolls and circles interrupting straight lines are characteristic here. The blue-and-white is of various types. One is remarkable for the clean hard rendering of the Chinese peonies and rocks with showers of dots about them: this hand may be recognised on Liverpool delftware, and the porcelain is therefore probably Pennington's, like the often excellent punch-bowls with ships painted on them in blue or polychrome. Another type of blue-and-white is remarkable for an odd bright sticky-looking blue: the best pieces in this colour again show a delft-painter's style, with figures and plants rapidly sketched in with great vitality; a fine mug with horsemen is in the Schreiber Collection at South Kensington, where there is also a tiny cup with figures after the print of 'La Cascade'; a superb jug with a Chinese landscape remarkably rendered in a multitude of quick nervous touches was in the Hignett Collection. Other subjects in blue are by the hand of one of the polychrome painters who had a trick of rendering the foliage of trees by a cluster of circles. The blue-printing is heavy in execution with great masses of blurred dark blue: queer prints of strawberries and convolvuluses and borders of cell-diaper are distinctive. Sometimes red and yellow were added over these prints in the crudest fashion. Some tin-enamelled porcelain apparently made at Liverpool is so rare as to be scarcely worth mentioning. Another class ascribed to Liverpool, however, with cold glassy paste and Chinese subjects in colours, including a harsh pink, is important, since it has been ascribed on Enoch Wood's authority to Littler of Longton Hall (*q.v.*); but it shows the simple-minded borders mentioned above, and similar pieces in the Liverpool Museum have a traditional ascription to that city, so that it may reasonably be regarded as a local type, in spite of the Hanley record.

CHAPTER XIII

PLYMOUTH AND BRISTOL

THE hard-paste porcelain made by William Cook-worthy of Plymouth (*b.* 1705, *d.* 1780) and his successor Richard Champion (*b.* 1743, *d.* 1791) will always have an attraction for the English collector quite out of proportion to its aesthetic interest, since it represents the successful conclusion of a long and historic research into the materials and manufacture of true porcelain as made by the Chinese, exactly parallel with that conducted by Tschirnhausen and Böttger in Germany more than fifty years earlier. That the latter had already succeeded in the search does not from the sentimental point of view diminish the thrill of Cookworthy's quite independent and unsubsidised success. The Sèvres factory about this time was also endeavouring to make hard-paste; the search was there rather for a French source of the necessary materials than for the process, which was already known to the factory through the disclosures of German 'arcanists'. The Sèvres efforts were not successful until 1768, the very year in which Cookworthy took out his patent. In Germany the secret was known to a dozen factories by this time, and indeed the art of porcelain was already declining. The artistic impulse and the princely interest which had created the finest wares of Meissen and the others in Germany and of Vincennes and the earlier soft-pastes in France were already almost spent, and this accounts for and excuses the relatively slight artistic importance of the Plymouth

195

and Bristol wares. Their charm resides in their associations
and in the impression they give to an informed mind of
something new, achieved with great difficulty—the charm
in fact of the true primitive. For more than twenty years
Cookworthy had sought the materials described by Père
d'Entrecolles, and the eventual fruits of that long unaided
search must stir us to a respect tinged with something like
awe. Hard-paste, though not our national china, is now
too utterly familiar to excite the least part of the wonder
it aroused in our forefathers; we have handled it unthink-
ingly too many times. But it needs only a little imagination
to appreciate the difficult success represented by a piece
of the Plymouth porcelain. Its very imperfections make
this clear: its common misshapenness and discoloured
smoky glaze, as well as the obviously melted appearance
that proclaims it as the fire-won product of a fusible rock
and the most refractory of clays. It is a primitive of which
the English collector may be as proud as the German is
proud of his Böttger ware and porcelain.

The Cornish china-clay was discovered by Cookworthy
before 1758, perhaps as early as 1745, but the essential
china-stone (locally known as 'growan stone' and 'moor
stone') not until some much later date unascertained. The
district still supplies the Staffordshire industry, and immense quantities of the clay have in recent years been put
to a new use as a coating on the shiny paper used for 'half-
tone' illustrations, such as those in this book.

Cookworthy's manufacture was started on the granting
of the patent in 1768 by a company of his relatives and
some Bristol citizens, supported by Thomas Pitt, afterwards Lord Camelford, on whose estate the materials had
been found. At first the factory was at Coxside, Plymouth,
but after a little more than two years it was transferred to
Bristol, perhaps at the instance of Richard Champion, who

PLATE XIX

See pages 145, 191, 200

(*a*) JUG. PORCELAIN, PAINTED IN COLOURS. LOWESTOFT, ABOUT 1770

Victoria and Albert Museum (Tolson Bequest)

(*b*) TEAPOT. PORCELAIN, PAINTED IN COLOURS. BRISTOL, ABOUT 1775

Mr. Herbert Allen's Collection

(*c*) PLATE. PORCELAIN, PAINTED IN GREY MONOCHROME BY JAMES PENNINGTON WORCESTER (FLIGHT PERIOD), 1792

Victoria and Albert Museum

had been interested in the subject from the start and seems
to have been in charge of the factory after the transfer.
Several fully dated pieces and a drawing of a kiln (published by Owen) inscribed 'Last burning of enamel Nov.
27 1770' probably refer to the impending removal. In
1773 Champion finally purchased the patent rights from
Cookworthy, who was by this time an old man. The patent
expired in 1775, and its renewal was violently opposed by
the Staffordshire potters led by Wedgwood, who had found
a use for the materials in the improved cream-coloured
ware. In the extended patent granted him Champion was
allowed no more than the exclusive right to use the
materials in translucent porcelain; the others could use it
in opaque wares. This was a serious set-back to an over-
ambitious venture, never very sound financially, and in
1781 Champion was obliged to sell his patent rights to a
company of Staffordshire potters, who after a short interval began making hard-paste at a factory at Shelton,
called The New Hall.

To distinguish the Plymouth china from the Bristol is
not always easy, as the paste and glaze were essentially the
same in both. At Plymouth a factory-mark was adopted in
the form of the alchemist's sign for tin (also the astro-
loger's for Jupiter), resembling the numerals '2' and
'4' conjoined, but this was certainly also used at Bristol
during Cookworthy's proprietorship and is then sometimes
accompanied by a mark eventually adopted by Champion,
a cross in colour or gold. The pieces so marked perhaps belong to a transition period. Champion also
occasionally marked his wares with a capital 'B', and this,
too, is found together with the cross-mark. The
crossed-swords mark of Meissen was also copied,
and it is surprising to find this on two tumbler-shaped
cups, now in the British Museum, which were produced

before the House of Commons in 1775 in support of
Champion's application for the renewal of his patent. It is
remarkable that practically none of the figures are ever
marked. The solitary exception known to me is a *Sportsman*
in the Museum at Hanley, which bears the cross-mark in
blue enamel.

The porcelain material was rarely perfect. A brownish
smoke-staining is quite common in the Plymouth glaze,
and a very common feature throughout both proprietor-
ships is the 'wreathing' or faint spiral ridging of the
surface, due to unequal wetting in the throwing, and
the twisting askew of handles. This last defect is bound
to occur in hard-paste if the handles are straight when
attached; a deliberate twisting in the opposite direction
is required so that they may right themselves in the firing.
More subtle indications are the texture of the paste and
glaze themselves. There is a fused look about them, and
the close-textured glaze is often almost milky with bubbles.
If a chip has exposed the body it will show the conchoidal
and glass-like fracture characteristic of true porcelain, and
of course both glaze and body are very resistant to the
file. As Champion wrote in support of his appeal to
Parliament, 'The *Seve* and several other kinds [of soft-
paste] . . . when they are broke seem as dry as a Tobacco
Pipe, that is the case with all the *English* China; but the
Dresden, the *Bristol* and the *Asiatic*, China, have when
broken a moist and lucid appearance'. The firing of the
porcelain obviously gave great trouble. Though lime and
plant ash were used exactly in the manner described by
Père d'Entrecolles, it appears that the proportion of flux
in the Plymouth and Bristol paste was much less than in
the Oriental or Meissen, and a higher temperature was
therefore required to fire it. This was perhaps hard to
control and accounts for the fire-cracks, the half-collapse

of figures, and the warping of plates and dishes. The latter were often strengthened beneath with straight or 'S'-shaped ribs. Wedgwood was well aware of this weakness of the Bristol plates (shared, by the way, with the Chinese) and pressed this point to his own advantage in the patent dispute; the cream-colour could be made perfectly 'true' and regular in size. It is not uncommon to find sand and grit on the foot, and the porcelain often has a generally primitive appearance. Its great hardness and infusibility prevented the enamels from melting into the glaze in the muffle kiln as completely as on lead-glazed frit porcelains or the less refractory hard-pastes, and the colours have sometimes scaled off or stand out as a superficial incrustation. The Bristol is perhaps cleaner than the Plymouth, and often has a cold white and glittering appearance. In its favour was its great durability and strength. To quote Champion again: '. . . its texture is fine, exceeding the East India, and its strength so great that water may be boiled in it. It is distinguished from every other English China which being composed of a Number of Ingredients mixed together the principal part being glass occasions it soon to get dirty in the wear, renders it continually liable to Accidents and in every respect only an Imitation and therefore is stiled by Chemists a false Porcelain.' This then was the material made with so much labour by these West Country Quakers. I have described it at length, since the interest of the porcelain so largely lies in the material itself. Its decoration is of slight importance, historically and artistically. Two periods may be distinguished, the first being that of Cookworthy's proprietorship, the second, Champion's. These names would be preferable to Plymouth and Bristol, since the control of the first-named continued for three years into the Bristol period.

The inventor seems to have celebrated either his application for a patent, or the start of his manufacture, by making a mug and painting it in blue with his own hand. This mug is now in the British Museum; it bears the arms of Plymouth, the date 'March 14 1768' (some days before the patent), and the initials 'C F' presumably for 'Cookworthy fecit'. Such blue-painting, however, was never an important part of the productions and was practically confined to the Cookworthy period. The style was a copy of the Chinese with some curious additions in the way of *bucrania* and *Louis Quatorze* pendants. The blue-colour was almost always of a not at all unpleasant blackish tone. Some rare blue painting in a brighter colour and some equally rare printing of exceedingly poor quality, again in Chinese style, are seen on Champion's porcelain.

The factory styles in general seem to have been inspired by Worcester and Sèvres as regards the useful wares and vases, and by Longton Hall and Derby in figures. The Cookworthy figures are distinct in their *rococo* scrolled bases picked out in a peculiar brownish crimson. Under Champion the figures generally have rockwork bases in the Chelsea-Derby manner. The shapes of useful wares (Plate XIX, B) in both periods are often peculiar. A double-curved profile was favoured for the bodies of tea- and coffee-pots and also for handles, which were often longitudinally ribbed, and flattened on the inside only. The presence of Tebo at Bristol, and possibly also I think at Plymouth, is evident from his mark and the making of his favourite shell salts, some of which include new shells and are unusually well composed.

The Plymouth figures include several models—such as a group of *Boys with a goat*, two *Seated Musicians*, and some of the *Continents* and *Elements*—which almost exactly correspond with Longton Hall, and this curious circumstance is conjecturally explained by an assumed purchase by Cookworthy at Salisbury in 1760 of some part of the Longton Hall stock. Only the *America* among the *Continents* is known to me in the latter, and the set has generally been supposed to be original Plymouth work, but this cannot now be accepted. Like the little boys as *Elements* they are charmingly modelled in the Longton Hall manner. They can of course be distinguished by their different paste, and also by their being hollow under the bases. A grave *Shepherd* and *Shepherdess* and a large *Venus and Adonis* in the gold-anchor Chelsea style are probably original Plymouth or early Bristol modelling. Figures of birds and animals were done at Plymouth (not Bristol), but have no special originality.

Champion's figures are much less attractive and reproduce very closely the mawkish Chelsea-Derby style. There is, in fact, evidence that the same modeller was employed at both Derby and Bristol. Champion's letter of instructions to him, dated 1772, proposing the series of large *Elements*, was published by Owen, and refers to the artist's having modelled a series with the same subject at Derby, but his identity has not been certainly discovered. Mr. Frank Hurlbutt's assertion that he was John Bacon has no more to support it than the fact that the latter did some work for Derby. I think Pierre Stephan is a much more likely person: he is, in fact, recorded as the modeller of a set of Derby *Elements*; but this is again no more than a conjecture, and there is no positive evidence that Stephan was ever at Bristol. The Bristol *Elements* are fairly lively in movement but woefully dull in colour. The grown-up *Seasons*, for which also Champion's instructions survive, are equally good; but the large-headed smirking children also modelled as *Seasons* and those with dogs and musical instruments I find as detestable as their Derby relatives. The mark of Tebo on some of these figures was probably added in his capacity as 'repairer'. He was no doubt responsible for the vases with applied decoration and the like, and there is one curious instance of his use of the head of the *Winter* (which he presumably had 'repaired') for the spout of a jug. The Schreiber Collection includes specimens of all the important Plymouth and Bristol figures, acquired in most cases from descendants of Cookworthy.

Large vases were not much made at Plymouth. A *garniture* of five small ones is in the Schreiber Collection, painted with flowers in the characteristic Plymouth colours, which include a fine leaf-green (especially iridescent), a yolk-of-egg yellow, and an unusually juicy well-fluxed red. Champion on the other hand made a feature of vases, but they were seldom wholly successful. The Worcester influence was apparent in the 'Tebo' forms and in such decorations as the light scale-blue of one in Mr. Herbert Allen's collection. The best are painted by a hand, seen also on Worcester porcelain, probably of later date, which is supposed to be that of the 'Monsieur Saqui' or 'Soqui' referred to in Prideaux's *Relics of William Cookworthy* as 'an excellent painter and enameller from Sèvres', employed at both Plymouth and Bristol. His is the thickly stippled strongly coloured exotic-bird painting with shadowy distant trees, imitating the style of the Sèvres painter Evans. His work is found on cups and saucers as well as the big vases. His style was at one time put down in error to the portrait miniaturist Henry Bone (*d.* 1755) who is recorded as having been apprenticed at Plymouth. But neither his work nor that of William Stephens, another painter whose name is often quoted, can be certainly identified. The painters' numerals (in the marks) '1' and '2' attributed to them respectively cannot be relied upon as proof of their work, and two different numerals sometimes appear on associated pieces apparently by the same hand. One might surmise that the little landscapes and sea-shore scenes on late Bristol are such as Bone might have painted, but there is no proof of this.

The most ambitious table-wares bearing Cookworthy's mark are some huge tea- and coffee-pots with claret- or blue-coloured grounds marbled in gold. These were *tours de force* doubtless intended to surprise his Bristol friends. The modest wares of the more ordinary sort have little distinction. Painting of Chinese figures in 'Mandarin' style was probably copied from Worcester, as were the Japanese Kakiemon patterns and certain *famille verte* designs with monsters. These are all Plymouth types, again well represented in the Schreiber Collection. Champion's greatest achievements in this department were cabaret services in the style of Sèvres. It was his boast that his porcelain combined the virtues of both his great contemporaries, 'equalling the Dresden in strength' and 'in elegance perfectly resembling the beautiful manufacture of Sèvres'. There seems to have been less actual copying than at Derby, which was similarly inspired, but paradoxically there was also less definite individuality than at the latter place. A plate in the British Museum shows an original touch in its scrolled border; it belonged to John Britain, who was Champion's foreman. Green festoons and green husk were popular in many forms. One famous service was made by Champion for his friend Edmund Burke on his election as Member for Bristol in 1774; this has allegorical figures and the Burke-Nugent arms. Another was made for presentation by Burke to the wife of a prominent Bristol supporter, one Mrs.

Smith: this bears a monogram of two 'S's' and the favourite green festoons. The 'Robert Smyth' service (for the wedding in 1776 of the fifth Baronet of that name, of Colchester) has the monogram composed of tiny flowers in the style favoured especially in Germany at the time. Part of a service made for William Cowles, a neighbour of the factory at Castle Green, Bristol, is in the Schreiber Collection. This is painted with the typical mannered flowers of the period. Two principal hands may be recognised in this flower-painting. One shows a fluent style with emphasis on curving stems and leaves; the other crowded his flowers into a mass. As I have explained, we cannot (with the one possible exception mentioned above) identify the names of the painters. Perhaps they were among the 'lads of genius' who were offered 'encouragement' in an advertisement of 1775. Some charming borders made up of fantasies on architectural beading and *guilloche* pattern should be noted. Painting in monochrome or limited to one or two colours is always interesting for the emphasis on design imposed by the convention: a charming example is the blue enamel and crimson of some of Soqui's exotic-bird painting. (There is a specimen in the Schreiber Collection.) Little groups of Cupids and children in the Sèvres manner in grey, and flowers in pale-blue monochrome are also noteworthy. Besides the finer painted pieces much Bristol was made as 'cottage china' with simple decoration of sprigs and garlands in colours without gilding. This was the part of the Bristol tradition taken up by the New Hall factory, to be discussed in the next chapter. Transfer-printing seems to have been tried, but the hard glaze allowed it little success. A cream-jug in the Schreiber Collection has a *chinoiserie* print in Caughley style, and a large mug in the Broderip Gift at South Kensington has an early

PLATE XX

See page 209

(*a*) DISH. PORCELAIN, PAINTED IN COLOURS
STAFFORDSHIRE (MINTON'S FACTORY), EARLY 19TH CENTURY
Bethnal Green Museum

(*b*) CUP AND SAUCER. PORCELAIN
PAINTED IN COLOURS
STAFFORDSHIRE (NEW HALL)
LATE 18TH CENTURY
Mr. T. G. Martin's Collection

(*c*) DISH. PORCELAIN, PAINTED IN PINK
LUSTRE AND RED
STAFFORDSHIRE, EARLY 19TH CENTURY
Victoria and Albert Museum

Hancock print of children playing. Certain other mugs, of typical Bristol form, showing a heavy foot with circular recessed panel in the middle, are very roughly printed in black with birds and painted over in colours. Chinese figures treated in the same way are also found.

One singular Bristol type remains to be mentioned. This comprises the biscuit plaques with wreaths of modelled and applied flowers framing portrait-reliefs or shields of arms. Among the portraits are those of Benjamin Franklin, for whom Champion had a great admiration, and George Washington. They are remarkable for their exceedingly delicate workmanship, the flowers especially being wrought with the most minute attention to naturalistic detail. Their material is a rather cold white biscuit with a slight gloss. They are sometimes said to be the work of a Derby artist, on the strength of a pasted-on label referred to by Owen inscribed 'Specimen of Bristol china modeled by Thomas Briand of Derby 1775'; a specimen now belonging to Mr. Wallace Elliot, formerly in the Sheldon Collection, was believed by its late owner to be marked 'T. B' at the edge, but this was an error or fanciful misreading of accidental markings. There is no sure record of anyone of this name connected with the porcelain-factory at Derby or Bristol, but it is at least a remarkable coincidence that it should be the name of the person who exhibited a specimen of soft-paste before the Royal Society in 1742–43, as recorded on p. 110. The plaques have been very fully dealt with in a paper by Mr. Wallace Elliot. They should be distinguished from the closely similar pieces made by a later Bristol potter named Edward Raby, working at J. D. Pountney's Water Lane Pottery about 1845–50. These were sometimes on a blue ground, and were generally larger than Champion's. A pale heliotrope was only rarely used by the latter, as in a specimen in Mr. Wallace Elliot's collection. Specimens of both Raby's and Champion's plaques are to be seen to-gether in Mr. Herbert Allen's collection, on loan at South Kensington.

CHAPTER XIV

NEW HALL AND THE RUSTIC PORCELAIN
OF STAFFORDSHIRE

AFTER the presumed failure of Longton Hall in 1760 no porcelain was, as far as we know, made in Staffordshire for more than twenty years. I have already suggested that an explanation of this remarkable fact is to be found in the Staffordshire reluctance to take up so precarious a manufacture as that of soft-paste, and in its foreignness to the local methods. The obstacle to the making of hardpaste, on the other hand, was the patent held by Richard Champion, and this, as we have seen, was eventually acquired, in 1781, by a company of Staffordshire potters: Samuel Hollins, Jacob Warburton, William Clowes, Charles Bagnall, and Anthony Keeling. Operations were begun in the works of Keeling at Tunstall, but there were disagreements, and in 1782 a factory was started by the partners jointly at the New Hall, Shelton. The company were apparently as much interested in the sale of china-clay and china-stone as in the making of porcelain from them, and there is considerable doubt as to the extent of their operations in the last years of the eighteenth century. It has even been suggested that they did not make true hardpaste at all; a technique new to Staffordshire was evidently needed. A cup and saucer in the Brent Bequest at South Kensington, though clearly in the style of 1790–1800, bears the cross-mark usually supposed to belong to Bristol only, and suggests that some of the 'cottage china' put

PART III

NINETEENTH-CENTURY POTTERY
AND PORCELAIN

PLATE XXI   *See pages* 217, 222, 229

(*a*) FLOWER-VASE. PORCELAIN, PAINTED BY THOMAS BAXTER
WORCESTER (CHAMBERLAIN'S FACTORY), ABOUT 1815
Victoria and Albert Museum

(*b*) DISH. PORCELAIN, STIPPLE-PRINTED
IN BLACK
STAFFORDSHIRE, EARLY 19TH CENTURY
Victoria and Albert Museum

(*c*) PLATE. PORCELAIN, PAINTED IN
COLOURS. SWINTON (ROCKINGHAM
FACTORY), ABOUT 1825–30
British Museum

CHAPTER XV

NINETEENTH-CENTURY POTTERY
AND PORCELAIN

IT is sometimes said that to limit the study of European porcelain to the eighteenth-century wares, as is commonly done, is merely to follow that snobbish rule which requires a certain measure of antiquity as a necessary recommendation in works of art. But there is very good reason, in the case of the ceramic art at all events, for stopping short at the cultivated court of the Empress Josephine. The Napoleonic Wars mark a clean break with the artistic traditions of the eighteenth century and the beginning of an unblushingly commercial period of vulgar plutocratic taste. A further excuse for separate consideration here is the development of the Staffordshire bone-china and the consequent merging of porcelain and earthenware styles at the close of the eighteenth century. Josiah Spode II then established a formula for a practical and economical hybrid porcelain containing bone-ash, and this became a standard English body which has remained in use until the present day. Whether the entire credit for this should be put down to Spode is often disputed. Martin Barr of Worcester was certainly experimenting on the same lines, and Sir Arthur Church even declared that Spode's formula was common knowledge in Staffordshire at the time. The bone-china represented a great practical and commercial advance, but it made for a grievous monotony, and the charming multifarious soft-pastes had gone for ever.

The Staffordshire industry grew enormously in the first half of the nineteenth century, and English productions in cream-colour, blue-printed, and bone-porcelain flooded the world's markets. They are familiar enough, but their relative nearness to our time brings peculiar difficulties to their study, and doubtless that is why no serious attempt has yet been made to classify the wares of the century as a whole, or to provide the collector with the means of judging date and make by style. A great deal was un-marked, and even where marks have been used I have sometimes found the most astonishingly exact corre-spondences in design; patterns were evidently copied freely from factory to factory. It is obvious, therefore, that attributions cannot be given with the same certainty as in the case of much of the eighteenth-century porcelain. The centres of manufacture outside Staffordshire remained relatively unimportant, but were still numerous. Except, however, at Derby, Coalport, Worcester, Swinton ('Rock-ingham'), and Liverpool ('Herculaneum'), porcelain was little made outside the Potteries, but earthenwares of many sorts were not beyond the powers of an immense number of minor factories—in Yorkshire, farther north on the Tyne, Wear and Tees, in South Wales, and at Bristol. Proximity to coalfields had virtually become a necessity in this now fully industrialised pottery manufacture.

The following sketch, which will inevitably be some-what discursive, will be better understood if I suggest a division into periods corresponding to leading types or inspirations. The vast number of makers and artists and sorts of ware are bewildering, and in the short space at my disposal I propose merely to indicate the landmarks and describe as far as possible the sequence of styles without a confusing multitude of references to the names of potters and their dates; these are easily ascertainable if need be from the books of reference. The first twenty years of the nineteenth century may be called the Spode and English *Empire* Period; it was never as severely classical as its French counterpart, and as far as the fashionable wares (as distinct from 'peasant' pottery) are concerned was marked by an insensitive loudness and hardness of style and a general bad and vulgar taste. From about 1820 onwards a space of twenty-five years or so may be called the Rockingham or Revived Rococo Period; it was more amiable and sentimental than the early Spode, and perhaps less pretentious, but still much inclined to heaviness and over-decoration. The Revived Rococo coincides in date with the main body of the Gothic Revival (which may be traced back into the eighteenth century but hardly affected English ceramic art), and culminates in the Great Exhibition of 1851, which also saw the beginnings of that backward-looking New Eclectic or Museum Period which has not yet come to an end. The nineteenth-century stages may be typically represented by the various styles of flower-painting prevailing, in which the usual alternation of formal and natural is to be observed. Thus at the beginning of the century sprig patterns (especially the French 'cornflower') are found, according with the severe taste of the neo-Classical, which also dictated a literal naturalism (perhaps started in ceramic art by the 'Flora Danica' service in Copenhagen porcelain, made between 1789 and 1802); the named 'specimen flowers' of Pegg, Pardoe, and Absolon are typical. The Revived Rococo flowers were perhaps inspired by Billingsley's work at Nantgarw and Swansea; they were full-blown bunches and often gaudy in colour, and gradually hardened into the over-exquisite imitations of the mannered Sèvres flowers characteristic of the more pretentious wares of the Great Exhibition period: the Coalport flowers of William Cook are typical of the latter. The rage for Japanese art which began in the 1860's inspired a floppy naturalism. About 1870 the Morris movement brought stylised floral and foliate compositions in Gothic, Renaissance, and 'Persian' styles, and in the '90's and 1900's the *Art Nouveau* found an echo in England in a naturalism which contrived to be at once both sinuous and flat. Other types of flower-painting could of course be found in each period, but these were dominant.

Spode's porcelain is sometimes said to date well back into the eighteenth century, but little or none of it can be so early; the typical shapes were obviously inspired by the French *Empire*. The porcelain material was clean and white; in composition it was partly feldspathic like hard-paste, but with bone-ash replacing a proportion of the china clay; the glaze usually contained lead. Towards 1830 Spode followed Rose of Coalport in adopting a purely feldspathic glaze; and a special mark was used on pieces so glazed. Many of the wares were in fact marked with the name of the firm, but no distinctive Spode style emerges. Some of the slighter Japan patterns in red, blue, and gold or in the Kakiemon manner are neat and not without fancy; but many were heavy and overcrowded, and in my opinion hideous and vulgar with their show of rich gilding. Similar Japan patterns were made at Derby and by Chamberlain at Worcester about the same time, particularly about 1810–15; and variants still survive at the present day. The misuse of gold which was the chief vice of French and Russian *Empire* porcelain also afflicted the Spode wares, and we find masses of hard unpleasant gilding, some of it appearing more lavish by being done in relief by a process said to have been invented by Spode's chief enameller, Henry Daniel. Spode's porcelain is dealt with at length in Mr. Arthur Hayden's book and need not be further described here.

Worcester shared the early Spode style to some extent, but with greater accomplishment in such matters as figure-painting. The miniature-like all-over painting started by Sèvres in the eighteenth century and developed especially at Vienna under Sorgenthal was particularly well done at Worcester, where James Pennington did classical and other figures in the 1790's (Plate XIX, c) and later, and the versatile Thomas Baxter in the early part of the nineteenth century painted still-life pieces with shells and flowers as well as figure-subjects of all kinds (Plate XXI, A), latterly often in grey monochrome; his touch was light and not without feeling. He worked for both Worcester factories, as apparently did John Barker, to whom are attributed certain plates and vases painted with shells and feathers in a minutely naturalistic style very like Baxter's own. Humphrey and Walter Chamberlain did similar work, the former notably in sporting subjects. The characteristic gilt borders and grounds show most often classical anthemion or scrolled acanthus foliage and 'seaweed' pattern and vermiculation. About 1810 pearled and beaded edges imitating actual metal began to be popular. Some porcelain with a pattern of small geometrical panels, some coloured yellow, others filled with floral sprigs, made at Worcester about 1815, has for some reason become known as Church Gresley, where (or more precisely at Castle Gresley) an unsuccessful factory was started with the help of some Derby hands about 1794–95. The Gresley porcelain, if it was ever made, has never been convincingly identified. Other Worcester porcelain has also been ascribed in error to Isleworth, where no porcelain was ever made. The Worcester firm had become Barr, Flight and Barr in 1807, and Flight, Barr and Barr in 1813. In 1840 Chamberlain's was amalgamated with the original company, and seven years later the older works were given up. In 1852, after a period of decline, the firm became Kerr and Binns and began to revive, and in 1862 the still-existing Royal Worcester Porcelain Company was formed. A third factory had been started in 1800 by Thomas Grainger; it was Grainger, Lee and Co. in 1812 and was absorbed by the Royal Worcester Company in 1889. All these firms' names were used as marks and are a help in dating, the 'B F B' and 'F B B' impressed alone requiring elucidation. The unidentified Caughley-Coalport china of the early nineteenth century (see p. 190) is presumably still mistaken for Worcester; a plate at South Kensington marked 'Coalbrookdale' in full, in red, with painting of a basket of roses which I attribute to William Billingsley, is in the style of about 1810. It was perhaps painted in the period of the artist's wandering (referred to below) on china sold in the white, as was the factory custom, and for some special reason marked; or it was possibly done on the occasion of a visit to Coalport in 1811. Its material is grey and very similar to Worcester.

The old Derby factory went on until 1848, under Kean until 1811, under Robert Bloor until 1826, and was then managed until its closing by James Thomason and Thomas Clarke. The marks included a careless red version of the old Crown-Derby mark, the words 'Bloor' and 'Derby', and a crowned black letter 'D'. Later factories have claimed the title of successor: Stevenson and Hancock, later Sampson Hancock, used the old Crown-Derby mark, plus their initials, and a new factory was started in 1876 in the Osmaston Road, adopting the title 'Royal Crown Derby Porcelain Company' and a mark of two interlaced 'D's' under a crown. The early nineteenth-century styles included some good formal *Empire* scroll and foliage designs in colours, and borders and diapers of seaweed and other gilt patterns, together with the usual miniature-like painting of the time, here naturally showing a fondness for the traditional Derby style of landscapes; these, however, were now done in colours which were harder and more emphatic than in the eighteenth century. The identification of the hands responsible for the later Derby painting is very uncertain. Thomas Steele is known to have painted still-life groups of fruit in a very naturalistic style. George Robertson, Jesse Mountford, and Daniel Lucas are reputed to have been the best landscapists. The ugly Japan patterns, already mentioned, continued to be done into the 1830's and later.

The 'Derby landscapes', which were commonly inscribed on the back of the piece with the name of the place depicted, were also done at Pinxton, where a sensitive hand, believed to be that of Fidèle Duvivier (also an 'outside decorator'), is sometimes recognisable, and where John Cutts was a rapid and careless worker, in a style which he later took on to Etruria. The Wedgwood porcelain of this time, marked with the name printed in red capitals, is said to have been made only between 1812 and 1816. The same Derby-Pinxton style is common on the porcelain attributed to Enoch Wood, which was hard-looking and grey, and sometimes marked 'W(***)'; bow-fronted flower-stands or bulb-pots were characteristic in both Wood's and the later Pinxton, which came to an end in 1813. A very pleasant variant of the simpler Derby landscapes is seen in some brown monochrome work on a buff or rich red-brown glazed Staffordshire earthenware, sometimes bearing the impressed anchor-mark of Davenport of Longport.

Another sort of early nineteenth-century naturalism is represented by the specimen flowers, with botanical names inscribed on the backs, attributed to William Pegg of Derby. The same careful rather insensitive style was applied to cream-colour by a painter or painters at Swinton and by the independent decorator Absolon of Yarmouth, who also did simple inscriptions, sprigs, and starry patterns on Staffordshire and other wares bought in the white, sometimes marking them with his name in enamel colours, and by Thomas Pardoe at Swansea, Nant-garw, and Bristol. The last-named was also an independent decorator who signed the characteristic painting on two plates with bunches of flowers (not botanical specimens) at South Kensington, which are apparently of Worcester or Caughley-Coalport porcelain.

The stoneware of this period has been referred to in a previous chapter (p. 60). The Herculaneum factory at Liverpool made a drab-coloured ware commonly decorated with lines and formal borders in coloured enamels, and this mode of decoration was general in the period, as at Castleford and on the Wedgwood black basaltes, which in one well-known type, dating from about 1804 to 1810, was painted with formal chrysanthemum-like flowers in opaque colours. The Adams and Turner factories excelled in fine cream-coloured and buff stoneware jugs in characteristic early nineteenth-century shapes (Fig. 11), often with a band of chocolate enamel on the neck. Turner's ware sometimes bears the mark of Mist, a dealer, who was his London agent.

Lustre-painting is commonly said to have been introduced to Staffordshire by an invention of the first Josiah Wedgwood and is dated back by Church to 1792, but I have never seen a piece with a date before 1800, and most by their shape and style are clearly later. The 'silver'

PLATE XXII   *See pages* 224, 225, 228

(*a*) DISH. PORCELAIN, PAINTED IN COLOURS. SWANSEA, ABOUT 1815–20
Victoria and Albert Museum

(*b*) PLATE. WHITE EARTHENWARE
PRINTED IN DARK BLUE
STAFFORDSHIRE (ENOCH WOOD'S
FACTORY), ABOUT 1825–30
Victoria and Albert Museum

(*c*) CUP AND SAUCER. CREAM-
COLOURED EARTHENWARE
PRINTED IN BROWN
STAFFORDSHIRE (WEDGWOOD'S
FACTORY), ABOUT 1830–40
Victoria and Albert Museum

(platinum) lustre was used either 'all over' to simulate actual silver objects in the style of the time, or with decoration of white scroll or leaf patterns in reserve produced by painting in a 'resist' medium. The pink lustre (from gold) is commonest in painted patterns over a white slip, but when applied directly over a red body gave a ruddy hue like polished copper. The Wedgwood firm

FIG. II. JUG. ADAMS STONEWARE

added this pink lustre in a curious way 'all over', on some vessels in cream-colour in the form of large shells, recorded to have been borrowed for the purpose from the British Museum in the early part of the nineteenth century. The best styles of painting in lustre have already been described in connection with the rustic porcelain of Staffordshire. Coloured enamels added to crude reliefs on jugs and mugs are later in date (about 1820 onwards) and much less attractive; similar work was done on earthenware at Swansea and at the Northern potteries of Sunderland, Newcastle, and the neighbourhood. A distinctive but scarcely admirable use was made of lustre-painting at the latter: crude washes, scribbles, and marbling of pink lustre were added to artless and often amusing transfer-printed figure-subjects and inscriptions, which by their lettering and the style of costume depicted appear to date chiefly from the first quarter of the nineteenth century, though the opening of Sunderland Bridge, so often celebrated on the jugs, takes the possible date back to 1796. The Sunderland and Newcastle earthenware was soft-looking and unresonant and of a dull cream-colour or dead white.

The early nineteenth-century overglaze transfer-printing was usually in stipple done by the 'bat' process, in which a flexible sheet of soft glue replaced the paper transfer and would take up more delicate engraving than the latter. Excellent landscapes, flowers, and figure-pieces in black done in this way appear on the Worcester, Spode, and other Staffordshire wares (Plate XXI, B), and some pretty prints in a dark brown of shells and seaweed are found on early Minton.

A new material of the period was the so-called stone-china, a hard, dense, and heavy glazed earthenware usually of a greyish tone. Spode introduced his variety in 1805; the famous 'ironstone' of C. J. and G. Miles Mason, alleged to contain slag of ironstone, was patented in 1813. There were many other makers. The characteristic decorations were bastard *famille rose* patterns mainly in pink, blue, and red in flat washes over printed outlines, simple and unpretentious but terribly heavy. Degraded Imari patterns in the style of the Derby-Spode-Chamberlain 'japans' are very numerous and dreadful. Exact copies of the late Chinese 'export' blue-and-white were made in Spode's stone-china, and some of the heavy dishes in this style roughly glazed over the brownish body beneath are at times hard to distinguish from the actual Chinese, which had been copied from English models, perhaps even from the Spode wares themselves. The stone-china reached the height of its popularity in the 1820's, when the well-known angular jugs of Miles Mason were first made. It was cheap and durable and remained a stock line for many years. The 'ironstone' patent was bought first by Morley and then by Ashworth, whose wares, according to Jewitt, 'include priceless Art treasures deserving to be in every home of taste'. Ridgway's of Cauldon Place also made much stone-china, and the same author claimed for their *toilettes Victoria* and other productions that 'they achieved results never before attempted or attained as to magnitude and finish of goods'. But these were mid-nineteenth century. A feature of the 1820's was the revived *chinoiserie*, of which the Brighton Pavilion decoration of 1815 was an early example; figures and relief-decoration are sometimes found, as on a large white Staffordshire vase given to the Victoria and Albert Museum by Mrs. Willoughby Hodgson. Painted pseudo-Chinese figure-subjects with printed outlines are more common, and indeed have hardly yet disappeared from the cottage type of china. They are rarely of fine quality.

Underglaze blue printing was a favourite decoration on English pottery and porcelain in the first half of the nineteenth century, and the Staffordshire earthenware so decorated is one of the largest classes, distributed over the whole world. It was especially fashionable after about 1820 and so falls largely outside our first period. Much of it was anonymous, but rare marked pieces sometimes enable the specialist student to assign it to such prolific makers as Turner, Spode, Rogers, Enoch Wood, William

Adams of Greengates (Tunstall), William Adams of Stoke, A. Stevenson of Cobridge (1810–18) and his successor James Clews (1818–30), R. Stevenson and Williams, also of Cobridge, Shorthose of Hanley (who also made and marked porcelain about 1800–10), Wedgwood, Davenport and Stubbs and the latter's successors the Mayers, all of Longport, and J. and W. Ridgway of Cauldon Place and elsewhere, besides Leeds, Hull, the Don and Brameld potteries at Swinton, and Liverpool ('Herculaneum') in the North, and Bristol and Swansea in the West. Some of the printing was in a heavy, dark, but intense blue newly introduced in this period by Enoch Wood and quickly taken up by others. The subjects of the prints were at first mainly Chinese in the Caughley manner (which originally inspired this Staffordshire work), and later were typically romantic pastoral landscapes with ruins or mansions. The starting of the railways provided some subjects, and the great American market for this sort of ware led to the engraving of historic American scenes, including especially, of course, the kind of 'view' favoured in the English market. Foreign—especially Italian—landscapes were also done, sometimes with the title printed on the back in the foreign language. To the period about 1830–40 belongs the familiar printed mark in a foliated or flowery cartouche, with the name of the pattern—'Shiraz', 'Indian Bird', or 'View of London', etc.—sometimes but not always accompanied by the maker's initials or name. This type of mark was of course not confined to the blue-printed. The ample florid borders of shells and flowers (Plate XXII, B) of about 1825 onwards, and the rather earlier and very charming manner of framing the distant view with the abundant foliage of trees and herbage in the foreground, are to be noted especially. New colours for underglaze printing gave new resources; a pleasant brown appears about 1835–40 on the cream-colour of Wedgwood, in lively prints of foreign towns and shipping (Plate XXII, c), and on the wares of Copeland and Garrett (1833–47), successors of Spode; the underglaze chrome green was also brought into use towards 1850, and these and other colours gave an effect-ive because not quite naturalistic polychrome (somewhat in the manner of the contemporary Baxter prints) that is particularly associated with the names of F. and R. Pratt of Fenton, who received a medal for this kind of work in 1851. All this underglaze printing of about 1820 to 1850 counts as thoroughly original work. It represented a new addition to ceramic technique, and has a romantic quality that is often charming. But with this we have passed on to the second of the periods proposed, the origins and inspiration of which must now be considered.

While the second Josiah Spode was developing his bone-porcelain in Staffordshire, William Billingsley, the Derby hand already mentioned as the maker of the earlier Pinxton porcelain, was trying in various parts of the country to obtain financial backing for the manufacture of his white and translucent soft-paste, meanwhile making a living by decorating other white china obtained from various sources, France included. He was successively at Mansfield, Torksey (pronounced 'Torsey') in Lincoln-shire, and Worcester, working as a decorator, with his son-in-law Samuel Walker, who busied himself with designs for kilns, one of which he built while at Worcester. Billingsley and Walker seem to have actually started a company and factory at Torksey, but it was short-lived, and the few pieces traditionally ascribed to it are not remarkable; an experimental-looking large cup and saucer at South Kensington with a good pedigree are in fact totally unlike Billingsley's other porcelain. Eventually at Nantgarw in

South Wales in 1813, with the help of a William Weston Young, he made a new start with his costly manufacture, and a considerable body of pieces survive with the mark of the place-name impressed in the paste. Seeking Government help, Billingsley was in 1814 brought to Swansea at the instance of Lewis Weston Dillwyn, who had become owner of the Cambrian pottery in 1802. Here the Nantgarw paste was tried for a time (and, it is believed, marked with that place-name), but was found too extravagant. Dillwyn tried to improve it, by adding first more china clay, then soapstone, to the formula, indicating the latter change by adding to the impressed mark of 'SWANSEA' single or crossed pairs of tridents. But the work was still not a success, and Billingsley and Walker went back to Nantgarw in 1817. At the same time Dillwyn gave up Swansea, but porcelain continued to be made there until 1824, and the earthenware manufacture was not closed down until 1866. At Nantgarw the work was taken up again with further help from W. W. Young. Much of the Nantgarw and Swansea porcelain, early and late, was sent to London for decoration by the enamellers working for the big dealers—Mortlock, Pellatt and Green, Daniell, and the rest—and their preference for Billingsley's fine and translucent milk-white china began to injure the similar trade enjoyed by Coalport, which as we have seen certainly supplied porcelain to the decorator Baxter and doubtless to other independent enamellers, such as Fidèle Duvivier and Thomas Pardoe, and to many of the dealers direct. This led John Rose, the Coalport proprietor, himself to engage the services of Billingsley, with a subsequent improvement in the Coalport paste and the taking up there of the Nantgarw-Swansea tradition. The style of the latter, I think, marks the beginning of the florid Rockingham-Coalport manner, after which we have named our second period. Following Billingsley's departure in 1819, Young continued Nantgarw until 1822; it is also said that at a later date (1838) he made up the 'Nantgarw' body and sold it dry in casks to a Staffordshire potter, S. Daniel of Stoke. Nantgarw and Swansea are eagerly collected to-day, but much that passes by the name is undoubtedly Coalport or Staffordshire. John Rose, in fact, had Billingsley's formula, and his porcelain at times came very close to the Welsh, subtle differences of style being often the only indications of its later date. The outstanding quality of the Nantgarw itself is its translucency. Only a few easily recognised relief-patterns were used for the borders of the numerous plates and dishes; these anticipate the Revived Rococo. The forms generally were simple and vases few. The local decoration was of the simplest kind—sprigs and sprays of roses and artless *chinoiseries* in colours with little or no gilding were usual. Billingsley's own flower-painting is rarely found on it. On the best Swansea (which was normally marked with the name in red or impressed capitals) the forms and decorations were more elaborate and pretentious, and large classical vases were often made. The hands responsible for the painting are as much discussed as those of Derby. For the latest views on the subject of the hard, mannered flowers of 'de Junic', the laboured bird-painting and landscapes of Colclough and Beddow, and the facile and monotonous wild flowers now attributed to Evan Evans and David Evans, the reader is referred to Mr. Isaac Williams's catalogue of the collection in the National Museum of Wales at Cardiff. But I hold that the landscapes with flowers in the foreground are usually not by William Pollard but by Thomas Baxter (who was at Swansea from 1816 to 1819), as affirmed in a law-suit regarding the Swansea china, when a plate now at South Kensington was produced in court, and that the

fluent 'botanical' flowers on both earthenware and porcelain in the style of Pegg of Derby are for the most part by
Thomas Pardoe, who was originally of that place, and are
not by W. W. Young; this is the view put forward by the
late John Ward, and it is supported by the handwriting
of many of the inscriptions. Young was an illustrator of
books on natural history and topography; his laboured style
is seen in some naturalistic butterflies and birds and in
figure-pieces on Nantgarw china and Swansea earthenware. Much of the Swansea decoration was of formal
patterns in the *Empire* style in gold, often with the addition
of touches of a characteristic dark green copied from the
contemporary Paris porcelain. The Swansea gilding was
excellently done, with delicate lace-work patterns (Plate
XXII, A). The London decoration is harder to classify.
Elaborate figure-pieces and landscapes are found in addition to the bouquets, which were often very full and
strongly coloured.

The Nantgarw-Swansea and the London decoration of
the period 1815–25 set the fashion later followed at Coalport, at Swinton in Staffordshire, and also at Derby and
Worcester. I have called this the 'Rockingham' style, since
it was carried to its most extravagant lengths at that factory. It was Revived Rococo setting in by way of reaction
against the severities of the neo-Classical and *Empire*.
The 'Rockingham' Works themselves had existed at
Swinton in Yorkshire since the middle of the eighteenth
century, but did not make porcelain until 1820 or later,
eventually receiving a subsidy from the Marquis of Rockingham and taking his name in 1826; they were closed in
1842. The porcelain made was clean white bone-china
not distinguishable from the best Staffordshire. The mark
was a griffin passant printed with the name 'Rockingham'
and that of the proprietors, Brameld; but much was left

PLATE XXIII   *See pages 236, 238, 239*

(*a*) CANDELABRUM. PORCELAIN, DECORATED IN TURQUOISE BLUE AND GILT
STAFFORDSHIRE (MINTON'S FACTORY), ABOUT 1865
Victoria and Albert Museum (Florence Bequest)

(*b*) VASE. PORCELAIN, WITH
DECORATION IN IMITATION
OF LACQUER AND IVORY
WORCESTER (KERR AND BINNS)
ABOUT 1870
Bethnal Green Museum

(*c*) VASE. EARTHENWARE, WITH
DECORATION IN BLUE AND GOLD
BURSLEM (DOULTON'S FACTORY)
ABOUT 1885
Bethnal Green Museum

unmarked. The florid new *rococo* shared with Coalport and the rest in this period entirely lacks the nervous delicacy of the eighteenth-century style. It is coarse and energetic where the other was quick and flamelike. At its amusing worst its extravagance takes such forms as the two enormous 'Rockingham' vases at Wentworth House and South Kensington, with huge paw feet beneath a monstrous body smothered in applied oak leaves and twigs, the whole surmounted by a lid with a knob in the form of a rhinoceros. The flower-painting on this vase (by Edwin Steele) is also typical: hot in colour and laboured in handling, but not without a vulgar abundance and excess that reveal an unmistakeable vitality, if little taste. The flowers on the plate here figured (Plate XXI, c) are also probably by Edwin Steele, whose manner was derived from the Derby style created by Billingsley. The gilding was of course profuse. Coalport shows much the same florid taste, but had a more translucent porcelain, following Billingsley's advent, and rather lighter colour and slighter decoration prevailed. Davenport's of Longport, apparently the most versatile of the Staffordshire factories, was capable of fine wares in the best Derby, Swansea, and Rockingham manners, but absurd *rococo* vases are also found with the firm's mark; Ridgway, and Mayer and Newbold, also produced excellent porcelain in this style. Minton's were of rather less account in porcelain at this time; a typical decoration with their mark of crossed 'S's' has a deep blue ground with bold gilt foliage and reserves with flowers usually in strong hot colours. In the Minton and Boyle period a foliated mark with 'M & B' was used with the usual pattern name, such as 'Amherst Japan', etc. Worcester was heavier, and in the 1810's and 1820's massive pearled edges lavishly gilt had been the rule on the 'dress services' in which Binns took such pride, and these continued to be characteristic. Chamberlain's porcelain had been grey and wavy surfaced at first, and much still remained so, but finer bodies (such as the 'Regent China') were introduced as the firm became more prosperous. The ordinary Chamberlain ware was usually unmarked. At Bristol, on Ring's cream-coloured ware of about 1820–50, William Fifield, junr., painted bouquets of roses, etc., in a style obviously suggested by the contemporary porcelain, as well as landscapes with buildings in the style of the contemporary water-colours. Derby had supplied the best Rockingham painters, including Thomas Steele and his sons Edwin and Horatio, and the styles of the two factories had much in common in this period still. The Derby china itself had by now lost its distinguished quality and approximated to the Staffordshire. Coloured grounds were of course very popular everywhere. Chrome green enamel provided a new shade, more opaque and yellowish in tone than the fine copper green of the eighteenth century; this was especially popular at Derby and Rockingham. Spode introduced a hideous bright 'matt' blue, a lifeless pink, and a dull heavy claret colour; in one of his most expensive patterns a hard gilt scale pattern was painted in gold over a dark blue with flowers in reserve; some fawn and grey grounds were much better. A deep, wet, slightly violet-toned dark blue was peculiar to Rockingham. The commonest ground at Chamberlain's was also blue. It is often a matter of great difficulty to distinguish the showy porcelains described in this section. In diagnosis it is useful to remember that Spode and Copeland and Derby were usually marked; Coalport is very translucent, often with a rather light yellowish green prominent in the painting and frequently with pink printed outlines; Chamberlain's ordinary porcelain has a characteristic undulating surface, while the Rockingham is sometimes thought to be recognisable by its flower-painting when it is by a man with a fondness for tiny vetch-like sprays projecting from the bouquets; this is, however, the hand of Edwin Steele, who with his father and brother seem to have worked in Staffordshire as well as at Derby and Swinton.

Figures had of course continued to be made since the eighteenth century. Those still done in porcelain at Derby were mostly mere repetitions of the old, with a few new subjects, such as the Dr. Syntax series, added. Their colour was harsh, over-strong, and paint-like, and the gilding brassy and hard. The figures made at the Rockingham factory in general share the Derby style. Some Staffordshire earthenware and porcelain figures continued the Wood and Neale traditions; others, particularly those made in earthenware by Walton and by Salt about 1820–1830, were amusingly crude copies of Derby porcelain, with elaborate *bocages*. Obadiah Sherratt, and Lakin and Poole, made others in similar style, but usually without the bocages. Some of the latest and most original were made at an unidentified factory (perhaps Sampson Smith's at Longton) apparently in the 1840's and later. They are 'crude' in modelling, but excellently simple, and sparingly coloured in dark blue and clean fresh enamels generally including orange, pink, and red, in graded washes. The young Queen Victoria and the Prince Consort give the period; while some characteristic tartan-clad Highland lasses have led to the mistaken attribution of the whole class to Scotland, where much less clean and pleasant figures were certainly made in the same style. Some of the Rockingham figures are similar, but more sophisticated. To the same class belong the toy cottages and figures of dogs with roughened patches of 'vegetation' and 'fur', which are often indiscriminately called Rockingham, though undoubtedly for the most part made in Staffordshire. It is

231

often difficult to assign a place of origin to these. Mention should perhaps be made here of the trivial biscuit figures of George Cocker (*b*. 1794, *d*. 1868), who worked on his own account as well as at Derby (whose style he adopted), Worcester, and Minton's.

The stoneware of the Rockingham Period included no novelties of importance unless we may count as such the popular spirit-flasks made about the time of the Reform Bill of 1832, at Denby, Brampton, Chesterfield, and elsewhere in the Midlands, and at Lambeth in London (by Doulton, Stiff, and Stephen Green). These have the tops in the form of the head and shoulders of the Duke of Wellington, Richard Cobden, Daniel O'Connell, and other statesmen and politicians. Some red, green, and black wares, in fantastic Chinese or Revived Rococo forms, with glossy (actually varnished) surface, have usually been called Isleworth and their commonest mark, 'S & G', interpreted as that of Shore and Goulding. But they are now known to be productions of a Bohemian firm, Schiller and Gerbing of Bodenbach; the similar wares marked 'W S & S' come from 'Wilhelm Schiller und Söhne' of the same place, or 'Wilhelm Sattler und Söhne' of Aschach near Kissingen. Glossy black wares of similar appearance were, however, certainly made in England, as for instance by Cyples of Longton, whose mark occurs on some of them. Wedgwood, the Adams, the Ridgways, and others, of course continued to make black basaltes, blue jasper, and most of the eighteenth-century types of coloured stoneware, often in the old moulds, but also with forms and subjects modified to suit the *Empire*, romantic, sporting, or florid taste of the later times. The fashion of enamelling brown or black unglazed stoneware in opaque colours continued, as on the very bad but numerous productions of Lowesby (about 1835).

Some half-glossy plain white porcellanous wares (akin to the 'Parian', to be mentioned presently) were popular towards the middle of the nineteenth century and are especially associated with the name of Charles Meigh of the Old Hall, Hanley. One of his works in this material, a jug surviving in great numbers, is an outstanding example of the taste of the Gothic Revival in English

FIG. 12. JUG. MEIGH'S STONEEWAR

ceramic art. It has straight sides and crowded relief-decoration, with a frieze of figures of apostles under pointed arches (Fig. 12). Others have classical subjects treated in the same manner. But the more numerous jugs and vases in this white material are grotesquely shapeless, entirely covered with moulded reliefs, the monstrous lumpy handles also bearing figures or the like in relief. The same fashion of course extended to the brown-glazed stoneware of the Midlands and London. Many of the Meigh type of jugs bear a mark of a diamond or lozenge, with letters and numerals and the word 'Regd' in relief, the meaning of which is not generally known. It is not a factory mark, but records the registration of the pattern at the Patent Office, and one of the letters gives a key in cipher to the date; I understand that the Patent Office can also by a little research ascertain from another of the letters the name of the maker, and will do so for a fee. This 'Meigh style' was well represented at the Great Exhibition and in one sense was the last word of the Rockingham Period. But the more prosperous firms making porcelain at the time of the Exhibition were concerned with a much more sophisticated art.

Awareness of the triumphs of Sèvres had never died out in England since the eighteenth century, and as it happens there is more fine Sèvres porcelain in England than in any other country. Its exquisite finish and obvious luxury made it a model well within the comprehension of the uncultured plutocracy of the second quarter of the nineteenth century. Thomas Baxter had prided himself on his exact copies of Sèvres, and later on one T. M. Randall became a notorious redecorator of old Sèvres china, and himself made, at Madeley in Shropshire, for ten years or so from 1830 a soft-paste resembling the French. Even later he seems to have inspired the Minton copies of Sèvres with the turquoise ground. It became the boast of the Coalport, Copeland, and Minton factories that their copies of Sèvres could hardly be distinguished from the originals. With the perfecting of this typical achievement the Great Exhibition ushered in the Age of Museums, bringing home to the manufacturers an awareness of Art, especially the art of the past. Some technical advances of the time were, however, noteworthy, and included the underglaze printing in many colours of Pratt and others, already mentioned, and the Parian porcelain body.

The introduction of unglazed white 'Parian' porcelain, a variety of hard-paste, by Copeland's about 1846, following researches after the formula for the Derby biscuit, stands as a landmark; it made possible the enormous development of modelled figure-decoration applied to vases and even to table-wares, as well as a new fashion for independent figures in the manner of marble sculpture. Minton's and Copeland's were the leaders in this kind of work, which was largely represented at the Exhibition. Renaissance styles came more and more into favour, and the exaggerated *rococo* and bastard styles of the 1830's and 1840's cleared a little to a new sort of Classical which was hardly ever simple and never severe. From this time onwards the English potter was caught up by wave after wave of fashion, reacting all too easily, and never creating a sincere or original style of his own. The Exhibition was filled with pottery and porcelain in 'Moorish', 'Indian', 'Cinquecento', and every other style known to the nascent art-scholarship of the time. A general optimism was abroad, and it was felt that modern science and machinery in the service of a taste familiar with the 'best examples of the applied art of the past' must inevitably bring an all-surpassing excellence. The result has been an almost complete failure, as much from a lack of artistic conviction as from any other cause; the new technical resources have been insincerely employed in mere imitation. In the succession of styles observable between the fifteenth and eighteenth centuries there is to be noted a broad play of action and reaction with florid Gothic or *rococo* extravagance alternating with Classical severity, over long periods. But after the ferment of the Industrial Revolution which occupied the first half of the nineteenth

century came an eclectic period of mere fashions, suddenly
changing, apparently without roots, with the artists, or
rather manufacturers, concerned chiefly to sell their goods
and thinking of art as a mere dress to make them more
saleable. The customary term 'applied art' is significant
here. This was (and is) the age of the designer, replacing
the craftsman. In the decades just before and after the
Great Exhibition there were Greek fashions which
brought 'Grecian' styles of painting in Staffordshire: at
Swansea from about 1848 to 1850 were made by Lewis
Llewellyn Dillwyn and his wife the feeble copies of Greek
vases known as their 'Etruscan ware'; Greek styles even
affected the blue-printed earthenware. At Worcester in
the 1860's were made versions in porcelain of Limoges
enamels, painted by T. J. Bott. Minton's, directed from
1849 by Léon Arnoux, exactly copied the Palissy and
Henri Deux wares and in general followed the French
Renaissance taste, often enough with a woeful lack of
understanding (Plate XXIII, A). All the coloured grounds
of Sèvres—the *rose Pompadour* ('*rose du Barry*'), the apple-
green, and especially the turquoise—were copied with
fair exactness and great technical perfection. Parian
figures were modelled by Jeannest, Carrier-Belleuse, and
other Frenchmen, and Sèvres-like painting was done by
many skilful artists. Standing apart from the French re-
finements and porcelain style were the imitation of English
mediaeval encaustic tiles made by the subsidiary firm of
Minton, Hollins and Co. A technique new to England
was brought by M. L. Solon, who joined Minton's during
the Franco-Prussian war in 1870, bringing the Sèvres
pâtes d'application, which he renamed *pâte-sur-pâte*. In
this, delicate reliefs were modelled in translucent slip on
dark grounds. Solon's style was a sentimentalised French
Renaissance. Copeland's were less French but equally

PLATE XXIV   *Pages* 238, 240, 242

(*a*) DISH. EARTHENWARE, PAINTED IN RUBY AND YELLOW LUSTRE
BY WILLIAM DE MORGAN. ABOUT 1885
Victoria and Albert Museum

(*b*) VASE. STONEWARE. MADE
BY EDWIN MARTIN (MARTIN
BROTHERS) AT SOUTHALL, 1903
Victoria and Albert Museum

(*c*) VASE. STONEWARE. MADE
BY BERNARD LEACH AT
ST. IVES. ABOUT 1930
Victoria and Albert Museum

devoted to the Sèvres exquisiteness and to Parian, in which figures by John Gibson and J. H. Foley, amongst others, were designed or adapted for them. At Coalport, for the Great Exhibition, William Cook painted trophies and flowers in precise imitation of Sèvres, and Chelsea vases were also copied. An elaborated Sèvres naturalism in flower-painting was skilfully practised by C. F. Hürten at Copeland's at a rather later date, while in the '60's and '70's a new and freer style of figure-painting in colours, with browns predominating, was brought to England by Émile Lessore, a Sèvres painter who worked for a short time with Minton's in 1858, and subsequently until his death in 1876 for Wedgwood's. Thomas Allen at Minton's was a worker in the same manner.

A singular use of glazed Parian is to be noted in the wares of Belleek in Co. Fermanagh, in Ireland, where a pottery was started in 1857. Vases in naturalistic shell forms were especially characteristic, but busts and table-wares were also made, all covered with a slimy nacreous lustre, produced with a bismuth compound, on which the factory greatly prided itself. Jewitt in fact wrote of the wares in 1878 that they 'have an almost unearthly appearance of liquid beauty'.

All Europe was taken by storm by the Japanese art made known in Europe on the opening of Japan to trade in 1859, and henceforward a new asymmetry and naturalism began to modify the revived-Renaissance manner. It is hardly necessary to say that the Japanese pottery and porcelain in question was largely the degraded over-decorated and -gilded 'Satsuma' and other export types rather than the subtle, grave, and sombre pottery in true Japanese taste. At Worcester this Japanese influence was especially strong, affecting not only the painted designs but encouraging the use of gold in various colours and textures,

dull or bright, in imitation of lacquer ware (Plate XXIII, B).
An ivory-like porcelain material, actually of much beauty
in itself, shows the same influence. Here at Worcester as
in many other potteries came the Moorish styles, popularised at the exhibitions, and we find ogee, horseshoe, and
arabesque filigree gilding used to deck out the highly
wrought luxury wares. At Worcester a feature was made
of elaborately pierced porcelain, and this continued to be
made until recent times: George Owen was a famous and
very skilful practitioner in this. The common porcelain and
earthenware of the period show the same styles cheaply
rendered in transfer-printing and coloured wash. A lax
touch, wet thin colour, and a fondness for long wavy leaves
and rushes, mark the more ordinary flower-painting of
the '70's, while the landscapes and figure-pieces show a
kindred soft and smeared-over quality.

An interesting type of decoration taken over by Wedgwood's in the 1860's from the French factory at Rubelles
(where it was known as *émail ombrant*) employs a design
impressed in intaglio relief and flooded with translucent
glaze, usually green. It gives a design in light and shade
in which the most deeply impressed parts appear darkest.
The principle is the same as in the well-known 'litho-
phanies' made at Berlin and Meissen (and also at Llanelly!)
from about 1825 onwards; here the design, usually a re-
production of a famous picture, impressed in a biscuit
slab is seen by transmitted light.

About 1870 a museum-taught admiration for 'Persian'
and 'Rhodian' (actually Turkish) pottery and Italian
maiolica brought bold foliate designs and stylised figure
and animal subjects in the Pre-Raphaelite (more properly
the William Morris) manner, with clean strong colours and
ruby and golden lustre. William de Morgan was a noteworthy figure here (Plate XXIV, A) despite his grievously

imperfect technique. But F. Moody and others, working for Minton's, had already done similar Italian Renaissance decoration in lustre in the 1860's. The powerful influence of Walter Crane was felt far and wide, in pottery as in other crafts, and designs in his styles, which ranged from 'Rhodian' flowers and foliage to children's picture-books, quickly acquired a sort of academic respectability which they still retain. About 1885 an extraordinary fashion for monochrome turquoise glazes inspired imitations made at Minton's, at the great tile-works of Maw and Co. at Broseley, and by de Morgan. The monochrome copper-reds of the Chinese, the *sang de bœuf* and *flambé* glazes, similarly attracted attention; and though the technical problem was here very much greater, it was solved with success in the 1890's and later by Mr. Bernard Moore and by Mr. William and Mr. Joseph Burton working for Pilkington's Tile Works at Manchester.

In the 1880's the firm of Doulton of Lambeth and Burslem devoted particular attention to stoneware, reviving and elaborating the grey, blue, and purple Rhenish styles. The vases so made show an astonishing taste, with elongated and distorted forms decked out with bizarre excrescences and overloaded with decoration, carved and modelled. Some simpler vases were decorated with incised free-hand designs by artists allowed to sign their names: Hannah Barlow's animal subjects are well known, but others were no less skilful. Painted designs generally continued the naturalistic style referred to above (Plate XXIII, c). George Tinworth was a prominent modeller at Doulton's, doing groups and single figures often on a small scale, with a mean and trivial effect. Robert Wallace Martin, oldest of three well-known brothers, served an apprenticeship here, working in the techniques just mentioned. The joint work of the three Martins has enjoyed great fame in recent years, and they are often spoken of as the first masters of modern English pottery art. Their salt-glazed stoneware was in essentials the same as Doulton's but with more varied glazes, in colourings usually of sub-dued tone; the incised decoration of their earlier pieces is seldom vital and often perfunctory, and the modelling of R. W. Martin, though skilful, has a kind of facetious humour which many people find distressing. Their best work was done after they had visited the Paris Exhibition of 1900; thenceforward, with a recollection of the finer Japanese wares to guide them, they devoted themselves to simple shapes, in many cases appropriately suggested by fruits and gourds, and to subtly wrought indefinite slips and glazes (Plate XXIV, B).

The Paris Exhibition of 1900 saw the triumph of the movement called in France and England *L'Art Nouveau*, and in Germany the *Jugendstil*. This was thought at the time to be one of those inspired 'returns to nature' by which the arts are from time to time saved from decadence. Now, in 1933, it is clear that it was an abominable hybrid between Japanese naturalism and the scrolled forms and foliations of European, especially French and Italian, Renaissance ornament. The Impressionism of its chief French exponent, Émile Gallé, was admirably suited to his technique in glass, and may have inspired the indefinite cloudings and lustre-painting of some of Pilkington's wares; but much of Gallé's own painted and incised pottery, like his work in other materials calling for pre-cision (such as wood and metal), is to our eyes absurd and incompetent, though contemporaries could write of him as '*poète, fraternel à la création entière*'. In England the movement chiefly resulted in a school-taught curliness that still survives and has continued to be regarded as essentially 'artistic' in Staffordshire and elsewhere.

Whatever its faults, the original *Art Nouveau* was a distinctive style, instantly recognisable. Its absurdities and unfitnesses largely resulted from its being design imposed, something which the craftsman was ordered to make from a paper plan, not design suggested by the tools and materials, or even adapted by them. A conviction of the wrongness of this proceeding is part of the modern artistic conscience and must form the subject of some concluding remarks here. That conviction would have been unthinkable in 1851, and even to-day is hard indeed to reconcile with the methods of the factories. That the latter should abandon the imitation of handwork and boldly take advantage of the special capabilities of the machine is scarcely admitted at present. An entirely new type of design has emerged in this way in architecture, and it may be suggested that in pottery too the power of endless repetition of the machine should be used, or at least symbolised, in frankly machine-made commercial productions.

A conviction of the blessedness of handicraft is not, however, exactly a recent phenomenon. William Morris preached it long ago, but his follower in pottery, William de Morgan, was content to make designs which he handed over to Joe Juster and Charles and Fred Passenger to copy on his wares. More recent efforts, including those of the Martin brothers already mentioned, have been much more consistent and logical, and a new race of artist-potters is at work to-day, making and decorating their pots from start to finish. Such work cannot of course 'compete' with the factories: it is a luxury product, and this economic circumstance gives an air of unreality to an art so often inspired by peasant wares. A wide gulf indeed separates the artist-potters from the factories; and with the former clearly rests such ceramic virtue as exists to-day. The dominant influence is Chinese and the fashionable material stoneware. Forms appear reasonable again and 'well-proportioned': the bizarre eccentricities of the 'art-pottery' of the 1880–1910 period (such as the abominable Linthorpe and the rest) are rightly contemned. Mr. Michael Cardew has assimilated the virtues of English peasant wares. Mr. R. F. Wells, one of the first in the Chinese field, has a complete mastery of the grey and opalescent glazes of the Canton stoneware, but is negligent of form. The blunt strength of Mr. Staite Murray is in sharp contrast with the nervous vitality of Mr. Bernard Leach (Plate XXIV, c); both have highly personal styles. The Chinese technique has now no secrets for these artist-potters, though some of the most successful reproductions made by others are dry and empty in form and decoration where their Chinese models are tense with life. Other fashions of the time have inspired other styles: the modern figures of Miss Gwendolen Parnell with their wit and amazing cleverness easily lead a large field, but even she has not achieved the first necessity in porcelain, which is a sensuously beautiful material. Here the Meissen and Copenhagen modellers, Scheurich and Malinowski, have the advantage. In the factory work, one looks almost in vain for true novelty; but Messrs. Carter, Stabler, and Adams have achieved this in recent years in a smooth-surfaced matt opaque-glazed stoneware painted with lively designs in an entirely modern palette of colours on a creamy ground. Somewhat similar wares made by Pilkington's are noteworthy for modern black and grey pigments of great beauty. It is through such technical advances that new ground is won for the ceramic art.

COLLECTING

COLLECTING

IT is well known that success in forming a collection calls for more than knowledge. Taste, for example, is naturally a first requisite; it cannot be taught, and it is proverbially useless to argue about it. But in spite of the warning I have endeavoured in these pages to show how many and various are the kinds of beauty possessed by the English ceramic wares, and with an appeal to the collector to despise nothing that is good of its kind I propose to leave the matter. It is no less difficult to speak of another necessary attribute in the collector, usually called 'flair', a word too often used to cover an ignorant dogmatism on the subject of makes and dates. Yet there is a gift by which not only the origin of a piece may be immediately known, but the existence, for example, of a rare and beautiful specimen in a dark corner may seem to be mysteriously sensed. The recognition of factory and period is indeed an act that may become apparently instinctive, from long familiarity with a large collection and constant study of documentary pieces, coupled of course with good memory and perception of colour, rhythm, and handling; but 'flair' of the other kind can hardly be taught.

The purposes, desires, and so forth, which govern the formation of a collection are so various that general advice is apt to be pointless, if not impertinent. Just as artists have often attributed to their work qualities quite other than those for which posterity values them, so collectors often set out to do one thing and achieve another;

one may hope that aesthetic considerations, conscious or instinctive, govern the formation of most collections. Few people, I imagine, visit the delightful Willett Collection at the Brighton Museum with the notion of studying 'crime', 'domestic incidents', and so on, in English pottery, as its creator intended. 'Associations', absorbing enough in one generation, prove impossibly dull to the next. Lady Charlotte Schreiber professed to be assembling her great collection of English pottery and porcelain, eventually given by her to the South Kensington Museum, as a representative series rather than for its beauty; but it is now valued much less for its comprehensiveness than for its nowadays almost unattainably fine quality.

But the published *Journals of Lady Charlotte Schreiber* is, as it happens, a collector's classic, almost the only book of its kind, and concerned as it is with this very subject of English pottery and porcelain may be warmly recommended. The search, the joy of possession, the discovery of the long-sought rarity that fills a gap, all this and more are set forth with a charming mid-Victorian directness and naïveté. The prices paid in her day—covering a period from about 1869 to 1885—are of course no indication of present values, and even relative values have greatly changed. On this subject of prices little can usefully be said here. Even sale-room figures may be deceptive. So much depends on condition; while the whim of a rich buyer may send the price of a specimen or a class up to a level out of all proportion to normal value. Then there are booms. A post-war boom sent up the price of Bow figures to a level at which a pair representing Summer and Autumn was sold for 3780 guineas, and even quite ordinary Chelsea and Derby fetched something like ten times its utmost present market value. Dr. Glaisher's death a few years ago has reduced by half or more the price of English slipwares and blue-dash chargers, for which he had been willing to pay almost any sum if a specimen took his fancy. The present fashion for figures of birds is another case in which abnormal prices are ruling. Then there are broad changes of taste; red-anchor is now more esteemed than gold-anchor, and the Worcester 'scale-blue and birds' has given pride of place to apple-green, and so on. Quite apart from all these factors, the recent industrial depression brought down the prices of all but first-rate things to a ruinous point. A few sales of the last year or two may, however, be referred to, with reservations, and the following may be taken as a rough indication of the range of prices prevailing for the chief types of English wares. There is now (January 1933) an unmistakeable tendency for prices to rise, if slowly.

Nothing can be said regarding the prices of the mediaeval pottery, save to mention that the day has gone by when a fine jug could be bought from a navvy for a few shillings. The London supply from excavations is nearly exhausted and prices may be expected to rise. Slipware of fine quality will always command a high price. Toft or similar dishes, if in reasonable condition, will generally run into three figures. At the Harland Sale in 1931 large posset-pots fetched about £40 to £70, while an exquisitely feathered small one went for only £14. At the Taylor Sale in 1930 a moulded Staffordshire dish fetched £36, and a good Barnstaple jug went to £15, but the Devon and Sussex wares are usually much cheaper than the best Staffordshire. The prices of delftware defy summarising: fine tulip dishes could be had at the Taylor Sale for £10, but the less attractive ones with royal figures surprisingly cost more. Prices at the Harland Sale had risen somewhat. Good Lambeth jugs and bottles cost from £10 to £50. The Bristol and other eighteenth-century wares, unless inscribed, seldom rise above £10 apiece, and are usually very much less. Stoneware is not of much account, unless it can be linked with Dwight. None of the latter's figures or busts have come up for public sale in recent years; but two marbled bottles at £10 and £84 (Harland) illustrated the uncertainty due to a particular collector's interest, while two 'Dwight-Elers' red mugs and a cup went for £21, £23, and £3 : 3s. respectively. Fine Nottingham jugs and tankards could be had for £6 to £10. Among later Staffordshire the following (taken from the same two sales) are fairly typical: 'Astbury' figures of a piper and a lady, £40 and £56; 'Astbury' jugs, £13, £35, and £6 (with two others!). Whieldon figures of fine quality as much as £72 and £130; less important ones £6 upwards; Whieldon plates not more than a pound or two, but teapots about £10, or for rare pieces £20 to £50 upwards. Salt-glaze table-wares are expensive only if enamelled; teapots may then cost £10 to £30; figures range from cats at £10 to pew-groups at £260 (Taylor). The more ordinary Wood figures and Toby jugs may be as little as £3 to £5, but important pieces like the St. George in the Taylor Collection fetch £50 or more, and the finest early Toby jugs as much as £100. At the W. J. Lee Sale in October 1932 two fine small Wood figures fetched £35 each, but many others, mostly later, in enamel colours, sold in lots at £5 or so. Wedgwood ware is now completely out of fashion, and even the finest vases may sometimes be had at sales for a tenth of the price they fetched fifty years ago; an excellent 'agate' vase went for £7 at the Taylor Sale. Single pieces of cream-colour are worth shillings only, though centre-pieces naturally cost more and painted Leeds teapots may fetch £5 or so.

Prices in porcelain range even more widely. Gold-anchor vases, especially if sold from noble houses, where many still remain, generally fetch prices running into hundreds of pounds; and the more showy Worcester vases may cost nearly as much. Fine services of mazarin-blue or claret colour have also fetched several hundred or even a thousand pounds. At the Viscountess Harcourt Sale in 1927 a beautiful mazarin service with gold decoration numbering twenty-eight pieces fetched £756. Whether such prices would hold at present is of course very doubtful; but fine pieces tend even now to hold their price. The current prices for the more ordinary English porcelain may be indicated by reference to two sales, held at the end of 1932, of the Hignett and W. J. Lee Collections. A Chelsea goat-and-bee jug then fetched £15 : 10s.; a raised-anchor Kakiemon 'nurl'd' dish, £10, others less; two cups and saucers by the 'fable-painter' (one cracked), £3 : 15s. These relatively moderate prices generally hold for small pieces of early Chelsea, but large pieces—dishes and tureens—may run to £50 or £100, and fine gold-anchor plates with coloured grounds, if in good condition, are still worth as much as £10 or more. Chelsea figures in good order are among the most costly of all English porcelain, but no rules can be given for them. Bow is not generally expensive. A good *famille rose* mug went for £5 at one of the sales mentioned; a less attractive one with leaves in relief, £7 : 10s.; and a beautiful plate with a river landscape and a dish with richly coloured leaves and fruits, £10 each; a pair of large powdered-blue dishes, £16, but miscellaneous blue-and-white much less, often under a pound on the average of each lot. Figures in fair condition cost £10 or more, but may be even less. Inscribed and dated Lowestoft still enjoys a vogue; prices between £11 and £41 were reached at the W. J. Lee Sale, in some cases for very plain pieces; other Lowestoft not inscribed usually costs only a pound or two apiece. Derby figures and useful ware are not among the more expensive porcelain, and early figures rarely exceed £10, the commoner 'Chelsea-Derby' figures £5 or £6, and specimens of the useful wares, unless exceptionally large or rare, not more than £1 apiece; two good Boreman landscape plates went to £4 : 5s. at the W. J. Lee Sale, where, however, a rare blue-and-white coffee-pot sold for £13 : 10s. Longton Hall prices are somewhat higher than these, but only in rare cases exceed £10 apiece for table-wares. Figures in good condition are more expensive. Worcester prices are high for the more showy sorts. 'Apple-green' is now the fashionable colour, and two cups and saucers with this cost £12 in November 1932; a yellow ground dish £26; and a pair of plates with the once supremely coveted 'scale-blue and birds' ran to £50 at the same sale. The earlier and finer things are still relatively cheap. A sauceboat with the rarest and most exquisite 'Lowdin's' figure-painting cost only £12, and a plate with figures in a landscape £14. Armorial and other pieces by the painter of the Lord Sandys mug may cost £20 or £30. A mug with the brilliantly coloured Chinese figure-subjects of about 1760 went for £9. Transfer-printed and blue-and-white pieces of ordinary quality and small size may cost shillings only; a signed and dated Hancock Frederick the Great of 1757 fetched no more than £4 at the Hignett Sale. Important large blue-and-white vases may be expected to cost more, and a small dish with the absurdly sought 'Eloping Bride' Chinese subject was sold in November 1932 for £37! Liverpool and Caughley are even less expensive than the ordinary Worcester they imitated. Plymouth and Bristol have rarity value, and figures in fair condition will generally exceed £15, and ordinary Plymouth table-wares may perhaps run to £4 or £5 apiece; Bristol, if not from some historic service, as a rule costs much less. No generalisations are possible about nineteenth-century porcelain, but it may be mentioned that Spode of the '1166' pattern (scale gold and blue ground) is commercially valuable, and up to £10 or even more may be given for marked Nantgarw and Swansea plates.

These prices, it must be repeated, are for the most part those prevailing in a slump period, though considerable increases are not to be expected. Furthermore, they are taken from the results of public sales, and cannot of course hold where dealers' profits have to be added. Strong-minded buying at public auctions with predetermined limits rigidly adhered to has much to recommend it, but it requires sure knowledge and much alertness on the part of the collector.

It is more and more evident that on the plane where the highest prices rule condition counts for everything; and the last-shilling man who is compelled to regard his collection as an investment will do well to observe this. Rarity values must also be considered: Derby *Miltons* and *Justices* or Staffordshire lustre or Chelsea-Derby table-wares, however charming aesthetically, will never fetch high prices. For this reason the collector will do well to frequent the sale-room, and observe for himself the condition of the objects sold, and note the rarity or otherwise of their appearance over a period of years. There can be no better training of eye and hand than the examination of specimens thus open to view, especially when the would-be collector has few opportunities for the handling of actual pieces. Museum study, however instructive in other ways, cannot give this essential experience. And this brings us to the difficult subject of forgeries.

Forgeries are of many kinds, few of them recognisable except through a perfect familiarity with the appearance of the genuine specimens. Some may indeed be accused by an ignorant bringing together of an early style with a late mark, or one factory style with the mark of another, as in the case of the hard-paste forgeries of the figures formerly called Chelsea but now known to be Derby; these are always supplied with a gold anchor, which the originals of course never have. As far as porcelain is concerned, the collector is well on the way to safety if he has merely learned to distinguish hard-paste from soft. It is by no means only the pretentious and costly types that are forged. There are copies of early Worcester sauceboats in the starch-bluish-white glazed porcelain used by a well-known Paris firm for its 'reproductions' of Chinese wares; these have a tell-tale pin-hole in the handle. Then there are the fakes of Lowestoft—'Abraham Moore' etc.— which are a sort of hard-paste, with names and dates copied from early lists of inscribed pieces. The versions of the so-called Chinese-Lowestoft are hard-paste like their Chinese originals. (It should perhaps be mentioned here that there was an old belief, based on a mistake of Chaffers, that the Chinese armorial and rose-painted export porcelain was made or decorated at Lowestoft; but no hard-paste was ever made there and the wares in question are wholly Oriental. Robert Allen, manager of Lowestoft and independent decorator, added his name unaccountably to a Chinese teapot in the Schreiber Collection, and this may have helped to create the legend.) Hard-paste forgeries of Bristol are perhaps more difficult to detect; they are too thin and white and clean, but I have seen them figured in a book on collecting as genuine specimens. On the other hand, a 'Plymouth' mug, supposed to be early soft-paste from that factory, with the mark in crimson, lately brought to my notice, was an obviously modern piece, with impossibly wet and careless exotic-bird painting. The mid-nineteenth-century copies of Chelsea made at Coalport and Tournay have deceived some experienced collectors: the goat-and-bee jugs of Coalport, like the gold-anchor marked vases from the same factory, are altogether too clean and white; the Tournay gold anchor sometimes has impossible nineteenth-century subjects, but is a true soft-paste and therefore dangerous. Attention to the mark will sometimes be a protection against forgeries of the Welsh porcelain. Anything but an impressed mark in Nantgarw must always be regarded with suspicion; *etched* marks are certainly wrong. The red 'SWANSEA' is on forgeries often written in careless italic capitals easily distinguished from the genuine.

Not all forgeries are wholly modern. There are, for example, the added yellow grounds, dates, etc., as on an otherwise genuine Lowestoft teapot at South Kensington: these were probably supplied to gratify the passion of the well-known collector Robert Drane for important unique and 'historic' pieces. Then there are contemporary forgeries: the anchor-marks and crescents on old Bow and Derby, the crescents on Lowestoft, and the many un-licensed uses of the crossed swords were all intended to deceive. Sometimes reproductions have been honestly made by the inheritors of old moulds, engraved plates, etc., as in the case of the later Wedgwood jasper and the nineteenth-century Derby porcelain; some little mugs and jugs with rather fuzzy Hancock prints, of which there are examples at South Kensington, are certainly not Worcester and may be nineteenth-century Staffordshire revivals. Some modern bone-porcelain table-wares with a well-known Chelsea-Derby blue-and-gold pattern are not in the old forms, but have been provided with the Chelsea-Derby mark and must therefore count as forgeries. Perhaps honest Staffordshire are some not uncommon re-

productions of Bow blue-and-white and *famille rose* plates
(sometimes with the arms of Lovett), which are very exact
copies of the Bow form and colours but are accused by an
impossibly hard 'pig-skin' paste and glaze, not unlike
some Spode wares. Their origin is much disputed, and I
am inclined to believe them to be even more modern than
some authorities have contended. The faking of earthenware is in general more difficult. Cream-colour, clean and
bright, with 'important' subjects (portraits of famous
persons, etc.), is, I believe, much made for America, and
there is Czecho-Slovakia lustre-ware of cream-colour type.
The tin-enamel technique is no longer in use in England,
and forgeries of delftware are usually foreign, from
Northern France or Holland. The Napoleonic subjects
figured by Pountney as late Bristol were certainly made in
France, and recently. The old Northern French wares are
often very like the English, with horsemen, etc., and are
sometimes seen to be 'wrong' as Bristol and are therefore
suspected. Lead-glazed earthenware of course presents
no technical difficulties. There is a forgery of slipware
made by a man named Sanders figured in Hodgkin (No.
61), and this undoubtedly deceived Solon, whose remark
in his *Maiolica* that no forgery of Gubbio ever deceived an
expert is accompanied by a plate figuring an unquestionable forgery—a warning against over-confidence in this
matter. There are forgeries of Staffordshire figures with
wrong colouring, with underglaze tones too bright, or
with enamels including modern colours such as chrome
pink; the imitation Astbury and Whieldon models are
much heavier than the genuine ones. The absurd Castle
Hedingham ware (late nineteenth century) with its thick
applied Elizabethan dates is sometimes mistaken for late
mediaeval ware, especially after the always indistinct applied 'castle' mark has been chipped away, as it so readily

can be. The not uncommon old salt-glaze enamelled in modern times is often accused by a discoloured black-speckled glaze, due to mismanagement of the kiln temperature and to the unremoved accumulation of grease on the surface of the old ware, which has only become apparent in the refiring: the same phenomena are familiar on the redecorated old white Sèvres. The well-known London 'clobberer' of the second quarter of the nineteenth century, whose embellishments of Chinese blue-and-white are so familiar, sometimes turned his unwelcome attentions to old English porcelain. There are at South Kensington, Worcester, Chelsea, and Lowestoft specimens disfigured by him.

But the surest safeguard against deception must always be a deep and wide appreciation of aesthetic qualities—of the various sorts of sensuous charm in ceramic materials, of vitality in painting, and of rhythm, strength, and delicacy in shaping and modelling. A collector who has cultivated such a sense will in any case obtain an authentic first-hand satisfaction in his possessions, and will be far less likely to be deceived by forgeries than if he should first set out to discover by some rule-of-thumb whether a proposed purchase is genuine, and therefore valuable, and only afterwards wonder if it is beautiful.

A SHORT BIBLIOGRAPHY

I. Earthenware and Stoneware

General

Jewitt, Llewellynn, *The Ceramic Art of Great Britain*. London, 1878.

Solon, L. M., *The Art of the Old English Pottery* (Second edition). London, 1885.

Hodgkin, J. E. and E., *Examples of Early English Pottery*. London, 1896.

Hobson, R. L., *Catalogue of the Collection of English Pottery in the British Museum*. London, 1903.

Burton, W., *English Earthenware and Stoneware*. London, 1904.

Turner, W., *Transfer Printing on Enamels, Porcelain and Pottery*. London, 1907.

Church, Sir Arthur H., *English Earthenware*. London, 1911.

Burlington Fine Arts Club, *Catalogue of an Exhibition of Early English Earthenware*. London, 1914.

Grabham, O., 'Yorkshire Potteries' in *Yorkshire Philosophical Society, Annual Report*, 1916; also Arthur Hurst, *Catalogue of the Boynton Collection of Yorkshire Pottery*, published by the same Society, 1922.

Rhead, G. W., *The Earthenware Collector*. London, 1920.

Rackham, Bernard, and Read, Herbert, *English Pottery*. London, 1924.

Rackham, Bernard, *Catalogue of the Schreiber Collection*, vol. ii. London, 1929.

English Ceramic Circle, Transactions (1933–   ).

Mediaeval

Hobson, R. L., in the *Archaeological Journal*, vol. 59 (1902), p. 1.

Slipware

Lomax, C. J., *Quaint Old English Pottery*. Manchester, 1909.

Hemming, Mrs. Celia, 'Sussex Pottery' in *The Connoisseur*, xxiv (1909) and xxxiii (1912), p. 15.

Roth, H. Ling, in *The Yorkshire Coiners and Notes on Old and Prehistoric Halifax* (p. 239). Halifax, 1906.

Maiolica and Delftware

Downman, E. A., *Blue Dash Chargers*. London, 1919.
Pountney, W. J., *The Old Bristol Potteries*. London and Bristol, 1920.

Stoneware

Church, Sir Arthur H., on Dwight, in *Some Minor Arts*, London, 1894, and 'Early English Stonewares' in the *Burlington Magazine*, vol. xii (1908), p. 293.
Parker, Alfred, 'Nottingham Pottery' in *Transactions of the Thoroton Society of Nottinghamshire*, 1932.
Honey, W. B., 'English Saltglazed Stoneware' and 'Elers Ware' in *Transactions of the English Ceramic Circle*, i (1931–32) and ii (1932–1933).

Staffordshire

Shaw, Simeon, *History of the Staffordshire Potteries*. Hanley, 1829.
Rhead, G. W., *Staffordshire Pots and Potters*. London, 1906.
Wedgwood, J. C., *Staffordshire Pottery and its History*. London, 1914.
Earle, Cyril, *The Earle Collection of Early Staffordshire Pottery*. London, 1915.
Price, R. K., *Astbury, Whieldon and Ralph Wood Figures and Toby Jugs*. London, 1922.
Luxmoore, C. F. C., *Saltglaze: With the Notes of a Collector*. Exeter, 1924.
Read, Herbert, *Staffordshire Pottery Figures*. London, 1929.
See also W. B. Honey, as above, and F. Falkner, below.

Wedgwood

Meteyard, Eliza, *The Life of Josiah Wedgwood*. London, 1865.
Jewitt, Ll., *The Wedgwoods: being a life of Josiah Wedgwood*. London, 1865.
Meteyard, E., *Wedgwood and his works*. London, 1873.
Meteyard, E., *Memorials of Wedgwood*. London, 1874.
Gatty, C. T., *Catalogue of a Loan Collection of the works of Josiah Wedgwood exhibited at Liverpool*. Liverpool, 1879.
Rathbone, F., *Old Wedgwood*. London, 1893.
Church, Sir Arthur H., *Josiah Wedgwood, Master Potter*. London, 1903.
Burton, W., *Josiah Wedgwood and his Pottery*. London, 1922.
Barnard, Harry, *Chats on Wedgwood Ware*. London, 1924.

Later Staffordshire, Leeds, etc.

As for *Staffordshire* above, also

Kidson, J. R. and F., *Historical Notices of the Leeds Old Pottery*. Leeds, 1892.

Gatty, C. T., *The Liverpool Potteries*. Liverpool, 1882.

Mayer, J., *History of the Art of Pottery in Liverpool*. Liverpool, 1885.

Turner, W., *The Ceramics of Nantgarw and Swansea*. London, 1897.

Turner, W., *William Adams, an old English Potter*. London, 1904.

Falkner, F., and Sidebotham, E. J., *Catalogue of a Collection of English Pottery Figures lent to the Salford Royal Museum*. 1906.

Entwistle, P., *Catalogue of Liverpool Pottery and Porcelain*. Liverpool 1907.

Falkner, F., *The Wood Family of Burslem*. London, 1912.

II. PORCELAIN

General

Jewitt, Ll., *The Ceramic Art of Great Britain*. London, 1878.

Nightingale, J. E., *Contributions towards the History of Early English Porcelain from contemporary sources*. Salisbury, 1881.

Bemrose, W., *Bow, Chelsea and Derby Porcelain*. London, 1898.

Burton, W., *English Porcelain*. London, 1902.

Church, Sir Arthur H., *English Porcelain*. London, 1904.

Hobson, R. L., *Catalogue of the Collection of English Porcelain in the British Museum*. London, 1905.

King, William, *English Porcelain Figures of the Eighteenth Century*. London, 1925.

Rackham, Bernard, *Catalogue of the Schreiber Collection*, vol. i. London, 1928.

Honey, W. B., *Old English Porcelain*. London, 1928.

English Porcelain Circle (later, *English Ceramic Circle*), *Transactions* (1928–   ).

MacAlister, Mrs. Donald (ed.), *William Duesbury's London Account Book 1751–53 (English Porcelain Circle Monograph)*. London, 1931.

Chelsea

King, William, *Chelsea Porcelain*. London, 1922.

Blunt, R., (ed.) *The Cheyne Book of Chelsea China*. London, 1924.

Bryant, G. E., *Chelsea Porcelain Toys*. London, 1925.

Bellamy Gardner, H., 'Chelsea Porcelain' in *Transactions of the English Porcelain Circle*, i (1928), p. 16; ii (1929), p. 23; iii (1931), p. 55; iv (1932), p. 22.

Bow

Mew, Egan, *Old Bow China*. London, 1909.

Hurlbutt, F., *Bow Porcelain*. London, 1927.

Toppin, Aubrey J., 'Bow Porcelain: Some recent excavations' and 'Some early Bow Muses' in the *Burlington Magazine*, xl (1922), p. 224, and liv (1929), p. 188.

Lowestoft

Spelman, W. W. R., *Lowestoft China*. London and Norwich, 1905.

Kiddell, A. J. B., in *Transactions of the English Porcelain Circle*, iii (1931), p. 7.

Longton Hall and Early Staffordshire

Bemrose, W., *Longton Hall Porcelain*. London, 1906.

MacAlister, Mrs. Donald, 'Longton Hall Porcelain' in *Apollo*, January 1927, and 'Early Staffordshire China' in *Transactions of the English Ceramic Circle*, i (1933), p. 44.

Derby

Haslem, J., *The Old Derby China Factory*. London, 1876.

Hurlbutt, F., *Old Derby Porcelain*. London, 1925.

Allam, E. Percival, 'The Artist-Modellers of the Old Derby Porcelain Factory' in *The Connoisseur*, lxxxii (1928), p. 29.

MacAlister, Mrs. Donald, 'The early work of Planché and Duesbury' in *Transactions of the English Porcelain Circle*, ii (1929), p. 45.

Tapp, Major W. H., on Billingsley and the Brewers, in the same, ii (1929), p. 62; iii (1931), p. 85, and iv (1932), p. 75.

Williamson, F., *The Derby Pot-Manufactory known as Cockpit Hill*. Derby, 1931.

Worcester

Binns, R. W., *A Century of Potting in the City of Worcester*. London and Worcester, 1865.

Hobson, R. L., *Worcester Porcelain*. London, 1910.

Hobson, R. L., *Catalogue of the Frank Lloyd Collection of Worcester Porcelain*. London, 1923.

Elliot, Wallace, 'Soft Paste Bristol Porcelain' in *Transactions of the English Porcelain Circle*, ii (1929), p. 6.

Kentish Town

Toppin, A. J., in *Transactions of the English Ceramic Circle*, i (1933), p. 30.

BIBLIOGRAPHY

Caughley

Roberts, C. Clifton, in *The Connoisseur*, liv (1919), p. 187; lv (1919), p. 223, and lvii (1920), p. 143.

Hobson, R. L., in *Transactions of the English Porcelain Circle*, iii (1931), p. 66.

Liverpool

Gatty and Mayer, as above.

Rackham, Bernard, and Honey, W. B., 'Liverpool Porcelain' in *Transactions of the English Porcelain Circle*, ii (1929), p. 27.

Plymouth and Bristol

Pountney, as above.

Radford, Lady, 'Plymouth China' in *The Devonian Year Book*, 1920, p. 31.

Hurlbutt, F., *Bristol Porcelain*. London, 1928.

Elliot, Wallace, 'Bristol Porcelain Plaques' in *Transactions of the English Ceramic Circle*, i (1933), p. 23.

Staffordshire

Hayden, Arthur, *Spode and his Successors*. London, 1924.

Thorne, A., *Pink Lustre Pottery*. London, 1926.

Nantgarw and Swansea

Turner, as above.

Williams, I. J., *Catalogue of Welsh Porcelain in the National Museum of Wales*. Cardiff, 1932.

INDEX

263

269

INDEX

THE END